Pavement in the Sun

House himself

Jack House

Pavement in the Sun

Hutchinson of London

HUTCHINSON & CO (*Publishers*) **LTD**
178-202 Great Portland Street London W1

London Melbourne Sydney
Auckland Bombay Toronto
Johannesburg New York

★

First published 1967

This book has been set in Baskerville,
printed in Great Britain on Antique Wove paper
by Balding & Mansell Ltd,
of London and Wisbech, and bound by
Wm. Brendon & Son Ltd, of Tiptree, Essex.

Contents

Illustrations

Preface

The thing to do with an autobiography nowadays, as far as I can see, is to draw it out to as many volumes as you think the public, or the publishers, will stand. I've tried to do mine in one.

That means, of course, that I've left a lot out. I haven't gone into my private life much, having the quaint, old-fashioned idea that it's private. I have taken as my guiding light in this book four lines from *Epistle to a Young Friend*, by Robert Burns, a man I esteem greatly.

He wrote—

> Ay free, aff han', your story tell,
> When wi' a bosom crony!
> But still keep something to yoursel
> Ye scarcely tell to ony.

In the course of my newspaper and broadcasting life I have met many, many people who have said to me, 'What a life I've had! I could write a book.'

This is easier said than done, as I have just discovered. (You know, naturally, that the Preface is written by the author after the whole job's finished.) It has been all the more difficult for me because I have seldom kept any letters, cuttings, notes or files. Once again I have been dependent on that great institution, the Mitchell Library in Glasgow. Like many another writer. I don't know what I'd do without it.

I am disappointed in this book for one reason, now that I've had another look at it. I meant to say quite a lot of nice things about my friends—and it may come as news to some people that I have a great many friends. But, since I have chosen to tell the story of a large part of my life in as little space as possible, I have had to leave some people out or just mention them briefly.

This does not mean I have forgotten them. Their names are in my heart.

Jack House

Glasgow

Pavement in the Sun

The summer was always sunny when I was a wee boy in Glasgow. We lived in very respectable Kennyhill Square in the Dennistoun district, then on the outskirts of the city. Just round the corner from us was the even more bourgeois Alexandra Park Gardens. But a family there allowed their boys to run about in their 'Baries' during the summer months. 'Baries' meant wearing your bare feet. How we envied them.

The tar bubbled up on the pavement and you could pick some of it out and mould it into figures. The only trouble was that the tar stuck to your fingers. Then you had to go into the house at 7 Kennyhill Square (a two-room and kitchen flat) and admit to your mother that you'd been playing with tar. And after some hard words, she'd get out a lump of salt butter and proceed to clean your hands. Butter was the only thing which took the tar off.

We had an open space at the back of Kennyhill Square which was known as The Field. It was bare in the centre because of the games of football played there. But it was surrounded by clumps of bright green grass, and you could pitch a tent. Any kind of material would do. It was in one of these tents that I first heard about the Facts of Life.

A Big Boy (he must have been at least twelve to our eight or nine years) said he'd explain to us how our fathers and mothers produced babies. But he'd only explain to those who learned the Deaf and Dumb Alphabet, which he had mastered. Perhaps I was precocious (or perhaps I was very anxious to know the secret), but I learned the Deaf and Dumb

I

Alphabet in double quick time. Indeed, I can still do it to this day.

The Big Boy then took me into a lonely corner of The Field and told me the awful things that fathers and mothers did together. It was several years before I discovered that he was quite wrong. He was just about as innocent as we were, and wasn't in the class of the boys at school who carried around a marked copy of the Bible, so that they could turn to the dirty bits at a moment's notice.

At the time, however, I just disbelieved this Big Boy. I had a great talent for believing what I was told by my parents, and I had already fought a friend of mine who said that Father Christmas was really just your father. I am the eldest of nine children, so that I had quite a lot of experience of babies arriving in our family. And I knew perfectly well that Dr Mackinlay brought each new baby along in that black bag he carried when he visited my mother.

But I have strayed somewhat from the pavement, which we all preferred to The Field. The pavement was in front of the four closes which made up the odd side of Kennyhill Square. A close, in case you don't know, is an entry to a tenement building. On each floor there were two facing flats, eight in all since it was a three-storey tenement. The numbers were 1, 3, 5, and 7, so that we were on the odd side of the Square. My family lived at 7 Kennyhill Square, looking straight at the entrance to St Rollox Bowling Club— the bowling green separated the odd and even sides.

I have said that it was a respectable place. It certainly was. The tenements were solidly built of bright red sandstone and the closes were proudly described as 'wally'. That meant that the entrance and the stairs up to the first landing were tiled. After that the scheme of decoration petered out into paint. To have a wally close right up to the top landing was rich indeed.

There were a great many boys and girls in Kennyhill Square—at least, there were on the odd side; we hardly knew anybody on the even side. And on the warm summer evenings we'd all be out there playing games or talking or chasing the girls. We played Leave-O (called by the lesser breeds

'Relieve-O'), Run a Mile; Kick the Can; Birds, Beasts, Flowers and Fishes; Hopping Charlie; and Robinson Crusoe.

Robinson Crusoe was a good game, but it could be played only when a new boy arrived in the Square. The new boy was designated Robinson Crusoe and posted on the top landing of one of the closes. He was instructed that, when the leader shouted from the foot of the close, 'Robinson Crusoe, give us a call, please give us an answer', he would reply 'Cooee!' and then run down the stairs shouting, 'It was me! It was me!'

Below him, on each landing, stood a boy at the ready. When the leader shouted his Robinson Crusoe call, each boy pulled the bells of the two flats on the landing and ran downstairs. And then the unsuspecting Robinson Crusoe descended, just as people were opening their doors to the summons, shouting 'It was me! It was me!'

It was on that pavement in Kennyhill Square that I first fell in love. I was ten at the time and my inamorata was a girl of twelve. She had an exotic attraction for me, because she was English and knowledgeable. Her name was Viva Pringle, and she was the daughter of the proprietor of Pringle's Palladium, a picture house in Dennistoun which became a dance hall. But it wasn't her superior status in life which impressed me. I just thought she was beautiful.

The Pringles lived in Alexandra Park Gardens, and that meant that I could look from our kitchen window up at Viva's kitchen window. How full was my heart when, after gazing at that magic casement for quarter of an hour or so, I would see Viva actually appear and even give me a wave. She was the queen of our circle and decided that we all should have a nickname, which she herself would bestow. I can't remember anybody else's nickname, but the one she chose for me was 'Tusks', because of my protruding front teeth. Strange to say, it never caught on.

Alexandra Park Gardens overlooked Alexandra Park, and every summer we went into the park to listen to the band or watch the concert parties. Naturally, I couldn't afford the tuppence to get into the enclosure, nor could Viva. So we stood outside the railings and watched from there. Once or twice, when I was really in the money, I bought a penny programme and so became acquainted with the works of the masters—at least, those masters whose works were suitable for brass or military bands.

I was not only younger than Viva, but also slightly smaller. So I stood nearest the railings and she stood just behind me. It seemed fair enough. On one such occasion Viva suddenly said, 'Jack, may I ask you a personal question?' I said certainly she could. 'Well,' she said, 'when did you wash your neck last?'

This, coming from the woman I loved, had a great effect on me. I started washing my neck the very next morning, and kept on doing it until the parting of the ways.

That came when Kennyhill Square learned one day that Viva had disappeared. She had not only disappeared, but her coat had been found on the bank of the Monkland Canal. The police were called in, dragging operations were started, and Viva's younger sister told us with every sign of enjoyment that one of the detectives had explained that, even if dragging was not successful, the body would float within a few days.

However, Viva had left her coat on the canal bank just to worry her family. She had actually gone to her grannie's home in some strange place like Hamilton. Her father, the motion picture entrepreneur, went to collect her. Back in town, he told her to wait outside a tobacconist's while he bought some cigarettes. When he came out, she had disappeared again. This time she went to her auntie's on the South side of Glasgow. And there she was once again discovered and her father brought her back.

I can still recall standing at the parlour window of our house in 7 Kennyhill Square, and hiding behind the muslin curtain as Mr Pringle brought his errant daughter home, holding her firmly by the hand this time.

I never saw Viva again. First of all, my respectable soul was outraged at such carryings-on. Secondly, I realised she was not the girl for me. And at the age of ten I had surely time to look around once again. In any case, Mr Pringle moved the whole family from Alexandra Park Gardens, and shortly after that gave up the Palladium Picture House.

I have often wondered what became of Viva. Such a femme fatale must have had a wonderful life. I'd never have been worthy of her anyway.

2

Although I regard the once delightful Glasgow suburb of Dennistoun as my calf country, I have got to admit that I am not a Glaswegian at all. I was born on Wednesday, May 16th, 1906, just in time for tea, at 13 Deerpark Gardens, Tollcross. The significance of this is that Tollcross was still a village outside Glasgow at that time, and was not absorbed into the city until 1912. So I am an incomer and can only claim to be a Glaswegian by adoption.

When I read the Octaves of Sir Compton Mackenzie and the reminiscences of some elderly ladies, I marvel at their early memories, and their capacity for total recall. I can remember very clearly my very first day at school, but I had reached the advanced age of five at the time. I have one or two confused memories of earlier days, when we lived in Onslow Drive in Dennistoun, but I recall nothing at all of my first three or four years in Tollcross.

Except one thing. For many years I had a clear picture at the back of my mind of a church at the corner of two roads. There was snow on the church roof and on the railings surrounding it. I thought this might be an early memory, but it seemed too much like a picture postcard to be genuine.

When I was about forty-five I was invited to open a Christmas Bazaar in a church hall in Tollcross. It was about a fortnight before Christmas and, surprisingly for Glasgow, snow had fallen. Near by was Brownlie Gardens, to which my parents had flitted after Deerpark Gardens, and I thought it would be pleasant to seek out the house after my bazaar opening duties were over. So I walked across and there, at the corner of the road, was the church with its roof covered with snow and the snow-topped railings around it, all exactly as I had seen in my mind's eye these many years.

My father was born in England and came to Scotland when he was a boy. He was brought up in Newton in Lanarkshire and, by the time he married, had got a job with the Steel Company of Scotland as a clerk. He met my mother, who worked in a baker's shop in Duke Street, Dennistoun, at social events in Christ Church off the Gallowgate of Glasgow. This was a Scottish Episcopal Church, for my father had been brought up in the Church of England, and my mother had come from Brechin in Angus, where the Scottish Episcopal Church is strong.

To his dying day my father kept a small cutting from a Glasgow newspaper describing how, at a Christmas party in Christ Church, the young man who was playing the part of Santa Claus was injured when his cotton wool beard caught fire from a candle on the Christmas tree. He was the young man.

Looking back, I see my father as a romantic. He sang in the church choir and he bought a small organ for our parlour. He couldn't play it very well, but he could accompany himself in comic songs which always seemed to have 'Hi-tiddley-I-tie' choruses in them. He never wearied of going in for competitions, and he once showed me a short story he had written for some contest. I thought it was a very good one.

He went in for silly jokes, such as pretending on a Glasgow tramcar that he didn't know my mother and his sister, so that they had to pay their own fares. When I had to study *Ivanhoe* and asked him about buying a copy he said, 'Ivanhoe already.' So, when the time came for me to take the book to school and I asked him for it, my father explained that this was a joke and what he meant was, 'I've an hoe.'

My mother was more practical. Of course, she was bringing children into the world at fairly regular intervals and she hadn't time to be much else than practical. She was a very good cook. She knew as many old songs as my father knew popular ones, and I learned them all.

The rest of the family circle consisted of my grandmother (my father's mother) who affronted us somewhat in Kennyhill Square by arriving on week-days with a shawl over her shoulders and a man's cloth cap pinned to her white hair. On

Sundays, though, she wore a black dress and a black bonnet. Her father had been an innkeeper in Wiltshire and she could remember the stage coaches driving into the yard.

My grannie had two daughters, Auntie Annie and Auntie Kate. Auntie Annie was handsome and dark and a school teacher. She thought I could be a genius and offered me the chance to go to Glasgow University. But at that time I was so fed up with school that I was determined to leave when I reached the age of fifteen. Now I regret that I did not go to Glasgow University. On the other hand, I don't regret leaving school at the age of fifteen.

Auntie Kate, when I knew her best, was a saleswoman in Treron et Cie. of Sauchiehall Street. It was a purely Glasgow firm in spite of its name and, like so many of the shops in those days, it specialised in a wonderful window display at Christmas. I remember being taken to see the great toy window, of which the outstanding item was a lion which nodded its head. As we were watching, the lion's head slowed down. Its nods were becoming almost imperceptible. All of a sudden my Auntie Kate appeared through a fold in a curtain and gave the head a sharp bash.

Immediately the lion started nodding like mad, and my Auntie Kate looked straight at us and gave us a wink. Oh, I was the proud boy, I can tell you!

We had also an Auntie Bella, who was a far-out cousin of my mother's in reality. She was small and energetic and Welsh, and she was married to a ship's steward who could play the mandoline. When I saw my very first pantomime— it was at the Theatre Royal but I can't remember the title— the principal boy came on and sang 'Let the Great Big World keep Turning'. I was absolutely positive that it was my Auntie Bella who sang that one number, although I didn't think she had appeared in the rest of the show.

We were a pretty close-knit family and we could have a party without inviting any outsiders. By the time I was twelve I had four brothers and a sister. It could have been five brothers, but one child died in infancy. I had very much the feeling of a pioneer, because, being the eldest, I had to do everything first.

About all I remember of our Onslow Drive days is that I went to a little wooden school where there was a big fire and we were given Plasticine to play with. Then there was an awful Pomeranian in the next close which barked at me every time it saw me. I have a very clear recollection of standing against the railings which marked our garden from the pavement and throwing this dreadful beast a piece of my Fry's Five Boys chocolate bar in an endeavour to placate it.

And then, of course, we faced the playing ground belonging to Golfhill Cricket Club, and there was a great occasion when I was sitting watching the game when a boundary ball hit me in the eye. I went around for days exhibiting my black eye and explaining how I got it.

But life really began for me when we arrived at 7 Kennyhill Square. Our house was on the ground floor—we always stayed on the ground floor because of the pram. You walked into the wally close and there we were on the right-hand side, with a glass door sumptuously decorated. Inside there was a square lobby in which my father installed a grandfather clock. There was a parlour (where the organ and a dining room table took up nearly all the space) and a bedroom on one side, and a kitchen and a bathroom on the other.

We lived in the kitchen, and used the parlour on special occasions only. The kitchen had a bed recess and, when things got crowded, we had a camp bed which I occupied for some years. The place seemed enormous to me and I was never conscious of any kind of overcrowding. I played with my toy soldiers in front of the bright kitchen range, when I wasn't reading or drawing. I read everything I could lay my hands on and, since my father was a member of a magazine club at Blochairn Steelworks, I had the opportunity to read the *Strand*, the *Pall Mall*, *Chambers'*, the *Windsor*, the *New*, the *Wide World*, the *Gaiety* and the *Royal* magazines.

I edited various magazines at home and got my brothers to contribute articles, stories and drawings. So drunk was I with my success that I wrote a short story and set it to the Editor of the *London Magazine* with a letter saying that I was thirteen and had no objection to being printed as a juvenile prodigy. (I think I had been reading *Nicholas Nickleby* at the time and had got a bit mixed up with infant phenomena.) Strange to say, the Editor of the *London Magazine* did not reply.

When I felt the urge to draw something, I went for the grocery messages to a shop in Alexandra Parade and stole a sheet or two of the paper used for wrapping butter. I was deeply conscious of the fact that I was committing a crime, but my artistic impulse was too strong for me.

My father was very keen that we should not devote too much time to these artistic pursuits. So we had porridge every night as well as for breakfast. He also bought us dumb-bells and boxing gloves and a book by the strongest man in the world, the Great Sandow himself. I was most impressed by the Great Sandow and followed his exercises religiously— that may be a cliché, but it's true.

One theory of the Great Sandow's was that you should have a cold bath in the morning and then put on your clothes without drying yourself. The heat of your body would do the rest. I tried this just once. I have had some un-comfortable experiences during my life, but I still look back on having a cold bath and putting on your clothes without drying yourself as supremely uncomfortable.

Later I read the life story of some famous runner or other. What impressed me was that this chap told how he had started training as a small boy by running everywhere he had to go. I dearly wanted to be an athlete of some sort, so, as I did most of the messages for the family, I ran them all. In-deed, the only time I stopped running was on my way to school. I realised there could be too much of a good thing. I didn't become an athlete of any sort—I have never been the slightest good at anything athletic. But I did develop my legs and, when I look at my rather peculiar physiognomy, my puny arms and my spreading paunch, I console myself with the thought that my legs are not so bad. I think also of the time at Haghill School when I was the leader of the Hairy-Legged Gang.

Though these were the days of Glasgow gangdom far beyond anything we have now, the Hairy-Legged Gang had no sinister implication. It existed entirely for exhibitionism. There was only one rule and that was that the boy with the hairiest legs was automatically the leader of the gang. As soon as I joined the group, I was elected leader. After that various challengers came along and the procedure was that we would go to a corner of the school playground, where the challenger and I would roll down our stockings and compare hairs. I remained leader until I left Haghill—although I realise now that I never led the Hairy-Legged Gang in anything.

In our house we celebrated everything. We started with the New Year and finished with Christmas, and in between we had Pancake Tuesday, the birthday of Robert Burns, all our own birthdays, the King's Birthday Holiday, St Andrew's Day and various other festivals. We did not observe Guy Fawkes' Night. This Guy Fawkes business was purely English and we didn't want to have anything to do with it. Our bonfire night was on the Kings' Birthday Holiday, which was usually in July.

Scottish summer nights are very long ones and that meant we had to wait up late for our bonfire, which was lit in The Field, of course. For weeks beforehand we collected wood, old chairs and bedsteads, anything that would burn, and stored them in the washing-houses which stood at the end of the back-green of each close. We were not taking any chance of having stuff pinched. On the day itself the bonfire was built up from the time we skailed from school, and a constant guard was kept on it because there were people living not far from Kennyhill Square who would have had our combustible material away in a twinkling if they got the chance.

At this time I had graduated from wearing a sailor suit, with H.M.S. *Indefatigable* on the ribbon of the hat, to a Norfolk jacket and shorts and an Eton collar of celluloid with a stick-in tie. I was ready to dash out to see the great bonfire lit when my mother called me back. She pointed out that celluloid was highly inflammable, so I must take off my Eton collar before I joined my friends round the fire. I was horror-struck but there was no alternative. I felt a social outcast as I walked into The Field with no collar or tie, but everybody was so enthralled with the bonfire and the fireworks that my nakedness went unremarked.

As I've said, we did not celebrate Guy Fawkes' Night (although it is widely celebrated in Glasgow now, such is the effect of growing Anglicisation over the years), and a lot of us did not celebrate Christmas either. In those days there was no general holiday on Christmas Day, though we were on holiday from school, of course. New Year's Day was what everybody waited for.

Everybody, that is, except the House family. Being 'Piskies' we did celebrate Christmas. We put up our stockings at the end of the bed on Christmas Eve and woke early on Christmas morning with the delicious sensation of something heavy lying across our feet. Father Christmas had visited us and we'd missed him again. My brothers and I did our best to stay awake each Christmas Eve, but never succeeded.

The other boys and girls in Kennyhill Square didn't get their presents until New Year's Day, and these were delivered by a peculiarly Scottish spirit named, as far as I could make out, 'Sandy Claws'. Later I worked out that this was a popular rendering of Santa Claus, a name which was never used in our house.

I think I went on believing in Father Christmas long after the average boy of my age. I wanted desperately to believe in him. As I have related, I once fought a boy who said that Father Christmas was only your father. But one day before Christmas my brother George, the next one to me, came into the bedroom with staring eyes and motioned to me to follow him. He led the way to the cupboard in one corner of the parlour. There, by standing on one of the plush-seated chairs, I was able to see on the top shelf a number of parcels which were unmistakably boxes of soldiers, dolls, and the like.

It was a great shock to me. I was horror-struck at the duplicity of my parents. I even wondered if, for some reason, Father Christmas had stopped coming down our chimney, and my father and mother were concealing this from us by giving us presents in his stead. Gradually I accepted the truth and got vicarious enjoyment in later years from the babies who came along and could get the Santa Claus indoctrination.

The only problem about Hogmanay and New Year was staying up late and trying to like port wine. The youngest members of the family were put to bed, but by the time I was twelve I was allowed to see the New Year in. This seemed very exciting but in fact it was a long wait for midnight. My mother was busy with the putting out of shortbread, black bun, sandwiches, cakes, oranges, apples, sweeties and biscuits. My father polished the glasses for the port. He was practically a teetotaller, but he considered it proper to provide port wine at the New Year.

Nowadays anybody can get the signal for the arrival of the New Year on the television screen. But then we did not even have radio and were a bit distrustful of watches. There was no need to worry, though. It was silent one moment, and the next the works hooters blew, the ships sounded their sirens from the distant River Clyde, a man in the next close came out banging a stick against a tin tray, and somewhere a piper started up with preliminary wails before he got into 'A Guid New Year tae Ane an' A''.

My father was always our first-foot. The first-foot is the first person who steps across your threshold on New Year's Day and he brings luck if he is a dark man. The custom is to wait until somebody calls, but one Hogmanay it was a man with red hair, and my mother swore that we had had bad luck the whole of that year. So, just to be on the safe side, my father, who was a bit bald but had once jet-black hair, went out some five or ten minutes before midnight and waited until the magic moment.

My mother would open the door and my father would enter shouting 'A happy New Year!' At the same moment as the door was opened, somebody would open a window, so as to let the Old Year out as the New Year came in. My father kissed my mother and handed her a piece of her own shortbread which he had taken out with him. He also had his bottle of port and a piece of coal. He dashed into the parlour and threw the coal on the fire, crying 'Lang may yer lum reek!' In this way he brought the three necessities to the house—food, drink and fuel.

After that neighbours came in, the man of the house

bearing a bottle in each case. As it was often whisky, my father would refuse the kind offer and ask his guest to have a glass of port. So the guest would just drink his own whisky and my father would sip his port. I got a glass of port, too, and I thought I'd never tasted anything so nasty. As soon as possible I got on to the ginger wine.

It was years before I appreciated port or any other kind of alcohol. When I was a boy, even a youth, I held my breath as I passed public houses because the smell was awful. Nowadays public houses hold their breath as I pass them. My conversion is another story, which I shall tell later.

While these celebrations were great events in our year, what I liked best was Sunday nights during the winter. We always had a special tea, with French cakes, and then we'd put the lights out and sit round the fire while my father told us a ghost story. The climax was always the same. Just as he reached the approach of the ghost, my father would lift the tongs (which he had concealed somewhere) and drop them on to the tiles of the fireplace. No matter how many times you'd seen and heard this done, it was still a delightful shock.

Of course, I believed firmly in ghosts. I had already seen one. I was sleeping in the bedroom at the time. There were three of us in the one bed. My brother George and I lay one way and my brother Jimmy lay the other. All of a sudden one night I wakened and there, in front of the white-painted wardrobe, I saw a tall figure in misty robes. Horns were growing out of its bushy hair and it had a moustache and beard and gleaming eyes which looked straight at me.

I was half terrified, half interested. I recalled that what you should do when you saw a ghost was to put your head beneath the bedclothes. So I did just that and, when I emerged again and looked towards the wardrobe, the ghost had disappeared.

I didn't say a word about the ghost next day. Indeed, it was years later that I mentioned it and we had flitted to the garden suburb of Riddrie by this time. When I told the family about my old ghost, my mother didn't laugh at all. She said that not so long ago she had gone into her own bedroom (we had three bedrooms at Riddrie to the one in Kennyhill Square) and just as she opened the door, she saw something disappear into the white wardrobe.

My youngest sister Dorothy still has that wardrobe, but it doesn't seem to be haunted any longer.

I was eight years old when the Great War broke out, and my principal memory is the intense patriotism which it aroused in my breast. I didn't know what it was all about. I just knew that the Goodies were fighting the Baddies and I was captivated by a comic paper which had a weekly instalment of the adventures of 'Kaiser Bill and Little Willie'. Then we got 'London Opinion' every week, and there were the cartoons of Alfred Leete to inspire us even more.

We had an elderly gramophone with a big brass horn and when the record of the Allied Anthems was put on, we all stood up—and I think some of us saluted too. Lord Kitchener was our hero, and the one absolutely clear memory I have of that war was the day that the news came out that Kitchener had been drowned. I remember standing in that wally close in Kennyhill Square watching my mother and her next-door neighbour, Mrs Scott, crying as they talked about the tragedy.

Then came the danger of air raids from the Zeppelins and street gas lamps were painted a dark blue and we had to dye our window blinds something of the same shade. It was all rather amateurish compared with the Second World War. Indeed, the only real impact that I remember was made by the rationing and the queueing. As I did the messages for the family, I knew plenty about queueing. I perfected a technique of looking pale and wan, so that some kind woman was sure to say, 'Let the wean get his first.'

I can't recall any hardships, but they must have existed, because I remember the excitement of the day that my Auntie Kate arrived with a small bag of potatoes. I can still see her and my mother kneeling on the kitchen floor and separating them into two piles—'One to you, and one to me —one to you, and one to me,' and so on.

There was some talk, too, of margarine being vastly inferior to butter. But, since I didn't like butter and thought of it only as a substance to take summer tar off my hands, I paid no attention. Incidentally, I have no idea at all what my mother used to take tar off our hands when butter was so severely rationed. Probably we just got a skelpit leathering and were told not to play with tar on the pavement again.

The big thing of the Great War to me was the spy scare. I had just graduated from *Lot o' Fun* as my Sunday morning reading to *The Scout*. I can still remember the very first cover of *The Scout* I ever saw. It showed a gallant Belgian Boy Scout hidden in the branches of a tree, spying on a couple of Uhlans below him. How I longed to be that kind of Scout.

But I had a difficulty. I had already talked to the Rev. Alex. McBain, assistant minister to his brother, Canon McBain, at Christ Church, and Scoutmaster of the church troop. And he said that I could only become a Scout on condition that I learned the catechism of the Scottish Episcopal Church (or is it the Episcopal Church in Scotland —I'm afraid I forget). Now my favourite book was *Scouting for Boys* by Sir Robert Baden-Powell and I knew all about the Boy Scout movement. Nowhere in *Scouting for Boys* was there a single mention of any catechism. So, even though my father did sing in the Christ Church choir, I decided not to join their troop.

I started an organisation of my own called the Wolves. It was a mixture of the Wolf Cubs and the Boy Scouts with some ideas of my own, and I recruited most of the boys of Kennyhill Square—at least, those who were younger than I was. I also wrote to Sir Robert Baden-Powell, explaining my new movement and suggesting that he might take it under his wing as part of the Boy Scouts. The Chief Scout did not reply.

As I went around Dennistoun I kept my eyes open for German spies. One day I was walking up the hill of Alexandra Park to the summit where the flagpole and two ancient cannon stood and on the way I passed a woman sitting on a park seat. At once I knew that she was a spy. She was tall and gaunt and pale and she was reading the *People's Friend*. She had a secretive look about her. The time was shortly after four o'clock, when I was out of school.

Next afternoon I went straight home from school, collected

my 'piece and jam', and ate it on the way to Alexandra Park.
I climbed the hill, more carefully this time. Yes, she was
sitting in the same seat, still reading the *People's Friend*. This
struck me as very suspicious indeed. My grannie got the
People's Friend and passed it on to us, and, since I read everything that came into the house, I was well aware that the
People's Friend could be read from cover to cover in one
evening.

Was the *People's Friend* just another kind of cover? What
was she concealing behind that seemingly innocent magazine?
I soon came to the conclusion that she was actually studying
secret messages which had been passed on to her by another
spy—perhaps the very newsagent who sold her the *People's
Friend*.

I decided I had better take my brother George into my
confidence. It wasn't much use tracking down a German spy
if you were the only one who knew about it. So I told George
of my suspicions and right away he agreed that I was right.
Two afternoons later we went up the hill in the park and
there she was, still in the same seat, still reading the *People's
Friend*.

Next day we did a proper job on her. We approached the
park summit from another angle, and crept down through a
plantation so that we could see her every movement. She
appeared to be immersed in the *People's Friend*. Nobody came
that way. We seemed to be alone in Alexandra Park with the
German spy.

Eventually she collected her bag and her gloves and rolled
up the magazine which she carried under her arm. We
followed her stealthily through the park and into Alexandra
Parade. When she stopped to look into a shop window, we
stopped too, and noted the shops she was looking at in case
she was getting secret messages from some arrangement of
boxes or tins or price cards.

She went down Meadowpark Street and into a close at
Roslea Drive. We noted the number. We hung about for a
time, but, as she didn't appear again, we concluded she
lived there. The entire operation was very satisfactory.

That, I'm sorry to say, is the whole story. Although we

went up the hill every afternoon, we didn't see her again. Perhaps her evil machinations were being carried on in another part of Glasgow. Or perhaps she had noticed two schoolboys skulking about in the undergrowth and following her home, and didn't particularly care for that kind of thing.

Having tracked down a German spy, I tended to lose interest in the subject. One day I was coming back from Whitehill School in Dennistoun with my bosom crony, Wilfred Horner. As we walked up Whitehill Street on the way home to lunch, a soldier appeared in full kit. As he came fornenst us, he thrust a package into my hand and said, 'You take that. I can't eat any more.'

I looked at the package. It contained more chocolate than I had ever seen at one time for years. 'We'd better divide this,' I said to Wilfred.

But Wilfred, besides being English, had impressed me as a deep thinker. He shook his head. 'How do we know', he said, 'that that soldier isn't a German spy and the chocolate is poisoned?'

I gazed at the chocolate with horror. We'd all heard these stories of German spies going around giving children poisoned sweets. A tug of war went on inside me. One side said, 'You like chocolate. What's wrong with a soldier giving you some?' The other side said, 'Of course it's poisoned. People don't give chocolate away nowadays.'

My Scottish instincts got the better of me. I wouldn't throw the chocolate away, as Wilfred suggested. I would take it home and think over the whole situation.

I kept that chocolate until I came home from school. Then I went into the parlour on my own and broke off a piece of the chocolate. In fear and trembling, I put it into my mouth. At the slightest sign of pain I was prepared to spit it out. But it tasted just like chocolate. I tried a second piece and this time I waited for several minutes before I had a third piece. I felt no sensation at all except the enjoyment of the chocolate, so I finished the whole lot myself. After all, I deserved it for being so brave.

I look back on my schooldays with a certain amount of affection and pleasure. But I doubt very much whether I really enjoyed them at the time. True, I liked all my classes in English and Literature and, about the age of ten, I came home from Haghill School to announce to my parents that I was 'the best compositioner in the class'. I think the only other subject I really enjoyed was the Art Class, and then only if we were allowed to draw 'what we liked'—in other words, use our imagination.

A drawing lesson in the schools I went to consisted of doing a pencil study of a blue vase on a white sheet of paper, or some other inspiring subject. When I go to schools today, especially primary schools in Glasgow, and see what the children are doing, I shed inward tears at the waste of time and spirit we had to face. And yet at school I decided I must be at least one of what I called the Three A's—Artist, Actor or Author.

My first school, as I have said, was the wee wooden one in Onslow Drive. I remember practically nothing of that except as I have said a bright coal fire and being allowed to play with Plasticine.

When we flitted to Kennyhill Square, I went to Haghill School, a mere two or three minutes' walk away. Perhaps the very nearness was the reason I was sometimes late. This was a terrible thing to happen. The late-comers—that's to say, everyone who arrived after nine o'clock to the second—were herded into a cloakroom. Then along came the second head-master, a sadist we called Daddy Milne. He wore a pointed moustache and looked like the worst kind of sergeant-major.

He terrified all of us, and when he barked out the question, 'Have you an excuse?', most of us couldn't even reply. Then he strapped us, one by one, and we went quivering into class to be reproached by our teacher. I say 'us' rather than 'me', because I could see the desperation on my fellow sufferers' faces.

We thought that Daddy Milne was terrible, but we were assured by the boys in the top class of the school that their teacher was far worse. His name was James Maxton, and he had married another teacher at Haghill. The boys in his class told us that he had the biggest strap that any school had ever known. It was supposed to be a 'Lochgelly', the toughest tawse made, and pickled in rum to make it even tougher. Since James Maxton was tall and gaunt and had a lock of jet black hair falling over his brow, he was a sinister figure to us.

We didn't know that the Maxton boys were, as we said then, taking a lend of us. Maxton was a pacifist. As I know now, he was being persecuted for his beliefs even when he was a teacher at Haghill. He did not believe in corporal punishment and he did not own a strap.

But I remember one day when we were all clattering downstairs at four o'clock, free at last, and Mr Maxton was standing at a corner of the stair, supervising the exodus. All of a sudden he glared at me and a long thin finger snaked out towards me. 'You, boy,' he said, 'Go into that room.'

I wasn't conscious of any wrongdoing whatever. All I knew was that the terrible Maxton was about to deal with me. I was trembling when, the last of the school having descended the stairs, he came into the class-room. I waited for him to produce his famous strap. I could feel it tingling on my palms already.

'Are you a donkey, boy?' he rasped out.

I muttered that I wasn't.

'Then after this don't behave like one,' he said. 'You can go.'

I couldn't believe my ears. I worked it out afterwards that he knew I hadn't been doing anything wrong and that he had no right to punish me. Of course, I still believed in the famous strap.

No so very long after that James Maxton became an M.P., but I didn't forget him. Around the age of fourteen I was still the supreme patriot and I realised who Britain's enemies were. I thought of starting a movement of my own to combat them. I bought a wee blue-covered notebook for one penny and on the first page I wrote:

People To Be Dealt With

No. 1.—James Maxton, M.P.

Years later, when I was a reporter in Glasgow, I covered meetings where James Maxton was the principal speaker. I think he had shot his bolt by then. All I really remember now is sitting at the Press table and looking at his boots, unpolished and scuffed, with one unloosed lace straggling over the stage.

If I may return to Haghill School, however, what I enjoyed most was getting out of it. I had a great desire to go to the pictures. Most of the boys in my class were forever imitating Charlie Chaplin in the play-ground. They would do the Chaplin walk round the janitor's house, waving one leg in the air every time they came to a corner. I felt very left out of it.

It was just the same with Hengler's Circus. The great joy of every boy at Haghill was the annual visit to Hengler's Grande Cirque in Sauchiehall Street, and you were a nobody if you hadn't seen it by the New Year. This particular time I hadn't seen it and I didn't know if I ever would see it.

But it appeared from my schoolmates' conversation that one of the great scenes in the Cowboys and Indians play which ended the show was when the Indians attacked up a gigantic ladder or staircase. Some boys said it was a ladder, others were certain it was a staircase, and that became the main debating point in our class for weeks. I was asked for my opinion. Well, I couldn't admit I had not seen Hengler's so I opted for the view of a boy I liked and said it was a ladder.

Some weeks later my father took the family to the circus and I saw that the Indians attacked quite clearly up a gigantic staircase. But I couldn't go back on what I had said and I spent the rest of the circus season affirming vehemently that it was a ladder, when all the time I knew it was a staircase.

It was about then that I realised that the truth is the best thing. You must have a very good memory to tell lies. Of course, I've told many a lie since then, but I've always regretted it.

I was involved in lies in going to the pictures too. My parents didn't approve of the cinema. However, a great Boy Scout serial was advertised at the Parade Picture House, better known to us as 'the wee buggy', and I prevailed on my mother to let me go every Monday afternoon to the penny matinee.

The Boy Scout serial was most satisfactory—I was a Scout

by this time, in the 37th Glasgow (Regent Place U.F. Church) Troop—but what was far more wonderful was a serial called 'The Clutching Hand', in which Pearl White was the star. The Scout serial went on for a mere eight weeks, but I never let on to my mother. For months I kept going to the wee buggy every Monday afternoon, ostensibly to see the Scouts capture the spies, but actually to watch what, first of all, the Clutching Hand was doing, and then to see the exploits of Harry Houdini in *The Iron Man*.

By the time I left Haghill Primary School and went to Whitehill Higher Grade School, deeper in Dennistoun, I was quite sophisticated and didn't have to tell so many lies. Indeed, I now enjoyed detecting lies in other people. I think I was a very smug wee boy.

At first I enjoyed Whitehill School, except for one awful problem. One of the masters in the junior school was known to us as 'Pimp'. It was said that, on one occasion, he had cried to his class, 'Stand up the boy who pimped.' My problem was that, suppose this teacher asked me to deliver a message to the headmaster and the headmaster asked me who it was from, all I could say was 'Mr Pimp.'

All my life I have been troubled with problems of this sort. I can't recollect a single one of them coming to fruition.

The headmaster was a Mr Fergus Smith, an Olympian figure with a rough voice and a white moustache and beard. We held him in great awe, though we all called him 'Spondee'. Not one of us knew why, and it was many years later that I learned that spondee is a foot of two long syllables, and this was an erudite way of referring to the fact that Mr Fergus Smith had two very big feet.

Of course, I was now involved in learning languages. Automatically we were taught French, by a wonderful character called 'Paddy' McGill. I regarded him with fascinated horror—fascination because he had written a book about French teaching (and we studied it, naturally) and also wrote reports of football matches for a newspaper on Saturday afternoons; horror because he drank, and would come into the class-room after lunch, set the class some problem, and go to sleep.

B

One thing he could not stand was the sound of a pencil dropping on a desk. So, when the bell announced the end of the French period and he was still sound asleep, the whole class would raise their pencils and drop them simultaneously on the desk. Paddy McGill would immediately start awake, ready to take vengeance. Then he'd realise that time was up and dismiss the class. We had a parody about him which went—

> The stag at eve had drunk his fill
> And left the rest to Paddy McGill.

All the same, he taught us some French. I remember when the City Bakeries shop in Alexandra Parade introduced a new dainty—the Gateaux Cake. Well, I knew that meant that it was a cakes cake, but it looked good and I suggested to my mother that I should buy one for the family tea. She agreed and I went into the City Bakeries and asked for a gateaux cake, pronouncing gateaux in the precise manner of Paddy McGill.

The salesgirl said they didn't have any such thing. I assured her that there was one in the window. She looked at me suspiciously and said I'd better point it out to her. So I went outside the shop and, as she came to the window, pointed at the gateaux cake.

I walked back into the shop triumphantly and the salesgirl looked at me with scorn. 'What you mean', she said, 'is a gatoox cake!'

When it came to the time for me to take a second language, the scholars of Whitehill School for the first time got a choice of something other than Latin and Greek. Why I shall never know, but I opted for German. Little was I to realise that many years later I would be one half of the Scottish team in the 'Round Britain Quiz' and Latin would have been much more helpful to me than German ever was.

Only a few of us took German, and I was one of a small band who sat in the very first German class, taken by a young woman teacher who seemed overawed at the enormity of the whole affair. It was just 1919.

The class door opened and the dreaded figure of Mr Fergus Smith appeared. He looked around us grimly. It was obvious that he thought us the scum of the earth.

'This is the German class,' he observed to the teacher, who was too frightened to do more than nod her head and mutter unintelligibly.

'Ah, well,' said the headmaster, 'I suppose you're taking German so that you can tell our late enemies what you think of them.'

It's a strange thing that, though I had three years of French and only two of German, I can understand (and even occasionally speak) German much better than I do French. Or maybe it isn't a strange thing.

I edited a class magazine in my first year and in my second year. The school started its own magazine in my third year, but I was so fed up with school that I refused to contribute. My one idea was to leave as soon as I was fifteen. As soon as May 1921, arrived, I announced that I was leaving when the school closed at the end of June.

Our English teacher was Dr William Merry, a man who had surprised us all by asking if we approved of what the Black and Tans were doing in Ireland and, when we said we did, told us we were a lot of savages. We couldn't understand him at all. British soldiers were always right.

However, one afternoon he went right round the class, asking each boy what he was going to do when he left school. What I wanted, above all else, was to be a writer—or an actor, or an artist, in that order. But how could I say such a soppy thing? The whole class would laugh at me. I thought desperately of some respectable job to choose and, when Dr Merry at last reached me, I stood up and said I wanted to be a bank clerk.

'A bank clerk?' he cried, in his high, querulous voice. 'What on earth do you want to be a bank clerk for?'

That evening I reported this conversation to my parents. My father thought I had answered very sensibly. He couldn't see anything wrong with my being a bank clerk. All I knew was that banks closed at three in the afternoon, and I was beginning to like the idea myself.

'You go back tomorrow', said my father, 'and ask Dr Merry what *he* suggests you should do.'

So I did, and Dr Merry was somewhat taken aback. He hummed and hawed for a while, and then he said, 'I'm told the best jobs are a chartered accountant or an engineer with electrical experience.'

We had a family council over that. It was agreed at once that I would make no kind of engineer, with or without electrical experience. And so, when my schooldays were over and my last long holiday started, I began writing letters of application to chartered accountants' offices in Glasgow. I abandoned all thought of getting on to a newspaper. In my day you did what your parents told you.

When I wore a Bowler Hat

My first job was as an office boy in the single-man firm of Thomas J. Yule, c.a., 69 St Vincent Street, Glasgow, and I saw nothing whatever wrong with going to it wearing a school cap and shorts. Going into 'longs' in those days was a sign of decadence with us. Even the big boys in the Sixth Year at Whitehill, the ones with incipient moustaches, wore shorts as a matter of course.

About the only thing that T. J. Yule, c.a., was notable for was that his was the last name in the Glasgow Telephone Directory in 1921. I took a certain pleasure in that, and it made up to me for the fact that my great ambition, to have my address as one of the stops printed on a tram-car ticket, was never likely to realised. How I envied anyone who stayed at 220 Cumbernauld Road, for example—if that, indeed, was the address on the green ha'penny ticket I remember.

The rest of T. J. Yule's staff consisted of Jimmy Brown, who had arrived a week or two before I did and had some idea of becoming a c.a. apprentice, and Annie Macdonald, typist. T. J. Yule had just started and we didn't have a great deal to do. Indeed, by the time my family had flitted to Riddrie and I was running a local monthly magazine called *This and That*, I was able to duplicate the entire issue in the office in my spare time.

I had a lot to do with the Boy Scouts too, having joined the 37th Glasgow (Regent Place U.F. Church) Troop. I was now going to the United Free Church of Scotland because the 37th Troop did not demand that I should know any catechism. Otherwise I might well have stayed with the Scottish Episcopal Church.

By the time I was seventeen, I was wearing long trousers and a bowler hat and getting 12s. 6d. a week (I'd started at 7s. 6d.), and I signed my indentures as a Chartered Accountant apprentice with T. J. Yule simply because that seemed to be the way my life was to be cast. After all, my father had to pay £50 for this privilege, so I couldn't do anything about it.

But that same week I met my Scoutmaster who asked me how I was getting on. When I told him I had signed my indentures he said, 'But I thought you wanted to be a journalist?' I said I still did. 'Well,' he said, 'why didn't you ask me about it? I could have got you a job on the *Citizen*.' Since the *Glasgow Citizen* was the evening paper my father took and I read it every night, this came doubly hard. I doubt if ever a c.a. apprentice started his apprenticeship so dead set against the job. And I had five years to go.

I spent most of my spare time writing. I edited amateur magazines. I entered for various competitions and soon had an unrivalled collection of cheap fountain pens which would not work. That was the favourite prize in those days. I wrote pantomimes for our Scout Troop to perform (and produced and acted in them as well) and little plays for our Wolf Cubs to present.

One competition I entered for was a daft little crossword run by the columnist 'Argus' in the *Citizen*. He wrote 'Odds and Ends' and I thought he was wonderful. I was sophisticated enough to realise that he must also be 'C.M.' who wrote the interviews with the stage stars who appeared in Glasgow at that time. I thought 'C.M.' stood for 'Citizen Man', but I was to find out fairly soon that it stood for Colin Milne, a man I was going to work with for years.

I won this competition. I looked up the result in the *Citizen* for January 12th, 1925, and there it was—'The winner is John House, Jr., 871 Cumbernauld Road, Riddrie, Glasgow.' I always signed myself John House, Jr., though everybody knew me as Jack. I thought that was the correct thing to do.

The prize from 'Argus' arrived, and what should it be but a big box of cigarettes, and I didn't smoke. Indeed, I have never smoked in my life though once, when slightly drunk, I attempted a cigar without success. I sent a letter of thanks back to 'Argus' and he printed it in his column. Blush-making though it is, I give it here, since it was my first contribution to any journal, other than those I ran myself.

> Dear Argus, I hasten to write you
> Conveying my thanks and delight.
> How often I wish I could sight you,
> Espesh'lly on Saturday night.
> Your foresight, moreover, is showing
> In the gift which you sent, for the joke
> Is that Cross Words, just like it, are going
> And soon they will end in mere smoke.

I don't know why, but I had the convinced idea that I could write verse. I wrote a lot of it for 'This and That.' But printing your own stuff and being printed in a 'real' paper were very different things. All of a sudden, I decided to be a free-lance journalist as well as a c.a. apprentice.

One evening I wrote a 500-words piece in half-an-hour and sent it to *Blackie's Children's Annual* (gone, alas, like our youth too soon!). A week later I received a letter of acceptance and a cheque for one guinea. With my training as a c.a. apprentice, I was able to work out that, if I wrote at the rate of 1,000 words an hour for eight hours a day, five-and-a-half days a week, I would make £102. 18s. a week, which was approximately £102 more than I was getting.

This spurred me to great efforts, and huge numbers of rejection slips. Still, I did manage to get into various newspapers and magazines, and I received an almost indecipherable hand-written letter of acceptance from Sir Owen Seaman, then editor of *Punch*. It was the only thing I ever had published in *Punch*, but I kept that letter from the editor for a long time.

Through A. W. N. Mackenzie, secretary of the Glasgow Boy Scouts Association, I met a Cubmaster named Theo Brown, who had been writing plays for his Wolf Cubs. We got together and produced four plays each, and these were accepted by the firm of nautical and Scout publishers, Brown, Son and Ferguson in Glasgow. The senior member of the firm was James R. Brown and he was Convener of Publicity for the Boy Scouts in Glasgow. I was assistant convener.

We were on a 10 per cent royalty on a book which sold at 1s. 6d. but the first cheque we received came to more than £50. Just about the time the cheque arrived, I was summoned by the studies expert of the Glasgow School of Accountancy, from which I was taking a correspondence course, to explain why my studies had been falling off lately.

I told him I had been rather busy writing a book called *Eight Plays for Wolf Cubs*. He looked at me with scorn. 'What on earth did you do a thing like that for'? he asked. 'For £50,' I replied. I noted his eyes glaze slightly and he brought the interview to an abrupt finish. I think he was going off to write a book of plays for Wolf Cubs. Incidentally, I am still receiving a pound or two a year from that book I wrote nearly forty years ago. I wish I could say the same for some other books I've written.

I wrote for everybody and anything. In one of P. G. Wodehouse's recent novels there is a picture of a free-lance journalist who could and did turn his hand to anything. That was me. And, though manuscripts kept coming back like a song, I sold enough to make a small account in the Dennistoun Branch of the Glasgow Savings Bank. I might still have been banking there had it not been for *Poppy's Paper*.

Poppy's Paper was a weekly magazine for women, and it disappeared, perhaps deservedly, a long time ago. It specialised in short stories about love. I decided to have a bash at this, for I had always admired Christine Jope-Slade and Berta Ruck in my mother's copies of *Home Notes* and *Home Chat*. I couldn't tell you why I chose *Poppy's Paper* for my own efforts. Maybe it was an inborn sense of values. At any rate, *Poppy's Paper* took what I wrote at one guinea per 1,000 words. My short stories were always 3,000 words long and appeared under the name of Elaine Armstrong.

All went well until *Poppy's Paper* introduced that sort of cheque which was also a receipt. On the back of the cheque was something to the effect that the author had sold first British serial rights of . . . and then the name of the great work was inserted . . . and you signed it across a tuppenny stamp.

So the day dawned when I had to go into the Dennistoun branch of the Glasgow Savings Bank, where I knew everybody personally, and hand across the counter a cheque on which was written, 'Why Did You Ever Kiss Me?' I blushed a lot in those days, and I was very red in the face as I explained that this was only the title of a story I'd written.

The next time I went into the bank, I heard the murmur go round—'Why did you ever kiss me?' It was too much. I gave up my career as Elaine Armstrong and never wrote another word for *Poppy's Paper*. (Maybe *that's* why it didn't last so very long!) And I also gave up my account in the Dennistoun branch of the Glasgow Savings Bank and put my money into an ordinary commercial bank in Renfield Street.

2

Somewhere along the line of my double life as a Chartered Accountant apprentice and free-lance journalist I got a brilliant idea. Communists were very sinister figures in the Twenties and we still looked on them as portrayed by Alfred Leete—swarthy European types, wearing a big black hat and a voluminous cloak which only half concealed the fact that they had a smoking, circular bomb in each hand.

My father got the *Daily Mail* every morning and it was usually hot on the Communist's trail. My brilliant idea was to join the Communist Party, discover their dark secrets and then reveal all in a series of articles, presumably to be printed in the *Daily Mail*. I decided that I had better do this in disguise, so I went along to Woolworth's in Sauchiehall Street and bought a pair of spectacles with ordinary glass instead of lens inside the rims. And, since I wore a bowler hat

at all times, I borrowed an old soft hat of my father's and felt
my disguise was complete. In self defence I can only say that
up to that time, I had never seen myself in profile.

I looked up the *Evening Times*, where the Communist
advertisements appeared, and saw that one was announced
for a coming Sunday in Partick Burgh Hall, to be addressed
by H. Pollitt. That was for me. On that Sunday evening I
donned my disguise of spectacles and soft hat and out I went
from 871 Cumbernauld Road, Riddrie. I must have walked
a good 200 yards before a chap gave me the nod and said,
'Hello, Jack!' But I reasoned that the Communists would not
penetrate my disguise and on I went to take the appropriate
tram-car to Partick.

It was, I recall, a bright summer's night and the setting sun
slanted through the long windows of the Burgh Hall on to H.
Pollitt and other Communists. It lit the notices saying 'No
Smoking' placed round the front of the balcony and illum-
ined the faces of the comrades who leaned over the balcony
smoking. I cannot honestly say that I was impressed by H.
Pollitt, or any of the other speakers. Perhaps my main reaction was one of disappointment, because I could see
nothing whatever that I could make a story out of, far less a
dynamic series of revelations.

The meeting ended with the announcement that we would
sing 'The Internationale', and half-a-dozen quavering voices
actually did attempt it. I felt they'd have done much better
with 'The Red Flag'. Then it was time for me to join the
party. Out in the entrance hall a man was sitting at a green
baize card-table. I went up to him and said I wanted to join
the Communist Party. He was delighted and asked my name
and address. I gave the name of Alfred Abbott care of House,
871 Cumbernauld Road, Riddrie, Glasgow, E.1. He wrote it
in a book, then on a card, gave me the card and said, 'That'll
be a shilling, please.'

I was astounded. I didn't know people actually paid to
become members of the Communist Party. Where was all
this Red Gold I'd been reading about? Not only that, but all
I had in my pocket at that precise moment was one shilling. I
handed it over, took the card, and then had to walk all the

four miles or so back to Riddrie because I had no money for the tram-car.

It was a disappointing evening. What was even more disappointing was that the only communications I ever received from the Communist Party were two invitations to whist drives and one to a dance. That was hardly what I was looking for. I did not go to the dance or the whist drives and I assume that my membership lapsed. By this time, in any case, I had discovered the delights of 'ghosting' articles for stage stars and the Communist Party was losing its glamour.

I thought no more about it until one evening, at a Boy Scout County Council meeting in the Elmbank Street headquarters, I was attending as assistant publicity convener when a letter was read from the Chief Scout, then Sir Robert Baden-Powell. This letter revealed that the Communist Party had declared war on the Boy Scout movement and would try to disrupt it in any possible way. The Chief Scout warned us to be prepared for anything, but particularly not to accept challenges to debate from the Communists. I think he had something there.

Anyway, I recalled my own Communist days and at the end of the reading of the Chief Scout's letter I got up and said that, speaking as a member of the Young Communist's League, the four of us were too busy to be doing anything about the Boy Scouts. This got a cheap laugh and I sat down, pleased with myself. At the end of the meeting my publicity convener, the James R. Brown who was to publish my *Eight Plays for Wolf Cubs*, came over and asked if it was really true that I was a Communist. I told him the story of how I'd gone to the meeting at Partick, paid my bob and got nowhere.

Next morning I received a postcard from James R. Brown. It said simply, 'Phone Harold Dickson, *Evening News*, re Communists v. Scouts.' I understood from this that Mr Brown, as publicity convener for the Glasgow Scout County Council, wanted me to put this Mr Dickson in the picture about the Communist campaign against the Scout movement. So I prepared some pretty stupid material and, when I went into my c.a. office, I 'phoned the *Evening News*. (I should explain that we didn't have a 'phone at 871 Cumbernauld Road.)

I got Mr Dickson, explained who I was, and started to read my prepared statement. He listened for only a few seconds, then said, 'Just a minute. Are you the chap who got up at last night's County Council meeting and said you were a Communist?'

Like a fool, I replied, 'Yes, I am.'

'And are you a Communist?' he asked.

Taken aback, I said, 'Yes, but—'

And the telephone line went dead.

That worried me a bit. It was all I could do to keep my attention on Chartered Accountancy for the rest of the morning. When I left the office for lunch I got to the corner of West George Street and Renfield Street and there was a newsvendor with a big *Evening News* poster. It said simply, 'Glasgow's Communist Scoutmaster'.

I bought a copy and found I was on the front page. Anyone who needs reassurance on this point need only go to the Mitchell Library in Glasgow and ask to see the *Evening News* for Thursday, December 8th, 1927. The headlines were in enormous type for the time. They read—'Scout Sensation. Glasgow Scoutmaster as a Communist. "For Espionage Purposes." Remarkable Statement.'

The story was 'by Harold Dickson.' It told how the Communist Party had declared war on the Boy Scout Movement and gave details of the Chief Scout's letter which had been read to the Scout County Council on the previous night. But, Mr Dickson went on to say, all the Communists' plans, as far as Glasgow was concerned, would come to naught because a brave young Glasgow Scoutmaster had joined the party for espionage purposes and would let the Scouts know all the Communists' plans in advance.

There was a good deal more guff of the same sort. It seemed to me that my Publicity Convener had sold me down the river. I didn't know then, of course, that Harold was famous for making wonderful stories out of practically nothing and the truth seldom worried him. Later I was to know him well and marvel at his imagination. Just at the moment, however, I was horrified—and worried about possible reactions from the Communist Party. I knew that, if they looked up the Glasgow Boy Scout Directory, they would not see the name of Alfred Abbott anywhere. But I had given my home address when I paid my bob and joined the Party at Partick, and there were three different entries which said House, 871 Cumbernauld Road, Riddrie, Glasgow, E.1.

I wondered if there might be a bomb through the window that night. But first, I thought I had better go up to Scout headquarters in Elmbank Street and have a word with the Association Secretary. So at five o'clock up I went and discovered that the Executive were holding a meeting—about me. I was invited to join them and spent a very mauvais quarter-of-an-hour indeed.

Then the Executive got down to deciding what to do about the matter.

All of a sudden one bright chap got an idea. 'Just a minute, Jack,' he said to me, 'You're not really a Scoutmaster, are you?' I said no, I wasn't, I was an Assistant Scoutmaster. 'Good,' said he, 'we'll deny it!'

And so a denial that any Glasgow Scoutmaster was a secret member of the Communist Party was prepared and sent to the *Evening News*. I went home, said not a word to my family about all this, and spent a sleepless night.

Next day I couldn't wait to leave the office at lunch to get the *News*. I found I was still front-page news. Harold Dickson gave first of all the denial of the Glasgow Boy Scouts Association that any Glasgow Scoutmaster was a member of the Communist Party. Below that appeared a statement by the Communist Party denying that any Communist was a member of the Boy Scouts. But Harold went on to say that the *Evening News* was in possession of the name and address of the gallant young Glasgow Scoutmaster and would publish them if necessary.

I spent another sleepless night. Next, day, thank God, there was a murder, or something else that took Harold off my neck, and 'Glasgow's Communist Scoutmaster' disappeared for ever from the pages of the *News*. But Mr Dickson would have been a very disappointed man indeed if he had learned about the sequel to all this.

The Editor of the *Citizen* received an anonymous note saying that, on the following evening at 7.30 a party of Communists were going to 'attack' Scout headquarters in Elmbank Street. Arthur S. Hedderwick was editor at that time and he conceived it his duty to pass the note to Scout headquarters without making any editorial use of it. Scout headquarters immediately got in touch with the police. You must remember that 'Red Clydeside' was still the label pinned on Glasgow, and even Glaswegians were inclined to believe it.

On that evening, about 6.30 a whole platoon of police arrived at Elmbank Street and were strategically placed throughout the building. They could not be observed from outside, of course. Some half dozen plain clothes men were stationed at either end of Elmbank Street, acting casual-like. Some of the top brass of the Glasgow Scout movement were also in the building, together with A. W. N. Mackenzie, the secretary, and a woman cleaner whose business it was to be there anyway.

About 7.25 p.m. a group of four worried-looking men entered Elmbank Street from the St Vincent Street end. They looked at the plain clothes men hanging about the corner and may well have observed the other plain clothes men farther up the street. At any rate, they went up the stairs to Scout headquarters and rang the bell. The woman cleaner answered the door and one young man said, 'Is the secretary in?' 'No,' lied the cleaner. The young man said 'Oh', and the cleaner closed the door.

The four of them stood on the steps for a minute and talked. Then they had another look at the plain clothes men and hurried down Elmbank Street and into the night. That was the end of the Communist attack on Scout headquarters.

Just think of what Harold Dickson might have made of that! But Arthur Hedderwick never let bug, and the Scouts kept mum. As for me, I decided that it would be safer to be inside a newspaper office than outside one, and determined that, as soon as my indenture was up, I'd leave chartered accountancy and get on to a newspaper staff some way.

3

By this time I was writing for anybody and anything. I'd had my first articles published in the *Citizen*. They were on Boy Scout subjects! I was the Scottish correspondent of *Film Weekly* and wrote a fine piece on how the talkies would never get anywhere in Scotland. I wrote for a monthly magazine called *The Amateur Theatre* and out of that I became Scottish man for *The Hotel Review*.

This was how I met F. Rupert Crew, who ran a literary agency in London and asked me if I'd like to 'ghost' articles for stage stars. Well, it wasn't called 'ghosting' because, although it's become so respectable today, it was regarded as hack work then. What I was asked to do was to provide 'signed' articles. That meant that each week I sent Mr Crew a list of stage people appearing in Glasgow during the following week, and suggested subjects I might interview them on. He ticked off the ones he wanted, I did the interview, then sent the article to the star, who actually did sign it. For this I might get as much as five guineas a time, less Mr Crew's commission, and that was big money.

So I was a C.A. apprentice by day and all sorts of people by night. I had discovered a simple way to avoid becoming a chartered accountant. I had already passed the C.A. Intermediate Examination and was now due to sit my Finals. But you couldn't sit your Finals without taking a Scots Law class at Glasgow University, and I found that all I had to do was to forget to matriculate and that postponed chartered accountancy for another year.

About this time, in any event, my father was having trouble at Blochairn Steelworks. He was now secretary of the company. I never got to the bottom of the trouble, but I gather that my father was being too generous to some of the workers. At any rate, he was demoted and then resigned and in the general gloom at home my avoidance of matriculation was hardly even noticed.

My first signed article was 'Is Variety Dead? by Arthur Roberts'. I was mad about the stage and I knew what a great comedian Arthur Roberts had been. He was in Glasgow at the old Metropole in a 'Veterans of Variety' show. The only other real star in it was Tom Costello and it was quite electrifying to see the old men and women sitting around the stage as in a minstrel show, and then come to life as they did their own turns.

I went to see Arthur Roberts in his theatrical digs near Eglinton Street and was shown into his room at the precise moment that he was sitting half naked, rubbing embrocation into his lower back. 'Get out!' he shouted and the landlady apologised to me. I stood in the dark hall until Mr Roberts was dressed and opened the door. He explained that he suffered from arthritis and then went on to tell me that variety was dead. This was the first time I had ever interviewed anyone and I was terrified.

However, I persisted and was Carl Brisson, Owen Nares, George Robey and a wheen of others. I was even Dora Maugham. I don't think anybody will remember her now but she sang vaguely saucy songs and was billed as 'The Worst Woman in America'. I was Annette Kellerman too. She had been a great swimming champion in the U.S.A., had appeared in several films, and was now spending her declining years appearing in music hall programmes, diving into a tank and doing swimming tricks. I interviewed her in her dressing room at the Empire Theatre. She sat in the shadow with a hat pulled down low over her face. Even so, I could see it was a ruin of a face and realised how much make-up she must have used in her performance.

I found that the more important the stage stars were, the nicer they behaved to me. Lilian Braithwaite was wonderful. She took immense trouble with me. I was Lilian Braithwaite on three occasions and I wish very much that I could read the articles now. As I look back, I think it's amazing that established actors and actresses should have been so kind to a fledging journalist still wet behind the ears.

Of course, it wasn't always beer and skittles. An aged star of light opera, Hayden Coffin, gave me a gracious interview, then pointed out that he signed articles only for money. But, of course, I didn't know whether I'd get any money or not. It depended on F. Rupert Crew's ability to sell an article signed by Hayden Coffin. I asked him if ten shillings would do, and he said it would. So I handed over ten shillings and lived sparingly for a week.

Then there was Ernest Thesiger, who received me in his dressing room in a semmit, a pair of trousers and a necklace. He insisted on giving me a photograph of himself wearing this necklace and suggested it would be ideal to go with the article. I took it home and burned it so that my parents wouldn't know the kind of people I was meeting in the theatre!

Easily my most dramatic interview was with Sir Frank Benson. His company were doing *Hamlet* at the Theatre Royal, and he had reached the age when he preferred to play the Ghost and let some youngster, such as Gerald Lawrence, play the Prince. I was shown into his dressing room and sat there feeling awful. I didn't think Sir Frank Benson was a great actor but he put the fear of death in me.

Suddenly the door opened and Sir Frank stormed in. Maybe it hadn't been a very good audience, but he was certainly in a temper. I'd asked him to talk about 'What is Wrong With The Theatre Today?' and he was just in the mood for it. He was wearing an elaborate suit of heavy armour. He was certainly the best-dressed ghost of Hamlet's father I have ever seen. His dresser started to undo the armour while Sir Frank thundered his opinion of the Theatre Today at me.

The trouble was that he couldn't stay still. When he got really roused about some iniquity of the stage he strode up and down the dressing room, with the unfortunate dresser scrabbling on his knees after him, trying to undo the leg-pieces of armour. This was bad enough, but every now and then Sir Frank would stop and demand, 'Read that bit back to me.'

Here I was in dire straits. I couldn't write shorthand, and it was my custom in doing these signed articles to make my own sort of notes, regardless of the actual words being spoken by the star. So, when Sir Frank Benson asked me to repeat what he had said, I could only make wild guesses.

Soon he made it obvious that he regarded me as the most ineffectual interviewer he had ever met. He got to the point where he would say something and then repeat it slowly, watching me get it down.

How glad I was when Sir Frank graciously indicated that the interview was over. I staggered out into the ordinary world and wondered if it wouldn't be better just to stay with chartered accountancy. But, strange to say, I wrote the article, Sir Frank Benson signed it, and it appeared in *The Daily Sketch*.

Since these days I have never been anybody else in print. But sometimes I look back and realise what a great time I had while other chaps were just going to night classes.

4

One of my troubles when interviewing stage stars was being offered a drink. Apart from the ritual glass of port at home on Hogmanay, I didn't drink at all. But in 1928 the call of the wild reached me and I suggested to my Scoutmaster, Evan Eccleston, that he and I should go to Paris for a week before going on to the international Scout Jamboree at Arrowe Park in Birkenhead. We had been at the first Jamboree at Wembley in 1924, and that was the first time I ever saw London. I was young enough to think it was wonderful then, although my only clear memory is of three of us walking along Fleet Street one August evening.

All Scottish Scouts at Wembley wore the kilt and, thus dressed, we had got about half way along Fleet Street when we were stopped by a middle-aged gentleman who wore a black jacket, striped trousers, a big hat, a come-to-Jesus collar and a bow tie. I'd like to say that he had a monocle as well, but that isn't true. Anyhow, he looked at us, indicated our kilts and said, 'What's that?'

We answered that it was the kilt, whereupon he asked, 'But why do you wear it?' We said, 'Because we come from

Scotland.' He replied, 'Good God!' and walked on.

Well, I suppose I was a bit more sophisticated four years later. I'd been in London once or twice and I thought it was time I conquered Paris. Evan was a student at the Glasgow School of Art, so he was all for it. We booked through Poly Tours, went to London by bus (which was an arduous journey in those days) and crossed to Calais. We boarded our train for Paris just as the dusk came down and soon it was announced that dinner was served.

So along we went, got a table, addressed our inadequate French to the menu and thought about drink. In Glasgow people who knew all about France had counselled us. 'You can't drink the water,' they said. 'It's bad and will give you tummy trouble. You can't drink tea, because the French can't make tea. You can drink coffee, but it gets awfully monotonous. The beer is sour and aerated waters are too sweet. The thing to do is drink wine. That's what the French do themselves and it has no bad effects.'

All this was in my mind when the head steward asked us what we would like to drink. I said boldly that we would like to drink wine. He smiled slightly and asked, 'Red or white?' This was a poser. I hadn't realised there was a choice. We solved it brilliantly by ordering a half bottle of red for me and a half bottle of white for Evan.

Until we entered the dining car we had been in a compartment full of French people who seemed a rather nasty lot to us. They were unfriendly and they talked too loudly and too long. But when we got back to the compartment after our wine, we found that, somehow or other, they had changed completely. They were very friendly indeed and they roared with laughter when we tried to speak French, just as we roared when they tried to speak English.

We arrived at our small, second-class hotel just off the Champs Elysees. As we were signing in and checking our bags, a fat man came up to us and introduced himself as the son of the proprietor of our hotel. He bade us welcome and said would we like to see a little of Paris that night. It was his job to do the ordering of meat, fish and vegetables for the hotel, so he went out about 11 p.m. and had a drink or two before going round the markets. He appeared to be about seventeen or eighteen and we looked on him with great respect, and said we would like to see a little of Paris.

As I see it now, he must have been a nice chap and he probably knew very little about the night life of Paris. He was just showing off a bit. But we were impressed and when he took us to one of the open-air cafes on the Champs Elysees, we realised that this was the life. But there remained the problem of what to drink.

We explained to him that we didn't drink alcohol at all at home. We were prepared to drink wine with meals while we were in Paris, but what should we do at other times? 'Ah', said our fat friend, 'it is simple. Sherry Cobbler!'

He ordered the drinks and I found myself with a fairly tall glass of light brown liquid with some cherries on top. Immediately I came to the conclusion that I had misunderstood his pronunciation and that this was a soft drink called Cherry Cobbler. So we stayed with Sherry Cobbler throughout our week in Paris and couldn't understand how it was that sometimes it was crowned with cherries and at other times with quite different fruit. Nor could we understand why, on a night of Sherry Cobblers, we were apt to go down the Champs Elysees jumping over the seats.

However, that is how I learned to drink, and I've never looked back. It was quite a change to go from Paris to Bootle where Evan had relatives, and attend the Scout Jamboree.

Before I leave my first visit to Paris, though, I must relate a Cautionary Tale. One afternoon we booked a bus tour to Versailles. It was, I recall, an open-air charabanc. The guide was an Austrian who looked like Adolph Menjou. He asked everybody in the bus to tell him where they came from so that he could work out the languages he was going to use. When he came to us, I thought that Scotland was too small a country to be mentioned in Paris and said we came from England.

'What part of England?' asked the guide.

'Glasgow,' I said, with a sinking heart.

'Ah, you mean you come from Scotland,' said the Austrian.

'That is not England at all. Vive Scotland! Vive Harry Lauder!'

This, I realise, is banal in the extreme. But it taught me to respect my own country. I realise full well that too many Scots make too much of Scotland when they go abroad. I'd rather they did that than betray their own country as I did.

5

I did so many damned stupid things in those days, though they seemed excellent ideas at the time. Of course, I've always felt that I'd like to try anything at least once, and that has led me into a lot of trouble in my time.

My family went to Joppa for a holiday—Joppa near Edinburgh, I mean, and I hung around Letta's Pavilion on the Portobello promenade because I was so stage-struck. I went to every change of programme, and I can still see in my mind's eye Harry Chambers, the Edinburgh comic; Jack Wakefield singing 'On the Road to Anywhere'; and the dashing blonde Embert Sisters with their saucy song which included the thrilling lines—

> They had one or two rows,
> Then he pulled off her blouse—
> They had a wonderful, wonderful time!

So, when an amateur night was announced, I decided to enter for it. I wrote a monologue especially for the occasion, in which, with a certain amount of insight, I cast myself as a bit of a saftie. I rehearsed it in Portobello Public Park before my brother George who said he thought it was all right. (This is high praise in Scotland and it sent my spirits up considerably.) I didn't tell my parents about this venture, and only a couple of my brothers accompanied me to Letta's Pavilion on the night.

When the amateur competition was announced, three of us went boldly forward. One was an elderly chap with glasses, who turned out to be a baritone. Then there was a very plain young lady who was a soprano. And there was me.

The elderly chap went on first and sang 'Dark Lochnagar' to moderate applause. Then it was my turn. Letta's pianist had asked what my opening music was and I replied that anything would do. And just as she was playing an entrance of some sort, a brilliant idea came to me. Every evening Harry Chambers ran on to the stage and shouted 'How's Club?' Don't ask me what he meant. All I knew that it got a round of applause.

So, when the entrance music ended, I dashed on to the stage and shouted 'How's Club?' It went badly. Then I started my monologue, and it went worse. I struggled on amid boos and jeers and suddenly I noticed a nice-looking young man sitting in the front row with a girl. He was gently waving his hand in an indication to me to get off the stage. That was enough. I went. However, in the wings Jack Wakefield patted me on the shoulder and said, 'They wouldn't listen to you, son.' He became an instant hero to me.

Another daft thing I did several times was to go into places where I had no right to be and pretend I was a foreigner if I was discovered. I managed this successfully when I trespassed through a farm at Stepps on the north-east of Glasgow. When the farmer, a nasty piece of work, raged at me, I replied calmly in French of a sort and all he could do was point at the nearest gate and wave me out.

My firm had an audit at a grocer's shop in Bearsden. So one day, at lunchtime, I went along to Bearsden Academy, strolled in and had a look around a little museum place one stair up. Along came the janitor, demanding what I was doing there. I replied in German and after a little he just shook his head and walked away. It was only later that I wondered what I'd have done if he had taken me to a teacher who could speak German. I could have ended in the nick that way.

However, these things didn't cost me anything, except pride in the case of Letta's Prom Pavilion. What did cost me money was my efforts to be a song-writer. I liked taking correspondence courses. I even enjoyed the School of Accountancy one because it included free lessons in psychology with the ordinary lessons. I'd had the Premier School of

Journalism course, which I thought was absolutely wonderful. So, when I saw a School of Song-writing Course, I entered as a pupil right away.

For some time I had been writing songs for my various pantomimes and other plays, but I thought it would be a great idea to make some money out of this gift of mine. Alas, I never did. But I did have a song published and how I wish I had a copy by me now. I saw an advertisement for a firm—called Kennedy, I think at this distance of time—wanting lyrics to be put to music. So I sent them two of my best numbers, ones which had actually been praised by the British School of Song-writing.

Kind Kennedy wrote back and said he'd buy the rights of one of the songs for half-a-guinea and that I would receive royalties as soon as it was published. For the other, 'Arizona Aeroplane', he suggested publication right away. But publishing a song was a grave financial risk and he asked me if I'd contribute three guineas to the cost of the music plates. Quick as a flash, I worked out that I'd only really be out two-and-a-half guineas and I'd have a song published. Also I'd get 100 free copies to my own cheek and, since the publication price was one shilling, I had only to sell these copies to make a profit, no matter what else happened.

I agreed with good old Kennedy right away. In due course I received my hundred copies—possibly the only hundred actually printed—and there was 'Arizona Aeroplane' in all its glory, as played by a famous band I'd never heard of, and my name as lyric-writer on it. Oh, I was the proud man.

I took 'Arizona Aeroplane' round two or three of the music shops in the East End of Glasgow. They were very kind and said they'd take half-a-dozen copies and see if they could sell them. But I never had the courage to go back and ask if there was any money owing to me. Kennedy had got another sucker.

Although I have no copy of 'Arizona Aeroplane', I can still remember the words of the chorus. Perhaps, before I give you them in all their sheer majesty, I should explain that the Twenties was a time when everybody was going

back to somewhere. I was much affected by songs like
'Swanee', 'Shufflin' Along', 'My Home in Tennessee', and so
on. It struck me that everybody was going by train or boat or
shuffle or even just walking, and that there was room for the
most modern method. So—

> Put me on that Arizona aeroplane,
> Aeroplane, right as rain.
> Let me fly into the deep blue sky—
> I got to get to Arizona 'fore I die.
> Home, sweet home, from the aerodrome,
> To see my folks again.
> You can tell the feller
> To wind up the propellor
> On that Arizona Aeroplane.

All the while my chartered accountancy droned drearily on.
But by this time my apprenticeship was over and my indentures had been run. By now I had left T. J. Yule and
joined a firm called Russ and Cree, who were considerably
more advanced. They were advanced enough to see that I
wasn't getting anywhere and one day, as we rode in a tram-
car down to an audit in Govan, one of the partners, J. R.
Davidson, said to me, 'Jack, do you really want to be a
chartered accountant?'

I said no, I didn't and he replied, 'Well, you'll have to
make your mind up.' I recall it was a fine morning in July
and I said, 'If I don't get a job on a newspaper by October,
I'll matriculate and take my law classes and sit my Finals.'
J. R. Davidson gave me a pitying look and that was the subject closed.

I reported this to my father and mother who took it very
badly indeed. Although they were Episcopalians, they called
in my Regent Place minister, the Rev. J. McCallum Robertson, to give me some good advice about staying with chartered
accountancy. I was considerably shaken.

But I had a breathing space and the first thing I did was
to write to the editor of the *Citizen* and ask if I could get a job
on his paper. By reply came a letter inviting me to see him. I
couldn't believe it. My knees were very weak indeed when I
climbed the stairs to the old *Citizen* office in St Vincent Place.

Arthur Hedderwick, the editor, was the third generation, if I remember rightly, of the family which had started the paper. He had been trained in the law, but he took over the editorship of the *Citizen* when his father retired. He was a nice chap, but he lived in Helensburgh and was a bit of a snob. To me, at that moment, he was a prince among men, a Northcliffe who was looking for a young eagle.

Mr Hedderwick said right away that there wasn't a job for me on the *Citizen*. But, he said, he liked the work I had been doing for the paper, and he hoped I'd continue to write for it. 'You have the light touch,' he observed gravely. "That's a very good thing to have—the light touch.'

I gulped my thanks, for I was as disappointed as hell. What good was 'the light touch' to a man who wanted to be on the staff of a newspaper?' I went back to the C.A.'s office and wondered if I should try the *News*. The previous Hogmanay I had achieved a minor triumph in having a whole-page article in the *News* entitled 'My New Year Resolution'. For this I had used the 'signed article' technique on the stars in the Christmas pantomies and musical shows. I'd gone to Harold Dickson and said that, after he'd made me 'Glasgow's Communist Scoutmaster', he owed me something. So the New Year resolutions of the stars appeared. I wondered if I should try this line of blackmail again.

But just a week later came another letter from Arthur Hedderwick, asking me to call at St Vincent Place. This time, when I achieved the presence, the editor said he had a job for me. Unexpectedly a reporter had left and the chief telephonist was being moved up. So would I like to be the chief telephonist, and could I write shorthand? I replied yes to the first question and no the second. No matter, said Mr Hedderwick, I could learn shorthand while doing the job. He recommended Gregg's system instead of Pitman's because, he thought, though there was no difference in the actual taking of notes, Gregg's was easier to learn.

I promised that I would contact Gregg's that very day. I was in the seventh heaven. He reminded me that I would be on three months' probation, and said that my salary would be £3. 15s.

First I told the partners of Russ and Cree that I was casting aside chartered accountancy for ever. They did not seem unduly worried. Indeed, they gave me their blessing. Then I went home and performed the much more difficult task of telling my father and mother. They were very gloomy indeed.

'How much did the editor say your salary was?' asked my mother.

'£3. 15s.,' I answered, rather proudly.

'That'll be a month,' she said, and I suddenly realised that Mr Hedderwick hadn't actually said whether it was £3. 15s. a week or £3. 15s. a month. At that moment I was highly paid for an apprentice C.A. and I was getting £1. 15s. a week. Was I going into journalism at a sacrifice? Oh, well, I didn't care. This was what I wanted to do.

Change to a Soft One

I spent my first week in the *Citizen* office waiting anxiously for Friday. When I opened my pay packet with trembling hands I found it was £3. 15s a week all right. This made a tremendous difference. When I was getting £1. 15s. a week, I gave £1 to my mother and spent the 15s in riotous living. Now I was able to hand over £2 a week and live like a lord myself.

£1 was a lot of money in 1928, and it was all the more important in our house, where my father was alternating between spells of unemployment and clerking jobs beneath his powers. But you were glad to get anything at all to do then. My sudden affluence was welcome and even my mother's brow cleared slightly, though she could not forgive me entirely for having thrown up such a dignified profession as chartered accountancy. I feel she thought, too, that I might not last long in journalism. My mother had the proper Scottish modesty about her children.

Mind you, she could have been right about my position as chief telephonist. I was totally unequipped for the job. I consider now that, if I had been editor of the *Citizen*, I would not have taken me on. In essence, the job was to take down in shorthand the 'phoned-in reports from all over Scotland, but mainly from our own reporters in Glasgow and the West. Then you transcribed these into long-hand (we had few typewriters then, and the telephone boys were certainly not allowed to use them) and took them through to the chief sub-editor.

As chief telephonist I had various other jobs to do, but the essential point was that I couldn't write shorthand. I was learning as rapidly as possible at the de Bear School in West George Street, and in three months I reached a speed of 100 words a minute, which was quite adequate for the job. But until then I had to take down reports in longhand with the few squiggles of Gregg that I knew.

I got into trouble on my very first day. My predecessor in the job, now a very new reporter, 'phoned in a story from a Glasgow police court. I took it down easily enough and placed it before the chief sub. To this day I can't tell you what was wrong with it, but some technical point was missing and I was judged guilty. I still recall the chief sub shaking his head and saying, 'I don't blame you. I blame the man who hired you.'

This didn't make me very happy. Nor did the situation by which we were regarded as the office boys to the reporters. A reporter had only to shout 'Boy!' and one of the four of us had to jump to it and carry his copy through to the subs' room or get him cigarettes or perform some other menial job. It was a bit difficult to take at the age of 22, but I decided that, if I wanted to stay in a newspaper, it had to be accepted.

It was many years later that I learned that I was actually resented when I took the job over. There were three tele-phonists already there, and the general feeling was that one of them should have got a move up and anyone new coming in would be at the end of the queue. And in came a chap from outside who couldn't even write shorthand! I was quite oblivious of this situation, which says a lot for my three compatriots, Jimmy McLaren (now motoring correspondent of the *Glasgow Herald*), Matt Irwine boxing expert for the *Evening Times* (now dead) and Johnny Boyd (now editor of the Stranraer newspaper).

As chief telephonist I had to be in at 7.45 each morning, when I met the early sub-editor who was going through the morning papers for suitable stories for our first edition. (The first edition of evening newspapers is partly a rag-bag of morning stuff, because it's seldom that enough news has happened to fill the paper at that time of day.) He cut the stories out and it was my job to rewrite the opening paragraph, put a new heading on the piece, and pass it through to the subs.

Saturday was my big day, in the winter time anyway, because that was football day, when the reporters' room was crammed with men brought in from outside, many of them teachers, to take down the football reports. Myself, I presided at the Exchange-Telegraph 'phone and it was my responsibility to shout out the half-time and full-time scores as they came in, so that my minions could write them in on the specially prepared score-sheets and we'd get them out to an avid public as soon as possible. There was no real radio coverage then, and the football fan depended on the newspapers. It was said that the *Evening Times* Saturday edition could reach half-a-million circulation on a day when Rangers and Celtic both won.

Once the final scores were in, I had to pay the extra men. I had a bag full of wee envelopes for this and I rather enjoyed it. Most of them got 7s 6d. for the afternoon's work. But it was somewhat embarrassing at Christmas time to find that some of these chaps thought it necessary to give me a Christmas present. If I remember rightly, I received five packets of cigarettes and a small box of chocolates.

One other job came my way for a time. I was appointed joke editor! On the back page of the *Citizen* was a column headed 'Varieties'. This consisted simply of one joke after another, in the order of the number of lines of each joke. To compile this column I was given copies of *Tit Bits*, *Answers*, and various other periodicals, and I had to cut out the jokes, paste them on to copy paper and send them to the case-room. They'd come back to me in the form of galleys and each day I'd select the jokes for next day's paper.

It was a time-wasting rather than a thought-provoking job and I gave as little time and thought to it as possible. But one day I was summoned by the chief sub-editor, whose nostrils flared when he was put out. They were flaring like mad when I went through. He pointed to one of the jokes and said, 'How the hell did *that* get in?' I read the joke—and I wish now that I could remember what it was—but could see nothing wrong with it. I said so.

'Don't you know the dirty version?' he demanded. I admitted I didn't. '**My God,**' he cried in anguish, 'how the bloody hell do you expect to run a joke column if you don't know the so-and-so dirty stories?'

That's how I lost my job as joke editor. It didn't worry me one bit.

Gradually I felt I was a newspaperman and so was inspired to throw away my symbol of serfdom, the bowler hat, and buy a dashing soft hat with a snap brim. I was writing occasional pieces for the *Citizen* (though I wasn't paid for them now!) and in my very first week on the staff I'd been given a reportorial job. It happened because so many people were on holiday and the assistant chief reporter was ill.

Nobody had told me anything about anything on the *Citizen*, a situation which was to exist throughout my service with the newspaper, and I assumed that a kindly bloke named Michael McArdle was the chief reporter. Actually, he was merely the senior reporter. The chief reporter was off on holiday. Anyhow, Michael McArdle came to me and said that John Logie Baird, the inventor of television, was in Glasgow and that I was to join him at the St. Enoch Hotel at 10 a.m. and accompany him to Glasgow University, where he would give a demonstration of his invention. Then I'd come back and write about it.

I was delighted and appalled at the same time. It was one thing to sit at home and write an article for the *Citizen*. It was a completely different thing to go out in the morning, see something and write an article about it immediately. I went down to St. Enoch Hotel full of foreboding.

In the lobby I met John Logie Baird. He seemed to me a small man, with a lot of hair, friendly eyes and a good deal of egg about his chin. He had obviously just finished breakfast. I can't tell how many other people were there, but I went up to Glasgow University in a taxi with John Logie Baird and two reporters. I gazed on them with awe. They were Jackie Robertson of the *Evening News* (later to become an editor of mine) and Eddie Anderson of the *Evening Times*. Each exuded efficiency. Indeed, they seemed slightly scornful of John Logie Baird. Maybe it was the egg on his chin.

At Gilmorehill we were conducted into the bowels of the earth. Baird was using two underground rooms for his demonstration. He wanted to prove that he could send an image from the first room to a screen in the second room. He had an old dummy, which looked as if it had once been a ventriloquist's doll. Well, he did it. I can't tell you why I wasn't more impressed. Probably it was my sheer ignorance of the amazing advance in this department of science.

What was really worrying me was my sheer ignorance in the department of reporting. Jackie and Eddie were harrying John Logie Baird with questions, and writing down the answers in shorthand. I had been given a reporter's notebook by the kind Mr McArdle, but I was writing weird notes in longhand. I was completely lost.

I waited until the other reporters left and then I explained to Mr Baird that I was absolutely new to the job and that I'd had some difficulty in following him. He smiled, went to a big bag and pulled out a magazine. 'There you are,' he said. 'That's an article I wrote for a non-technical journal. Possibly you'll get something out of that.'

I took it thankfully, hurried back to the *Citizen* office, didn't bother about lunch, and wrote like mad. I still remember that I called the article 'A Visit to a Wizard's Den.' It came out one edition before the *News* or the *Times*, which shows that Jackie and Eddie had the sense to have their lunch first. I was very pleased with myself. But then I have been lucky all my life.

My luck held on the *Citizen*. One day Arthur Hedderwick called me in and said, 'I've decided to make you a reporter. Mr House. But first of all, you will do six months as a subeditor'.

And so I bade farewell to the shouts of 'Boy!' Today I look on our telephonists in the *Glasgow Herald* and *Evening Times*. They don't have to bother with shorthand. They wear headphones and type the stories straight on to the machine. They are highly efficient men and women and quite a few of them get more money at the end of the week than the reporters do. When anybody shouts 'Boy!' they don't even lift their heads.

They belong to a powerful trade union. I trust I am not being denigratory when I say it's *not* the National Union of Journalists!

But I don't think they have the fun we had. After all, who has these days?

2

Life as a reporter was all I ever wanted. I now saw pavements in the sun all over Glasgow, and even in such astonishing portions of the outback as Paisley, Rutherglen, Kirkintilloch, Milngavie and Clydebank. You'll notice that I haven't mentioned my six months as sub-editor. That's merely because I think a sub-editor's work is lifeless compared with a reporter's. I don't regret my brief period as a sub—indeed, I probably learned quite a bit from it—but the only real journalism is reporting.

Admittedly, I had my teething troubles as a reporter. In the time-honoured way, I was sent out to cover two police courts in a morning without even the simplest instruction in what to do. I had never been in a police court in my life. Down I went to Govan and a kindly detective showed me the way up the door leading to the Press bench. I sat beside the only other occupant, who asked me what I was doing there. When I told him, he became kind too. He explained he was the representative of the *Govan Press,* a notable organ which has, on the front of its building in Govan, the busts of Gutenberg and Caxton, who founded printing; Robert Burns and Sir Walter Scott, who founded Scottish Literature; and Mr and Mrs John Cossar who founded the *Govan Press.*

'Don't worry,' said this kind chap to me. 'Just take notes when I do. And be careful of the law of libel.'

Such is fate that he got himself into a libel case that very morning. He inadvertently transposed the Christian names of two accused brothers. One had a list of previous convictions. The other had none. The 'innocent' one sued because

First House

Peeping Tom House

it was stated that he had previous convictions. I think the case was settled out of court.

I was luckier. At this same Govan Court I reported the case of a bookie who welshed at a Glasgow dog racing track. The poor chap had been having a bad night and, during the last race, it became obvious to him that he was on the losing end once more. So he made for the hills. The Police Superintendent who conducted the case for the prosecution said, according to my notes, 'When arrested, accused was found to have enough money to pay the bets.'

I was rather sorry for this bookie because he'd been menaced by a gang and I didn't blame him for running. I tried to phrase my piece in such a way as to show he was a decent sort at heart. But, as the German proverb says, ingratitude is the world's reward. The *Citizen* was hardly out ere a lawyer was after us for traducing his client, the bookie. The lawyer said we said that the accused had enough money to pay the bets of all his punters. The fact was that he had merely enough money to pay the bets of the two men mentioned in the charge against him.

I was summoned to the presence and Mr Hedderwick asked me to get my shorthand notebook, transcribe my notes into English and hand notebook and translation to the newspaper's lawyers. This was all very well, but I couldn't find my notebook anywhere. I knew nobody would believe that I'd lost it, least of all the bookie's lawyer. Just as I was beginning to give up hope, I found it lying beside a telephone. Since I wrote Gregg shorthand I had a certain advantage in the office. Nobody else could read my notes, as they all wrote Pitman. However, I transcribed the court case meticulously, handed it over to our lawyer, and never heard of the libel action again.

Some observant reader may ask, how was it possible to cover two police courts in the one morning? Since all courts started at the same time, this was manifestly impossible. But if they were not too far apart, such as the Marine and the Western, it was sometimes possible to get from one to the other and depend on the police to give you details of what you'd missed at the second court.

This double-timing never worried the *Citizen's* chief reporter, who was known as 'Milk' Smith to distinguish him from 'Beer' Smith, the chief reporter of another organ of opinion. He was a bland, Pickwickian gentleman and he would say unctuously, 'A good reporter should be able to duplicate himself—at least!'

We had a way of getting over duplication, however. Every morning the court reporters of the three papers met in a coffee-howff around 10 o'clock, not merely to drink coffee and enjoy each other's company, but to pass over the details of cases that the other papers had missed. Yes, we were rivals but there was no sense in being stupid rivals.

The *Citizen* was very much the poor relation among the Glasgow evenings. It had the smallest circulation. The *News* was the go-ahead paper, and the *Times* was the biggest. We used to say that, if the editor of the *Citizen* walked out into StVincent Place and was run over by a *Times* van, it would be reported first in the *News*.

3

Newspapermen were a friendly lot in Glasgow in the Thirties. We met at coffee in the morning and some of the macaronis (of whom I was one) also met in the Grosvenor tea-room in the late afternoon. Occasionally we went to pubs, and those were the days when there were still some magnificent pubs in Glasgow. I remember the Rogano in Royal Exchange Square—a vast, vaulted place whose walls were surrounded by barrels of sherry and port. There was a horseshoe bar, but the cognoscenti sat at little tables and the drinks were drawn from the barrels and brought over by waiters. On each table was a strange instrument which I discovered to be a cigar cutter.

Alas, one morning the charge hand tried to open the door of the Rogano and found that something was impeding him. He called for help and, when the door was forced, they found the body of the manager hanging from a rope behind it. Today Rogano is a completely changed place—a restaurant which none other than Nancy Mitford once described as the best she had encountered outside Paris. I like it today, but I remember the old Rogano fondly.

For a long time the *Citizen* pub was Cairns, at the corner of St Vincent Place and Buchanan Street. Since it was opposite the Western Club, it was known as the Eastern Club. In the days before I joined the paper, it was customary for the chief reporter to send a boy along to the Eastern Club to round up reporters for some unexpected job. But then reporters of the *Glasgow Herald* wore top hats, and it was said that, if the Press went along to a meeting and the *Herald* man didn't like the accommodation reserved for them, he'd just shake his head and the whole troop of them would walk out and leave the meeting unreported.

Reporters in the Thirties were not great drinking men—unless it was free, of course. There was the chap on the *Evening Times*, though, who was said to be keeping a pub somewhere because he was never in the office when the pubs were open. This was a libel, but he could hardly object because he went out of his way to be a character. For instance, he started his own Benevolent Society. He'd come up to you and explain that it cost a mere sixpence to join this organisation. So you paid over the sixpence and that was the end of that. The Benevolent Society had no other purposes than to benefit himself.

One evening I was late-duty reporter on the *Citizen*, which meant standing by until six o'clock or so in case something special happened which had to be covered. Our final edition went to press around four o'clock, and then a reporter, a sub-editor and a small case-room staff were left holding on. Final editions of the other evenings came in and I had to look at them to make sure we weren't being scooped.

This night we were. On the front page of the *Times* was a big story headed 'Rodeo Scenes on Broomielaw.' This described, in most exciting language, how a herd of Irish cattle being unloaded somewhere along the riverside had run amok. Bullocks had chased typists up closes. Men were lassoing animals right and left. I don't recollect if a bull had got into a china shop, but it probably did.

As late reporter, what was I to do? There was no question of going down to investigate along the Broomielaw. There simply wasn't time. I 'phoned the Marine Police and asked them if they'd heard about the rodeo scenes. They said they hadn't, but that didn't really surprise me, because something can happen round the corner from a police office and nobody ever tells them. Next I tried 'phoning various shops and offices along the Broomielaw. They were either closed for the night or the person who answered didn't know what I was talking about.

I went through to the late sub and reported my failure. He came up with a brilliant idea. 'You know we're now part of the Outram group,' he said and I nodded, because, although Arthur Hedderwick was still editor, he was no longer in complete control. 'Well,' said the sub, 'that means that the *Times* and us are really the one paper, so I think you should just lift the story from them.'

So that's what I did, and a few lines about the cattle stampede on the Broomielaw appeared in our Stop Press that night. The story appeared in every other newspaper too. It was only some time later that I heard that Willie Cumming, having been out of the *Times* office for most of the day, had suddenly appeared and, before his chief reporter could expostulate, had sat down and typed out his 'Rodeo Scenes on Broomielaw.' It was surmised that he had seen a herd of cattle being driven along that thoroughfare and his vivid imagination had done the rest.

It was claimed for Willie—if, indeed, he didn't claim it himself—that he was the man who put Britain off the Gold Standard in 1931. It was like this. When the British Fleet mutinied at Invergordon that year, various odd reports came in to the *Citizen* office that there was trouble there. But the only definite one indicated that some drunk sailors at a football match had booed their officers, and we left the story alone.

It was taken more seriously in the other newspaper offices, who sent out expeditions to the Far North. Today reporters would go by 'plane. Then it was either by car or train, and

train was out of the question. Just try taking the train to
Invergordon and you'll see what I mean. Willie Cumming
had just acquired a Bentley, and off he sped for Invergordon, where he found at once how serious the situation
really was, with red flags flying and officers locked in cabins
and sailors' committees taking over.

Willie went to the 'phone and, according to the story, was
faced with a divided loyalty. He worked for an American
news agency as well as the *Evening Times*, and he decided to
send his first message to the news agency. He'd hardly done
this, ere all telephoning in the area was banned. The other
newspapermen from Glasgow, hard on Willie's heels, found
they couldn't get through to their papers. Nor, of course,
could Willie to the *Times*. The only thing to do was to keep
driving south until they got to a 'phone box outside the
banned area.

This meant that the news of the trouble at Invergordon
reached American newspapers an hour or two before British
newspapers could get it. With this strange lack of news in
Britain, the Americans jumped to their own conclusion. The
old country was finished once again. Wall Street started
moving. And Britain went off the Gold Standard!

Did Willie Cumming really do it? Well, that's the story
which has been cherished in Glasgow newspaper circles for
more than thirty years, and I'd like to believe it was true.

My friend Harold Dickson, the man who made me
'Glasgow's Communist Scoutmaster', was maybe not in the
class of Willie Cumming, but he was a genius in his own
right. He worried the top boys in the Scout movement considerably because, since he had once been an officer, he was
quite capable of putting on his uniform and mixing with the
elite at big Scout happenings. He was forever writing stories
about the Scouts and when the Chief Scout decided that
Scottish Rover Scouts should give up the Balmoral for the
official Scout hat, Harold was in his element.

I revered the Chief Scout like mad, but I couldn't help
thinking that Lord Baden-Powell had taken the typical
English non-view of Scotland when he issued this edict. All
over the country, Scottish Rovers left the movement because

they would not give up their national headgear. I often think
that the English do more for Scottish Nationalism than they
ever know.

At any rate, Harold Dickson had a wonderful pro-
Balmoral story day after day. He reached his apogee when he
wrote 'Why should the Scottish Rover Scouts give up the
Balmoral, when Indian Scouts are still allowed to wear their
turbines?'

Harold was a man who specialised in contacts. When anything unusual happened, he'd 'phone all his friends to tell
them about it. That meant that each of his friends, when
something unusual happened in his area, telephoned Harold.
If only Harold had been able to write, he'd have been one of
the great reporters.

As it is, he is remembered by his friends for his idiosyncrasies.
One of the many jobs we reporters did without any extra
payment was to act as theatre critic every Monday night. In
those days there were so many theatres in Glasgow that it was
difficult to get them all covered. Harold, however, made
himself responsible for the Pavilion every Monday. The
Pavilion, still running, I am delighted to say, was managed
by a wonderful extrovert named Jock Kirkpatrick, who wore
full evening dress and a shining topper as he stood in the
foyer and greeted the more distinguished of his clientele.
Harold and Jock were close friends, and every Tuesday the
News intimated to an anxious world that the Pavilion show
was better than ever.

One Tuesday morning the sub-editor in charge of the
News theatre notices glanced over Harold Dickson's account
of the ongauns at the Pavilion on the previous night. He read,
'Outstanding among the acts was Randolph Sutton's light
railway.' This puzzled him somewhat, so the went through
to the reporters' room, sought out Harold, and asked him
what this meant. 'It's a great act,' said Harold, enthusiastic
as always. 'This chap Sutton has a miniature railway starting
on the stage and running up to the dress-circle and back on to
the stage again. Wee trains running round and round.
Absolutely wonderful.'

So the sub-editor passed Harold's notice and all was well

until the editor of the *Evening News* got around to reading his own newspaper. He sent for Harold and asked 'What is this light railway business? Were you really at the Pavilion last night?' Harold replied that he certainly was, but he had missed Mr Sutton's act because he was in Mr Kirkpatrick's room at the time. However, he knew everything was all right, because he had taken the details from the *Glasgow Herald*.

They looked up that morning's *Glasgow Herald* and there, sure enough, the Pavilion notice said, 'Mr Randolph Sutton achieved great success with his light raillery.'

4

Despite Willie Cumming and Harold Dickson, and one or two others whom it would perhaps not be wise to name, most of the Glasgow newspapermen were a straightforward lot, given to occasional peccadilloes, but otherwise a fairly blameless lot. Among my own particular friends was Angus Shaw, who came from the Hebridean Island of Luing and was fiercely Highland. He is news editor of the *Evening Times* today, and I'd describe him as the most completely equipped newspaperman I have ever met. Then there was Henry Lowrie, who now looks after the New York office of the *Daily Express*. And, rather younger than the rest of us, Stephen Watts, who went to London to join *Film Weekly* after he and I had started a monthly magazine called *The Scottish Stage*. We started it without any capital whatever. By some miracle it lasted a year, and then the Scottish Community Drama Association took it over and Stephen and I were left to pay the bills. It's just as well that bills were smaller then.

By this time I was immersed in the drama, one way and another. The amateur theatre movement was becoming so big that even the newspapers had to recognise it, and so I was appointed amateur theatre expert, covering the amateur

productions night after boring night, and writing a weekly
article under the name of 'Jingle', which I had pinched from
the character in *Pickwick Papers*.

I have already mentioned Colin Milne, then literary
editor of the *Citizen* and a great theatre man. At one time he
did all the interviews with stage stars. Now I was brought
into the act. When Colin Milne couldn't interview someone,
I did it in his stead. So I met Yehudi Menuhin, when he was
still a boy and his father did all the talking for him. Indeed,
the interview was punctuated with pleas from Yehudi that he
wanted to see Loch Lomond, the treat promised for him that
afternoon and being held up by reporters.

I met Thelma Todd, the school-teacher who became the
heroine of a Marx Brothers epic. She was a lulu. I asked her
what impressed her most about Scotland (I was always one
for the off-beat query!) and she replied, 'The fact that all the
reporters are so young!'

Charles B. Cochran, Anna Pavlova, Jack Buchanan, J. B.
Priestley, Anna Neagle, Bobby Howes—I met them all, and
marvelled that I should be allowed to mix in such society. It
was such a relief, too, to be writing my own stuff about them
and not having to try to get a 'signed' article.

But, ere I reached this advanced stage of sophistication,
I was called in by the redoubtable Mr Hedderwick, who,
more and more, seemed to be basing himself on the character
of Napoleon or Northcliffe, and asked, 'How would you like
to take Miss Pola Negri to lunch?'

What could I do but say I'd be delighted? I had seen and
admired Madame Negri on the screen for years, but I
thought she had gone a bit off the boil, particularly as she
was touring Britain in a one-act play. It was destined for the
Alhambra Theatre in the following week and the editor explained that I was supposed to take Pola Negri to lunch on
the Tuesday after the opening night. I wondered if my best
suit was good enough for the Malmaison, Glasgow's poshest
place for eating out. Thank goodness I now knew how to
order from a wine-list.

'You'll get the details from Mr Milne,' said the editor, so I
went along to 'Argus's room' and said I'd just heard the good

news about taking Pola Negri to lunch. 'Ah, yes,' said Colin, 'Did the editor tell you that you have to take her to Lang's?'

Lang's! There were two Lang's restaurants in the city, but the one Colin Milne meant was in St. George's Place. It specialised in sandwiches or all kinds, though there was also soup and an occasional hot dish. You just helped yourself to sandwiches, pulled yourself a pint of half-pint of beer, and at the end of your lunch you went to the cashier and told her how much you owed Mr Lang. She took your word right away. It was an excellent institution and carefully guarded by its 'regulars', so that if somebody was seen to be cheating, he was reported immediately.

The only trouble from any point of view of taking Pola Negri to lunch there was that it was for men only.

However, there was not to reason why. It was an order from the editor. I asked Colin Milne to fix me up with tickets for the Alhambra, so that I'd know all about the play and be able to chat gaily with Madame Negri as she munched her brawn sandwich amidst a crowd of Glasgow business men wearing their bowler hats. It was a tradition of Lang's that you kept your hat on while lunching.

Well, I went to the Alhambra. It was a variety bill, twice-nightly, and the *clou* was this one-act play, the title of which I mercifully do not remember. There were two characters in it. Madame Negri as some sort of queen or princess swept about the stage in a long velvet gown. Her lover—at least, I think he was her lover—was played by the late Reginald Tate, a very fine actor indeed. He did his best for the show, but it was dire. It got laughs where no laughs were intended. Some people in the audience walked out in the middle of it. The applause at the end was derisive.

I sat in my fauteuil (very swanky, the Alhambra always was) and cowered. I was committed to taking this leading lady out on the morrow. And to Lang's! Could anything in the world be worse?

Next day I put my Sunday suit on and spent a miserable morning waiting for noon, the magic hour when I was to pick up (if that was the right phrase) Madame Negri at her suite in the Central Hotel. On the very minute I walked into

the lobby of the Central and asked for Madame Negri. The
receptionist contacted her suite and had what was quite
evidently a puzzled conversation. Then she said, 'Miss
Negri's secretary will see you. Suite number so-and-so.'

Up I went to the suite, a reception room and a bedroom,
and met a worried looking young woman with spectacles.
'What exactly do you want?' she asked. I explained that I
had arrived to take Madame Negri to lunch. 'But she hasn't
had her breakfast yet,' said the secretary. 'And I know that
she's got no engagement for lunch today.'

I recalled that Colin Milne had said something about all
this being arranged by Madame Negri's publicity agent, a
Mr Blank, shall we say? So I mentioned Mr Blank's name.
'Oh, but we haven't seen Mr Blank for weeks,' said the
secretary. 'I think there must be some mistake. Just a moment,
please.'

She had all the morning papers before her and each one
was open at the Alhambra Theatre notice, which she had
marked with red pencil. I had already seen those theatre
notices. The kindest of them said that Pola Negri was 'adequate.' Could an actress be more insulted?

The secretary collected the papers and took them into the
bedroom. There were some low-throated mutterings and she
returned, looking positively scared. 'Excuse me,' she said, and
took a tray with a bottle and a glass on it into the bedroom.
Then I heard the sound of newsprint being torn apart and a
voice which I took to be Pola Negri's saying loud, nasty
things in a language I couldn't make out. You don't have to
understand the words to know that they're nasty.

After a while the poor secretary emerged again. 'I don't
think you should wait, Mr House,' she said. 'I think you
should make another arrangement with Madame Negri
yourself. But not today.'

I agreed with her heartily and left, feeling slightly shaky at
the knees. I went back to the office and told Arthur Hedderwick
all about it. He roared with laughter. I couldn't quite see the
joke myself. I also reported to Colin Milne, who then
admitted that Mr Blank had been considerably worried about
his job with La Negri, principally because the tour was going

so badly. He had gone on the drink himself and, presumably under the influence, had worked out the wonderful idea that a *Citizen* man (he really wanted Colin Milne to do it) would conduct Madame Negri through the city from the Central Hotel to Lang's *preceded by a piper*!

I have had to deal with the weird ideas of publicity men for years—I remember one who wanted me to arrange for a Glasgow gang to 'kidnap' Roy Fox's wife when that band-leader was appearing at the Empire—but lunch with Pola Negri beats all. Sometimes, though I wonder what would have happened if I *had* taken Pola Negri to Lang's.

5

If I have given the impression that my life as a reporter was all fun and games, it's the wrong one. You may have been brought up very quietly indeed, as I think I was. But you soon learn the facts of life as a reporter. I covered the police courts, the Sheriff courts and then the High Court itself, and in no time at all I knew a great deal about prostitution, homosexuality, abortion, bestiality, incest, rape, murder, blackmail, and a lot of other subjects which had not entered my life until that time.

I suppose it does something to you when you spend a hot Saturday morning and afternoon in a Glasgow police court, watching one after another of 22 prostitutes entering the witness box and giving evidence in the case of an Italian café owner who has been charged with running his place as a brothel. Especially when the Superintendent orders the bar to be cleaned with lysol because one of the witnesses has put her hand on it.

Then there was the 'dirty' cases, usually held in the South Court of the Justiciary Buildings when the High Court was in session. These were hardly ever reported in our clean newspapers, but a reporter had to be there in court in case the judge dropped dead or something unusual happened.

There was, of course, no need for every newspaper to have a man present. One observer was enough. So those of us who were detailed for the South Court would toss for it, and the man who lost sat through the case, while the rest of the boys stayed in the Press room and played cards.

One thing I did learn from these long sessions in court was that you can't judge any man's private sex life by his appearance. I don't know that this great discovery did me the slightest good, but I just set it down as an aphorism.

When I wasn't going to courts of justice, I was attending unemployment demonstrations and marches, and there were plenty of them in Glasgow in the early Thirties. Usually they were led by such stalwarts as Willie Gallagher, Harry McShane, Peter Kerrigan and other revolutionaries. I had seen that great agitator, John MacLean, leading a march along St Vincent Street, but that was while I was still a C.A. apprentice. Now, after more than 40 years, I can still see the glittering eyes in the grey face under the incongruous bowler. And I can still remember a fat business man standing beside me on the pavement, watching the bunnets and the mufflers go by and saying, 'Why don't they look for work?'

These were the days when Guy Aldred, the anarchist, was at his best, and would join up with the I.L.P., the Communists and the Tramp Preachers, a body of Christian activists who carried a cross and a red flag in front of them, in all sorts of demonstrations. Mr Aldred made it plain that he disagreed with all of them, but he couldn't resist a demonstration in those days.

It was my job one winter's afternoon to follow a demonstration from Blythswood Square, along Sauchiehall Street and down to George Square. I walked on the pavement, just behind the head of the procession, ready for incidents and arrests. Willie Gallagher has written about this procession and said that the bystanders cheered the demonstrators as they went by. I didn't hear any cheering. Indeed, the usual Glasgow way to treat an unemployed march—in Sauchiehall Street, at any rate—was to try to ignore it. The middle-class shoppers were apt to stand staring into shop windows until the demonstration passed.

On this day I accompanied the marchers to George Square and there trouble broke out. Several of the leaders, who had tried to speak in the Square, were told to move on and refused to go. They held on to the iron seats in the Square until the police prised them loose. There was a good-going rammy but the police won, and the demonstrators flocked down to Glasgow Green to hold a protest meeting at Nelson's Column.

At this meeting plain clothes police moved in and the trouble really started. The mounted police trotted into line at the top of the Saltmarket and charged down it. By this time I was back in the office writing my stuff, but a colleague of mine called Alex. Mackenzie was in the line of the charge and had to run up a close to avoid the thundering hooves.

Next morning I had to cover the appearance of the accused at the Central Police Court, where the public benches were full of followers of the Tramp Preachers singing hymns. I was standing at the side of the court, waiting for the Stipendiary Magistrate to enter when a plain clothes detective came up to me and said, 'Who are you?' I replied that I was Jack House of the *Citizen*.

'Well, you're a very lucky man,' he said. 'We got our eye on you in Sauchiehall Street yesterday and we thought you were one of *them*.' He didn't explain who *they* were, and I didn't ask. He just went on, 'We were ready to nab you if you'd taken one wee step out of line. But we lost you in George Square.'

I felt rather happy about that. If I'd suddenly been seized in George Square, I'd have had some difficulty in explaining that I was just a reporter at work.

All I recollect of the police court proceedings now was the real indignation of police witnesses who gave evidence that some of the demonstrators in Glasgow Green actually tore 'Please Keep Off the Grass' notices out of the ground and used them as weapons to attack the police. These must have been foreigners in the pay of Moscow Gold. No Glaswegian would have thought of touching a 'Please Keep Off the Grass' notice, far less tear it out of its proper place.

In my youth I had been squeamish and was apt to faint at the sight of blood. I soon got out of that because I had to cover so many horrible road and other accidents. To see a headless body at the side of the road after a motor-cycle accident or watch a burned-black miner brought up from the bottom of a pit is something that can only be done if you look at it in a professional way.

The trouble was that you got reactions afterwards. I remember a Hogmanay, December 31, 1929. I was the fairly recently appointed billiards expert of the *Citizen*. One day the chief sub-editor had said to me, 'What are your interests!' I made the stock reply—the theatre, the cinema, books— how often have I heard them trotted out! The chief sub-editor looked at me with scorn. 'What about sport?' he asked. I could only echo him and say, 'Well, what *about* sport?' I wasn't in the least interested in sport.

True, I had bought some golf clubs and played twice. I had a shot at tennis, and once won a competition at Alexandra Park because I was given such a wonderful handicap. I ran at various sports meetings. And I played cricket and football for the wee local teams in Dennistoun and Riddrie. But I did all this with no feeling for any game. The only thing I really enjoyed was walking.

So, when the chief sub-editor asked me about my sporting interests, I'd really nothing to say. However, he had something to say to me. 'You're a bloody fool,' he said. 'The only way to make money in newspapers is to go in for a sport.' I felt he had something there, because I remembered that, as chief telephonist, I had to make calls to various English and Irish 'phone numbers every Saturday night and read out the Scottish football results. For this service the chief sub-editor, who did nothing but furnish the telephone numbers, received a handsome fee for every result. He didn't even pay for the telephone calls. Certainly he knew how to make money out of sport.

Well, he took pity on me. I might be one of those effete types who liked going to the theatre and reading books, but he'd do his best for me. He made me the billiards expert. We had a miniature billiards table at home, and I knew a little about the game. This was long before the days of the inferior snooker, of course. Great men like Walter Lindrum,

Tom Smith and Joe Davis were playing billiards, and it was my job to describe the delirious delights of Lindrum knocking up hundreds in an afternoon at the old billiards parlour in West Nile Street.

On this Hogmanay in 1929 I was marked in the reporters' diary to cover the match between Walter Lindrum and Tom Smith in the McLellan Galleries in Sauchiehall Street. It was the second day and Lindrum had got himself into one of those impregnable positions of his, where he just kept scoring monotonously until he decided to miss and give the other chap a chance.

I was due at the Galleries at three o'clock in the afternoon, but first I had taken a girl friend of mine out to lunch at the Royal Restaurant in West Nile Street. It was a pleasant affair and I suggested to her that we should go to the pictures, to be exact, the Picture House in Sauchiehall Street, not far from the McLellan Galleries. I'd have to leave her around 3.30, go to the Galleries and find out the position of the billiards match, 'phone it to the paper, and then I could return to the cinema.

But she said no. I did my best to persuade her, but eventually I went disconsolately up to the McLellan Galleries for the billiards match. I had hardly taken my seat ere one of our sub-editorial boys rushed in, breathing heavily. 'There's a fire in a picture house in Paisley,' he said. 'Mr Smith says you've to go there at once.' I asked him for more details, but he knew no more than the message he had given.

There was a taxi-rank near by and I took the first one down to Paisley. I hadn't the slightest idea where to go, but on the main thoroughfare there was a crowd round a small, fourth-rate picture house called the Glen. I paid off the taxi, asked some questions and found that there had been a terrible panic at a children's matinee. A can of film had gone on fire in the projection room, which was just behind the ticket office at the entrance to the cinema. The projectionist threw the smoking can out into the foyer. Someone shouted 'Fire!' In a moment the children panicked. They rushed for 'Exit' signs which meant nothing because the doors were locked. They piled up on each other before those locked doors. Sixty-nine children died and thirty seven were taken to hospital.

I 'phoned the office, to find that most of these facts were already known. I'd thought I was working on my own, but the whole reporting staff of the paper had been sent to Paisley. I was told to go to the Royal Alexandra Hospital to see what I could find out there. On that winter's night I went into the grounds and followed a long queue of parents to the hospital chapel, which had been turned into a mortuary. And there I saw sixty-nine children, all dead, lying in rows. Those who had been identified had tickets tied to their clothing.

Fathers, mothers, brothers, aunts, sisters and uncles walked slowly past the dead children, who looked as if they were sleeping. Many people did not know whether their children had been at the Glen Cinema that afternoon or not. Some of the children who had escaped were so panic-stricken that they ran away and did not come home until late that night.

I telephoned what poor words I could to the newspaper office. Then, late at night, I went home to Riddrie for our Hogmanay celebrations. Up till then I had been professional, observing and reporting. But now, when we were going through the first-foot ritual and singing 'A Guid New Year tae ane an' a'', the reality of what I had seen came home to me. It has never left me. I can still see those serried ranks of dead children. I can still see that long, sad queue outside the chapel.

And sometimes I wonder what would have happened to me if I *had* taken my girl friend to the pictures that afternoon.

Many years later I was given a big volume on *The Cinema* to review. I can't remember the author's name, but he was an American and the book had been published in the United States originally. Among other things, the author dealt with the way the cinema had spread throughout the world. There was one single illustration to show Scotland's part. It depicted the miserable little front of the Glen Cinema —in fact, it was a photograph taken at the time of the disaster—and the caption revealed that this was a typical picture house in Scotland!

Ah, well, the time came when I gave up reporting and was transformed into the Assistant Literary Editor of the *Citizen*, working with Colin Milne, who was the Literary Editor. Between us we ran two gossip columns a day, did all the features on the theatre, the cinema, books, and anything else the editor thought up, ran competitions and laid out feature pages and the like. Any newspaper features department to-day would be horrified at the amount of work the two of us did. We never gave it a thought. We enjoyed it.

One of the last jobs I did as a reporter was probably the happiest I ever tackled. It was to tell the story of the day that work was resumed on the Cunarder 534 at John Brown's shipyard in Clydebank. For years the red hulk had loomed over the town. The depression on Clydeside was at its worst. Then suddenly it was announced that work on 534, to be-come the *Queen Mary*, would restart.

Early that morning I went down to Clydebank. The whole town was already out and about. An enterprising newspaper had engaged a pipe band and it was marching through the streets, followed by crowds. All of a sudden Brown's hooter blew. And then I saw a sight I shall never forget—men running to their work!

All this seems slightly unreal as I write it. You must have lived in those terrible times to appreciate what unemployment meant. I felt it only at second-hand, but that was close enough. When I read nowadays that the unemployment figure in Scotland is, say six and a half per cent, I remember that to an unemployed man, it's 100 per cent. If this sounds stupid and sentimental, I'm content that it should be so to you.

I suppose I was being sentimental when I was glad to be seconded from my post as Assistant Literary Editor to be-come a reporter for one afternoon—to help with the story of the launching of Cunarder 534. Almost the entire staff of the paper were on the job that day, and I was assigned to a small wooden hut at the outer end of Rothesay Dock, just to the east of the point where the liner would enter the River Clyde.

A ship of this size had never been launched in the Clyde before. When an English shipbuilder saw the breadth of the river at this point, he expressed surprise that any decent-size ship could be launched 'in this trout stream'. Actually, the Cunarders are launched stern first and they are aimed at the entrance to the River Cart on the other side of the Clyde.

There were all sorts of rumours as to how high the wash would be when 534 was launched. The bright chap who escorted me to the wooden hut, where a telephone had been installed so that I could keep in touch with the office, said, 'For all anybody knows, the wave could come right over this hut. I hope you're going to be all right.' I said I hoped so too.

At various times I 'phoned the paper and told them what I could see. Then I heard in the distance the sound of Queen Mary's speech coming over the loud-speakers, the noise of cheering and a great clanging of chains, and what looked like a tenement of steel came bearing inexorably down on me. I could see people on the opposite bank starting to run. Doubtless they thought the steel tenement was bearing inexorably down on *them*. Up came the level of the river in a great rush, but it didn't touch the top of my pier.

I have no doubt that I sounded rather incoherent to the telephonist at the office end but it was a mixture of awe and relief, to say nothing of pride, because we all felt that the 'Queen Mary' (I didn't learn the ship's name, incidentally, until I got back to the office) was a symbol of Clydeside.

Back I went to my Assistant Literary Editorship, but the gilt was wearing off this particular piece of gingerbread. I realised that Colin Milne had a long way to go yet as Literary Editor and that I was in a pleasant rut. I had a yearning to be a free-lance and I wanted very much indeed to restart *The Scottish Stage*, the monthly magazine which Stephen Watts and I had founded, but which had foundered. So I put up a plan to the Scottish Community Drama Association that I should run a new *Scottish Stage* for them, for an experimental period of one year. All I asked was a small fee and that half my rent, rates and etceteras would be paid by them.

When this was agreed I took a single room office at 35 Dundas Street, so that I could look out at Queen Street Station for inspiration. Also in my view was a pub called The Old Koh-I-Noor, which I adopted as my local. I was the

proud man indeed when I had a desk, three chairs, a telephone and a typewriter installed, and I watched a painter
inscribe *Jack House* on the glass panelled door, with *The
Scottish Stage* in somewhat smaller letters below it.

'Hey!' said the painter to me as he finished the job. 'Can
you tell me why they're cryin' a wee place like this the Jack
House?'

I mumbled that I didn't really know. But I've always
noticed in Glasgow that, as soon as you are inclined to be
puffed up with pride, there's somebody around to say something that puts your gas at a peep.

My Stage Career

The Scottish Stage lasted only the year of its trial. Then the Scottish Community Drama Association decided that, as it had lost something in the region of £100, it was not financially sound and stopped it. I thought they'd made a big mistake and should have tried it for another year. But, in actual fact, it suited me not to have to run the magazine. It gave me more time to write for money.

It was by no means the shortest run of any magazine edited by me. There had been, some time around 1933, the ill-fated satirical Glasgow weekly called *Well!* This was *Private Eye*, in a restricted field of course, thirty years before *Private Eye*. I kept suggesting to friends of mine that we should have a magazine 'to tell the truth about Glasgow'. Eventually ten of us had dinner in a beautiful Victorian restaurant called Sloan's Arcade Café. (It still exists, but much of the Victoriana has gone.)

We agreed to put up £5 each and write for nothing. All of us were journalists in Glasgow, with two exceptions. One was a young Glasgow lawyer who is now a professor and probably wouldn't thank me for dragging his name into this. He was there to watch for libel and write the gramophone record criticisms. The other was Allan MacKinnon, a Glasgow University student who had edited the *Glasgow University Magazine*, appeared in occasional broadcasts and wrote for the University annual revue, *College Pudding*. He and I were collaborating on radio scripts at this time, and he agreed to become 'official' editor of *Well!* since those of us who were on newspaper staffs wanted to keep our identities secret.

In fact, however, I edited *Well!* and on my staff I had Jessie Miller, who wrote for the *Evening News* and in the course of time became my wife, and George Millar, author of *Maquis*, *Horned Pigeon*, and various other distinguished books. George was then in the process of giving up the profession of architecture and learning the profession of journalism. He wrote a brilliant account of a Glasgow Corporation reception in the City Chambers, which I didn't print because I was frightened.

Our first number came out and attracted no attention whatever, except from Colin Milne, who was one of the ten who had put up £5. In order to fill up a small space at the foot of a column, I had written, 'Contemptuously tweaking the nose of the Editor of the *Evening Citizen* who says that nothing is unique, we state that this number of *Well!* *is* unique. It is the first number of any magazine to appear without letters to the Editor.'

I thought this was mildly funny. Colin was horrified. He pointed out that if Arthur Hedderwick learned that he was involved in *Well!* he might well get the sack. He wanted his £5 back, so that there could be no connection between him and the magazine. I gave him £5 and went on to get the second number out. It was quite a good one, but our printers reported that all our money was done. As we had agreed that our limit was £50, we stopped publication there and then. Anybody who possesses these two numbers of *Well!* should hold on to them.

Oh, by the way, Arthur Hedderwick never saw *Well!* as far as I know. That was the trouble. Hardly anybody saw it.

The Scottish Stage, on the other hand, was a completely respectable publication—even if I did have to write most of it. I couldn't afford to pay contributors. It was produced next door at 35 Dundas Street by Bone and Hulley, printers. This very small firm was run by John H. Bone, one of the family which included James Bone, the great journalist, Muirhead Bone, the great artist, and Captain Sir David Bone, the great seaman. John was the quiet one of the family, and all the quieter because he was almost stone deaf. When we were in the throes of producing *The Scottish Stage*, the whole building heard it because I had to shout so much.

I liked him immensely, and remembered that the first one-act play I had ever appeared in at Regent Place U.F. Church of Scotland was *The Crystal Set* by John H. Bone.

In these years I was immersed in the amateur and semi-professional theatre in Glasgow and the West of Scotland. It was a time when some writers talked glibly of a Scottish Renaissance, and the amateur theatre and such organisations as the Scottish National Players were part of it. Such great men as Tyrone Guthrie, James Bridie, Paul Vincent Carroll, W. G. Fay and Michel Saint Denis strode our streets in Glasgow.

Even before I went into newspaper life I was bound up in the amateur drama, for I followed the fate of the Ardrossan and Saltcoats Players who won the Scottish Drama Festival with J. M. Barrie's *The Old Lady Shows Her Medals*, then won the Howard de Walden Trophy for the whole of Britain in London, and finally crossed over to New York and won the David Belasco Cup there. I don't suppose there has been any other amateur dramatic company like it in the world. Its producer was James T. Woodburn, who later became a distinguished actor and played the part of John Brown in *Victoria Regina* both in this country and America, and its leading actor was Jack Lambert, a plumber who became a minor film star.

Woodburn had been brought up in the days when the local amateur dramatic company was produced by a coal-man, who would come straight from his work without washing and proceed to demonstrate to a young man the correct way to make love to a young woman. In this company every actor brought along his own prompter, and it was often difficult to get on to the stage because of the profusion of prompters in the wings.

Am I wrong in thinking that things were dafter in those days? Let's take Hugh McGettigan, now a pillar of the film business and father of Toni Gilpin, a television actress of some note. Hugh was an extremely good amateur actor in Glasgow. One night he went along to the Woodside Halls to see an amateur production of three one-act plays by some friends of his. As he was waiting for the performance to begin, the curtains parted and the face of a friend looked out, scanning the audience. When his eyes lit on Hugh, he indicated with his forefinger that Hugh was urgently wanted behind the scnenes.

So Hugh went back stage and was told that the company needed a man because somebody hadn't turned up. The middle play was one of those about Bonnie Prince Charlie (a computer would be needed to tell you how many of those I have suffered) and at one point four Highlanders had to bear on to the stage a bier carrying a dead man. Hugh was wanted as one of the tough Highlanders. He had no words to say, no movements to learn, and costume was simple because all he had to do was take off his jacket and his tie, roll up his shirt sleeves, change his trousers for a kilt (which they had waiting for him), and remove his socks and shoes. Maybe it was this simplicity of dress for the supers which made the Bonnie Prince Charlie plays so popular.

Having got ready for his part, Hugh was invited to join four other Highlanders, similarly arrayed in shirts and kilts, who sat round a table in the dressing-room drinking beer and playing cards. They played and drank for some time and then the producer poked his head in the door and said 'You're on.' At this one of the card players laid himself out on a stretcher. He was the dead man on the bier. Hugh and the three others seized a handle each and carried the body on to the stage, where Bonnie Prince Charlie was already orating.

They laid the bier down on the stage and stood behind it, as directed. All appeared to be going well until Hugh realised that, in his off-bier hand, so to speak, he was still holding a lit cigarette. Even though it was quite the practice for Bonnie Prince Charlies to go on wearing wristlet watches, Highlanders with cigarettes were considered out of place. His first instinct was to drop the cigarette and stamp on it. Then he realised he had bare feet!

Each time Bonnie Prince Charlie came anywhere near him, Hugh whispered, 'Send me off—for God's sake, send me off!' The cigarette end was getting shorter and shorter and he could feel the heat. At length Bonnie Prince Charlier got the message. He was a fellow of infinite invention. 'The papers!'

he suddenly yelled. 'Where are the papers?' Then he looked
straight at Hugh and cried, 'You, fellow! Seek out the papers,
and stay not upon the order of your going!'

Hugh had just time to dash off the stage and stub out the
burning end of his cigarette. He knew better than to go back on
again, because that would just remind the audience that
there had been some mention of papers. And audiences, even
those at amateur performances, hate to be confused.

Audiences at Scottish Community Drama Festival performances were soos wi' a different snoot. Although there was
an official adjudicator, the audience regarded themselves as
judges. I was there as a newspaper critic, so I had the delightful task of judging the players, the adjudicator and the
audience. As 'Jingle' of the *Evening Citizen*, I might well have
been described as the poor man's Walter Winchell. Oh, I
was a desperate character!

The Glasgow Drama Festival was a big thing in the early
Thirties. It could run quite easily for a fortnight, with three
or four one-act plays each night. Nowadays Glasgow seems
to be lucky to manage three nights.

I recollect some wonderful evenings in the old Athenaeum
Theatre, which now belongs to the College of Drama and is
no longer available for outside shows. The maximum length
of a one-act play, according to Festival rules, is forty-five
minutes. And so one night we had a performance of *The Lady
of the Camelias*, in which, as time wore on, Marguerite was
dying against the clock. She just made it. But not with the
adjudicator.

The greatest performance of my time was the Robert Owen
Players in *The Peerless Kinsman*. This was *Macbeth* cut down to
forty-five minutes. You may recollect that Duncan calls
Macbeth his 'peerless kinsman'.

The Robert Owen Players raced through *Macbeth* like
mad. They had chosen to present it on a bare stage, with
grey drapes at the back, opened to show a grey rostrum
with a dozen or so steps leading up to the top. The acting
was excruciating. The girl who played Lady Macbeth spoke
with a Glasgow accent that even a Scotch comic would consider a bit overdone. It was a genuine one, all the same. I

regret to say that the audience, particularly the sophisticated among us, started to titter.

As the play proceeded, various characters made their exit by way of the rostrum, which was the way into the castle or anything else the producer thought it might be. There was obviously something odd about this exit. Characters would go up, wobble a bit and disappear. Then one actor brushed against the drapes with his robe and left a gap between the curtain and the rostrum of about a foot. It was then apparent that there were no steps down from the rostrum and that characters who reached the top then had to take a flying leap down a good five feet on to the stage.

After that there was no holding the audience. Every time any unfortunate actor mounted the rostrum, they'd hold their breath as he balanced for the take-off. Then, as he launched himself into space, they'd cheer. People all round were wiping tears from their eyes. Brian Rix was never like this.

The Peerless Kinsman ended with the audience helpless. What interested me was how the adjudicator would tackle this debacle. He was Frank Sladen-Smith, an accomplished playwright and director of the Unnamed Theatre of Manchester. He seemed quite unperturbed as he strode on to the stage at the adjudication time. When he came to the Robert Owen Players, he launched a virulent attack on the audience. He said he did not propose to give *The Peerless Kinsman* a public adjudication because of the disgraceful way in which the audience behaved. Yes, he had that audience thoroughly ashamed of themselves.

I thought his technique was wonderful, but I wondered what had happened at the private adjudication behind the scenes. So later I asked him and, once he had my promise that I would write nothing in the *Citizen*, he told me that he'd wondered what on earth he was going to say in public about *The Peerless Kinsman*, until it occurred to him to attack the audience. Then, when the private adjudication took place, here were the Robert Owen Players, all lined up with smug looks on their faces because of the way the audience had been told off.

Frank Sladen-Smith told me that he didn't know where

to start. He looked along the row of eager faces and felt he couldn't possibly tell them the awful truth about themselves. His eye fell on the girl who had murdered Lady Macbeth.

'Ah, Lady Macbeth,' he said. 'You know, my dear, some of the greatest actresses in the world have had trouble with this part.'

'Izzat so?' she asked. 'Ah hidnae ony trouble at a'.'

2

I needn't talk. I made a fool of myself in the Scottish Community Drama Festival too. I am wont to boast that I have done everything in the Drama Festival. I have written a play, produced a play, acted, adjudicated and criticised in a newspaper. While there are others who can claim to have written, produced, acted, and adjudicated, I don't know of any other critic who attempted all these things.

The Regent Players (as we renamed The Regent Place U.F. Church of Scotland Dramatic Society) first entered the Drama Festival with a very good little play by the late Morland Graham called *C'est la Guerre*. Andrew Wilson, the adjudicator, placed us sixteenth out of thirty-two entries, which is a good average result. Andrew Wilson was an elderly actor and minor playwright whose full name was Andrew Patrick Wilson. When he directed a company in Ireland, he was known as Patrick Wilson. When he produced for the Scottish National Players, he was Andrew Wilson.

Then we tried a pretty ropey play entitled *The Lascar*. I can't remember who wrote it, but it was about a lascar who ran amok aboard a passenger liner in the middle of a voyage. He enters the Captain's cabin and holds everybody up at revolver point. Luckily a clean-limbed young Englishman present catches the lascar unawares and, by applying a little ju-jitsu (karate was unknown then), he subdues the villain. Curtain.

Well, I played the lascar. Our producer was a woman

teacher who, as far as I know, had never been to sea. We rehearsed well enough, but there were certain things we left to the night, when, as we all know, it would be all right on.

I wore an elaborate shiny brown make-up which, of course, I had never worn before. In the *Othello* tradition I had blacked myself almost all over. All went comparatively well until the moment came for the clean-limbed young Englishman, played by my brother George, to put the kybosh on me. We struggled together and, as we fought, I realised that my brown make-up was coming off on his tennis shirt and immaculate white flannels. In the midst of the struggle, I had to fire my revolver. But, though I had practised firing it, I hadn't tried it with slippy make-up on my fingers.

So on we fought, with my fine brown frame coming steadily off on my brother's flannels, with me frantically trying to fire the revolver, and my brother, not realising my predicament, hissing, 'Shoot, for God's sake, shoot!' At last I managed to shoot and the play was brought to a merciful conclusion.

The adjudicator was quite nice to us. But he pointed out that it was the first sea-going cabin he had ever seen where the captain's table was on castors. I think now that it was a wonderful idea, and I commend it to that 'Carry On' film company, who might well do 'Carry On, Captain' and have a big scene where the captain's table runs on castors all over the ship during a storm.

My final appearance in the Drama Festival was in a play which I wrote myself. I called it 'Press Room' and it was, oddly enough about the press room of the High Court in a Scottish town. Most of the characters were built on newspaper people I actually knew. The principal character was Harold Dickson, and I played him myself with, as Lord Woolton used to say, evident relish.

Later, owing to my friendship with L. A. G. Strong, it was published in a one-act play series by Methuen. As far as I know, it has been performed only once since publication. I don't even have a copy of this great work myself. When I asked Methuen about it the other day, they said it was out of print. That's maybe not so surprising after thirty years or so.

What is surprising, as I've said, is that I'm still getting
money out of 'Eight Plays for Wolf Cubs.'

It was rather difficult being a reporter and an actor at the
same time. My fellow reporters were very loyal. Angus Shaw
and Henry Lowrie actually came to see my performances
and, although they were rude about them, they were rude in
a friendly way. Neither of them had the slightest interest in
acting, but we were all much closer to the theatre then. Our
hero was Jack Buchanan, and many of us tried to model ourselves on him. Some managed to cultivate that dark brown
voice. Others copied his clothes. I recall a day in the Grosvenor Tea Room when a young lawyer burst in upon us
crying, 'It's all right! It's all right!'

When we calmed him down and asked him what was all
right, he replied 'To wear brown shoes with a blue suit. I've
just seen Jack Buchanan doing it in Renfield Street!'

For myself, though, I was more interested in the legitimate
theatre than the world of musical comedy. I went to everything that the Scottish National Players presented, first in the
Athenaeum Theatre and then in the Lyric in Sauchiehall
Street. I thought Morland Graham one of the most accomplished actors I have ever seen — and in this I was not far
wrong. I certainly considered Tyrone Guthrie the greatest of
all producers. Many of the people who were with the semi-
amateur S.N.P. went on to the professional theatre.

In particular, there was Elliot Mason, a massive, kindly
woman who taught Robert Donat how to speak Scots for
the film, *The Ghost Goes West*; R. B. Wharrie; Madeleine
Christie; Halbert Tatlock, the horror expert; Moultrie
Kelsall; James Gibson; Grace McChlery, the finest Maggie I
have ever seen in *What Every Woman Knows*; Hal D. Stewart
and his wife, who always called herself Jean Stuart (Hal did
very well out of *The Boy Friend*, which he managed for the
Players' Theatre); Meg Buchanan, who became Mrs. Mc-
Flannel of the radio series about the McFlannel family which
dominated Scottish listening for long enough; and a wheen
others.

I often wrote about the Scottish National Players and,
when I was producing something myself, I got the scenery and

costumes from their store. So I wasn't at all surprised to get a summons from Elliot Mason one day to got up to the S.N.P. offices and studio in Fitzroy Place to meet Tyrone Guthrie. We sat and chatted for about quarter of an hour and then I was dismissed from the presence. It was only afterwards that I suddenly realised that the great Guthrie was considering me for a part in the next S.N.P. production.

But it was a case of 'Don't call us—we'll call you', for I heard no more about it. I went to the next production and watched it with great interest, trying to work out which part I had been considered for. Perhaps it was my innate modesty, but I couldn't see a single one for which I'd be suitable.

I did, however, appear with the Scottish National Players. When they put on *What Every Woman Knows*, they needed a crowd for the election scene. I was not only asked to be part of the crowd, but also to recruit male members of the Regent Players for it. So every night for a couple of weeks, I was one of the leaders of the crowd and burst into the election room in the forefront of the struggling mass, which must have numbered a score at least.

This must have got me on to some sort of list, because the time came when I was asked to go up to the Theatre Royal (now Scottish Television headquarters) to help the Macdona Players. I was a great fan of the Macdona Players, who came to Glasgow every year to present a season of the plays of George Bernard Shaw. They were managed by a Mr. Charles Macdona, and their bright and shining star was Esme Percy, who had been playing Shaw heroes for so long that Glaswegians couldn't imagine anybody else in the parts. Among others I remember were Wilfred Lawson, George Merritt, George Bancroft and—I'm a little doubtful here—Roger Livesey.

For this season they were presenting *Man and Superman* in its entirety, as the posters say. That meant not only the Don Juan in Hell scene, but the one which precedes it in which the band of brigands capture the principal characters in the mountains. There are several small speaking parts among the brigands and these were to be played by amateurs, who would also make up the rest of the band.

I found myself on the dim stage of the Theatre Royal with
a group of young men, some of whom I had seen before in
amateur productions around Glasgow. To my pleased surprise I was picked out to try the part of the French Anarchist,
whose lines are few but good. To my even greater surprise,
I was given the part. And so I appeared in Shaw.

Today I can remember only two fellow actors in that band
of brigands. One was J. D. G. Macrae, later known as Duncan
Macrae, who played a Cockney part, and the other was
W. H. D. Joss, later a distinguished radio actor on the
Scottish Home Service. Willie Joss played a shepherd
brigand. He was clad in a woolly rug and little else and he
had to stand on a built-up mountain in the background. At a
signal from the stage manager in the wings he had to run
down the mountainside shouting 'Automobile! Automobile!' That was his entire part, and he did it very well.

I appeared in *Man and Superman* on three occasions altogether and after my opening night the stage manager was
good enough to say that I was just about the best French
Anarchist they'd ever had. I bet he said that to all the
French Anarchists! It was an arduous evening for the
audience, because the play started at 5.30 p.m. and went on
till at least 11 o'clock with a short interval for a meal.

It was also an arduous evening for Esme Percy, who had
not only to play the part of John Tanner, but also bear the
brunt of the Hell scene, in which he was Don Juan and make
the longest speeches I have ever heard in any theatre. There
are only three other characters in Hell with him, They are
his lady friend, her father and the Devil. In this production
they had static, and quite restful, positions. Don Juan was
the only person who moved about.

I watched this Hell scene from the wings each night. It
fascinated me. Hell consisted mainly of rocks and the static
characters had a rock each. Underneath these three rocks,
each had a prompter, rather in the style of the old Ardrossan
and Saltcoats Players. The only person without a prompter
was Esme Percy.

Any way you look at it, it was an amazing feat of memory
for an actor. I'm not surprised that the entire *Man and*

Superman is so seldom done. But the reason that the other actors had to have prompters was twofold. One was that Don Juan's speeches were so long that the Devil, for example, might well have missed his cue when it eventually came. The other was that, now and then, Esme Percy missed out a few hundred lines or perhaps transposed speeches in his rodomontade, and I'd then see the prompters under the rocks riffling feverishly through the book to try to keep the other characters on the right lines. You see, as long as Don Juan kept on talking, the audience felt he couldn't possibly be wrong.

My last appearance as the French Anarchist was during the Glasgow Fair Fortnight, the city's annual holiday which meant a lot more then than it does now. Our brigand ranks were much depleted and one or two of the speaking roles had to be taken by inexperienced actors. Well, I mean, I had already played the part for two nights and was word perfect! I had the feeling that our scene wasn't the success it had been originally, although Willie Joss still created his excitement when he skipped down the mountainside shouting 'Automobile!'

Our scene took place just before the long interval so, after it was over, I had plenty of time to change and go down to take up my accustomed position in the wings to watch the Hell scene. Along came Esme Percy in his Don Juan costume. I would like to think he recognised me, but I doubt it. However, what he did do was come up to me, throw one arm around my shoulders and say, 'Thank you so much, dear boy, for all you have done for us. You'll never know how much I have appreciated your help.'

I went home on air and waited for a contract from the Macdona Players. When it didn't come, I went back to writing plays in which I could appear myself.

3

As a critic of the amateur drama I ran into troubles which

I never experienced as a critic of the professional theatre. I suppose I was a trifle harsh sometimes. Some time ago a Glasgow business man who had been an amateur actor in his youth taxed me with this and, when I replied that I might be strict but I'd never been really hard on people, he produced a cutting of a criticism I had written of a church amateur drama group in Glasgow. It started, 'Every mistake which it is possible to make in amateur drama was committed by the Soandso dramatic club last night when they presented . . . . . .'

At various times amateur actresses I had criticised adversely threatened to slap my face. Lots of nasty anonymous letters came my way. Sometimes, when I criticised adjudicators in drama festivals, they would reply to me from the stage. It was wonderful.

I got into trouble with the amateur playwrights too. There were a great many in those days and I often wonder why there aren't more now. I was always crossing swords with Paul Vincent Carroll, and then he wrote *Shadow and Substance* and *The White Steed* and confounded me completely.

There were all sorts of experimental theatres in Glasgow, playing in places that would probably be banned by the authorities today. John Stewart started his Park Theatre in a house near Kelvingrove Park, and eventually it was translated into the Pitlochry Festival Theatre which is so successful now.

Molly Urquhart had a theatre of her own in Rutherglen, and I wrote a pantomime for it one Christmas. I recollect that my royalties for the three weeks' run came to just over £4. She had Eileen Herlihy (now Herlie) playing for her, and Andrew Crawford, and others who later made their name in the theatre.

I don't suppose anybody made much out of Molly's theatre, least of all Molly herself. I know that she and Eileen Herlie went down on their knees and washed out the theatre on several occasions, so as to save the hire of cleaners. They presented Paul Vincent Carroll's *Green Cars Go East*, a title which means nothing nowadays, but which was a sort of symbolic one then. Glasgow tram-cars operated on a colour scheme, and the East End was served by the green cars.

Teeth to teeth with Ken Dodd

Santa House

Eileen Herlie played the heroine, the school teacher daughter of a slum family, and where she showed she was a real actress was in her accent, just the right touch of the Gallowgate overlaid with the Jordanhill Training College for Teachers.

When he got into the money, Paul Vincent Carroll was fond of giving parties and, perhaps out of his Irishness, he always invited me along, although I had been his sternest critic. It was then that Eileen Herlie really looked like an actress. She wore odd hair styles and a face powder that made her look pale green. Paul's parties usually ended in most of the women present looking pale green, so perhaps Eileen was just showing the way. The trouble was that he thought men should drink whisky, and women should have a concoction of his own in which sherry and gin were mixed.

Eileen Herlie came to local fame through the Pantheon Club which, with the Torch Theatre Club and the Jewish Institute Dramatic Club, was among the leading amateur groups of the day. The Pantheon included my 'shepherd' friend, Willie Joss, and Molly Weir, who went on to be Aggie the Cook in the *Life with Lyons* radio series and is a television actress now. Nobody else, however, achieved the heights which Eileen Herlie reached in this country and America. I think I can boast that I am one of the few entertainment journalists of the time who has not since claimed he 'discovered' her.

My own favourite character was the miner playwright, Joe Corrie, now living, and highly regarded, in the new town of Glen Rothes. He never seemed to stop writing plays, mostly one-acters, and they were produced everywhere in Scotland. You could count on at least one Corrie play getting into the Scottish Community Drama Final each year.

His plays were translated into several foreign languages, including Russian. Eventually, Joe got word that a lot of rouble royalties were waiting for him in Moscow, so he arranged to go there. As soon as he arrived, all the royalties owing to him were handed over in one big bundle of roubles. He had never seen so much money in his life. Then it was explained to him that he would not be allowed to take

D

any of it out of Russia. And so Joe lived like a millionaire for a week or two.

He deserved it, for he had had a very hard time of it. He came from a mining family in Lochgelly, Fife, and he was determined to get out of the pits. He wanted to be a writer and he started with poetry. Some of it was published in Socialist and Co-operative magazines, but he made little money. Then he wrote a play and sent it to the Scottish National Players in Glasgow. He got an acknowledgment, but nothing else.

The weeks went on. He was drawing the dole and, apart from writing, his favourite ploy was to walk to the loch which gives Lochgelly its name. Here, on an afternoon, he'd meet three young unemployed miners practising all sorts of athletics. Years later, when he was touring with his own play company, Joe met a group of acrobats on the same variety bill. They called themselves the Three Aberdonians, and under that name had appeared at a Royal Command Performance at the London Palladium. But they were the three Lochgelly miners Joe had known in his young days.

There was no more word from the Scottish National Players. Joe Corrie gave up all hope. He was making nothing out of his writing. One day he decided to commit suicide. He walked to the loch and round it, trying to make up his mind to throw himself in. But he decided he hadn't the courage. He walked home and, as he came in sight of the house, he saw his mother standing outside waiting for him. When she saw him, she waved an envelope excitedly. The letter was from the Scottish National Players and said that *The Shillin' A Week Man* by Joe Corrie would be one of three one-act plays to be presented at the Lyric Theatre for a week.

There was also an invitation to meet Mr. Hugh Roberton of the Glasgow Orpheus Choir and Mr. David Cleghorn Thomson, Director of the B.B.C. in Scotland, for dinner in the Grosvenor Restaurant before the show. Joe was at once elated and downcast. He was a playwright after all. But what was he going to do about the dinner? His only suit was not too bad. At least, it could be cleaned and pressed by his mother. But his boots were in a shocking condition. However, he went out to one of those dumps you find round all mining villages and got hold of a discarded motor tire. From this he cut new soles and heels for his boots and nailed them on.

His distinguished hosts met him at the station and Joe was dumbfounded to see that Mr. Cleghorn Thomson was wearing full evening dress with a black cloak lined with scarlet silk. They took him up the marble staircase of the Grosvenor (another relic of my youth that is gone) and for the first time in his life he sat in an eating place bigger than a Lochgelly café. He couldn't understand the menu and he didn't know what to do with the cutlery, which seemed to stretch for yards on either side of him. However, he just said he'd have the same as Mr. Roberton and then, when it arrived, he watched which implements the conductor picked up and did the same.

And then the Lyric and his play and the applause. It was a great night for Joe. And here I should say, perhaps, that my second appearance with the Regent Place U.F. Church of Scotland Dramatic Club was in the eponymous role of *The Shillin' a Week Man*. He's the chap who collects one shilling per week from housewives who have been incautious enough to take goods from him, a primitive form of hire purchase which was much in vogue in Scottish mining circles in the Twenties and Thirties. The play consists in the efforts of the housewives to dodge him or to put him off in some way. It's simple, funny and disturbingly true to life as it was lived then.

Most of Joe Corrie's plays were written about people he knew in situations he knew, although occasionally he would write political satire or stark tragedy, and he produced a full-length play about Joan of Arc which was as good as Lionel Hale's *She Passed Through Lorraine*. He wrote a play about Robert Burns and one act of it was put out separately as *The Rake o' Mauchline*. Joe was so carried away by Burns that he took a house in Mauchline and did his writing there.

He married a London girl, who shared his political beliefs but kept her feet firmly on the ground. She must have done Joe a great deal of good. I'm glad to say Joe and his wife came to my wedding. He didn't come to the actual wedding service, because that was against his beliefs, but he said that they would like to be at the reception and what I believe is called the wedding breakfast in the best circles. The only thing he worried about was that he would wear no other headgear but his bunnet, his flat cloth cap, and he didn't know if that would be suitable. I assured him that it was, and I think he enjoyed the wedding.

But Joe's bunnet was dear to him. His meeting with Hugh Roberton introduced him to the great Glasgow Orpheus Choir, and he started going out with one of the girl singers. They got on very well together, but she was not at all keen on Joe's bunnet. She wanted him to wear a soft hat, as all the best people did then. Eventually it came to a show-down. Joe refused to give up his bunnet and they parted.

Years later, after Joe was happily married, he opened his morning paper at breakfast time one day and there was his ex-girl friend's picture and a story about how she had won some huge amount in the Irish Sweep. It struck him then that, if he had changed from a bunnet to a soft hat, he might well be sharing it.

I admire Joe Corrie more than I can say. Indeed, when a sodality of which I am a member, the Thirteen Club in Glasgow, ran a symposium on *My Most Remarkable Character*, I chose Joe Corrie. In his day he was a singularly successful broadcaster. I asked him how he did it. Joe said, 'It's quite simple. I just smile while I'm talking!'

4

It is my opinion that the Community Drama Festival in Scotland started to decline when the Press were asked not to criticise adjudicators until the Festival was over. As 'Jingle' of the *Citizen* I criticised adjudicators whenever I felt they needed it. Some of them resented this very much and complained bitterly to the S.C.D.A. But it made for excitement, and that is what is lacking in Drama Festivals today.

Of course, being a drama festival adjudicator is to be

placed in a particularly vulnerable position. I know, because I have done the job. The plays are over, but you have still to perform. And perform is the word. A festival audience expect some fun and fireworks from the adjudicator. The temptation, as I know only too well, is to play to the audience.

I have seen some famous men adjudicate. Tyrone Guthrie could be great, or he could be so perverse that he wasn't worth listening to. Sir Charles B. Cochran was the world's most artless adjudicator. He knew nothing at all of amateur drama. He amazed the panjandrums of the S.C.D.A. by applauding each play. And finally he picked a group from the Far North who were doing a simple Joe Corrie comedy.

Probably the finest adjudicator we ever had in Scotland was Michel St. Denis. Apart from his sound judgments, he was a great success because of his French accent. L. A. G. Strong was a nice chap, but didn't know anything about it.

After the Second World War was over, I was asked to adjudicate at various drama festivals. I couldn't resist the opportunity to show off. But I think I was quite a good and fair adjudicator and I tried not to hurt people's feelings. I had my troubles, of course. On one occasion I suggested that a producer had concentrated so much on production that he had forgotten the actors altogether, and gave as an illustration a production I had seen in Glasgow where the producer had rehearsed his players on a stage marked out in boxes. This was a Stanislavsky idea, and it had its points if it was correctly used.

So I talked about Stanislavsky and the trouble of following a method too rigidly. And then I went behind the scenes for the private adjudications with the various groups. This is the moment of truth. It's all very well to criticise them from the stage and get the response of the audience. It's quite a different thing to face, in a small room, a hostile dramatic club who want to know what you meant when you said so-and-so. In this particular case the group, led by the producer, filed in. And, when they were all settled, the producer said, 'You referred to Stanislavsky. What page of Stanislavsky?'

Then there was the occasion when I went to talk to a Women's Rural Institute team that I'd had to be candid about. The moment I appeared, they all burst into tears. Later I was told that they had decided never to enter a drama festival again.

I recollect, down at a drama festival in Galloway, criticising one of the actors for a too florid make-up, and then meeting him behind the scenes and finding he had been wearing no make-up at all.

Generally speaking, life as an adjudicator tends to give you a pretty low opinion of human beings. But the last adjudication I did was in Northern Ireland, and I had a singular experience there. The festival was held at Portadown and it was unusual because of its length and because one-act plays, full-length plays and even a Gilbert and Sullivan opera were included.

There were two slightly odd requests made of me before I was picked as the adjudicator. First of all, I was asked, in a delicate sort of way, if I was a Protestant. Portadown is the place where the cream of the Orange Order, the Black Lodge, was founded. Roman Catholics in Portadown keep very quiet indeed. Secondly, I was asked if I wore the kilt. My predecessor as adjudicator had been Finlay J. Macdonald of the B.B.C. in Scotland and, while he had appeared in normal dinner jacket for most of the festival, he arrived on the last night in the full fig of Highland evening dress. He had been the greatest success ever.

I was able to assure the organisers that I was a Protestant, but I had to admit that I hadn't worn the kilt since I was in the Boy Scouts. They took this very well.

The festival was a pretty straightforward affair, except for the performance of a potted version of *H.M.S. Pinafore* by a boy's school, until the last night. On this Saturday the presentation was a full-length play called *Many Young Men of Twenty* by a drama group from the other side of the Border. They were, of course, Roman Catholics and this was the first time that a group from Eire, far less Roman Catholics, had taken part in the Portadown Festival.

There was nothing in the rules of the Portadown Festival to stop Catholics from competing. I seemed to detect a slight air of daring about the organisers. The playwright, John

Keane, was well-known as a stirrer-up of things and a critic of the Government in Dublin. The team itself was from Dundalk which, though across the Border, is but a short car run from Portadown.

Well, there I was, sitting in the draughty hall, having totted up my marks for everything I had seen so far, and not thinking I had to worry very much about the next two or three hours. Then *Many Young Men of Twenty* started and I found myself watching something which was far beyond the standard of the rest of the Festival.

This is a play with songs and the title comes from the principal song which starts 'Many young men of twenty said goodbye.' Its theme is the way the country Irish send their children over to Britain to make money for them, and the effect on the children. It is very funny, and sometimes sentimental, and the Dundalk players made the most of it. Undoubtedly it was the best thing I'd seen on that stage in Portadown.

All the same, I wondered what would happen if I put a Roman Catholic play first in the Festival of a town where there were reminders at every second corner that King Billy had won the Battle of the Boyne and that the inhabitants disapproved of the Pope. Then I recollected that, among the large number of trophies and awards for the Portadown Festival, there was the audience's trophy. This was voted for by members of the Festival Association, and it was their opportunity to put the adjudicator in his place. Apparently it was quite common for the adjudicator to announce the best play and then for the audience to come to a completely different conclusion.

Ah, well, I was flying back to Glasgow next day and I wouldn't hear all the criticism of my choice. I went on to the stage and praised *Many Young Men of Twenty*. Then I read out my placings and, to my surprise and delight, the audience approved of my first to Dundalk.

Then it was time for the secretary to announce the audience's choice. I was certain that it was going to a team from Belfast, which I had placed second. But the Protestants of Portadown had picked the Roman Catholic entry. Not only

that, but I learned later that 80 per cent of the audience had
voted for it.

I was overjoyed. I felt that this might be a very small thing
in Northern Ireland, but it had its significance. Every time
today I think of the Rev. Ian Paisley, I think also of that
night I adjudicated at Portadown.

Comics in Kilts

I often think I'd have made a good Scots comic if I'd just had the guts to take a chance. Yes, I know I didn't do so well at my debut in Letta's Prom Pavilion, Portobello, but, if I'd persevered, I think I could have made the grade. Certainly, the late Tommy Morgan thought so, and he was such a successful comedian that he should have known.

Once or twice I did my party pieces in his presence and he said afterwards, though not to me, that I had a great sense of timing. So I might have been a rich man now—although judging by some of the Scots comics I have known, I could equally well have become an alcoholic or met an early death.

Scots comics are a race apart. Only a few of them are gagsters in the modern tradition. The real Scots comic is a great observer of the life around him and he translates it into terms of comedy for the stage. He uses various Scottish accents, mostly Glasgow for the simple reason that that's where the biggest concentration of population is in Scotland. But Harry Gordon kept to his native Aberdeen accent, and he was immensely popular in Glasgow. And even then, when it comes to Glasgow itself, Ian Sadler, who appeared in so many of my B.B.C. shows on radio, claimed that he could reproduce fourteen different Glasgow accents, each applying to a separate sector of the city.

The Scots comic is strong on satire, though it's inclined to be straightforward rather than subtle. His particular subjects for satire are the English and the Americans, apart, of course, from the Scots themselves. During the Second World

War, the Poles were popular as a satirical subject, and today the Pakistanis have taken their place.

There is a tradition of 'keeping it clean' among the Scots comics, although there have been some notable exceptions. I recollect meeting Will Fyffe, when he sailed into Glasgow from New York, having walked out of an 'Earl Carroll's Vanities' show. He explained to me that he was engaged as principal comedian of this revue, but his engagement was to appear twice or thrice in the evening in his own act. So, until the first night, he knew nothing of the content of the rest of the show.

Well, he didn't explain to me exactly what was wrong with it from his point of view. All he indicated was that his Calvinistic feelings were outraged and he felt he could not possibly take part in such an exhibition. So he threw up his part and all the money that went with it, and returned to Scotland.

One of the things he told me was that Walter Winchell, in his famous syndicated column, had stated 'Will Fyffe is a Jew'. Like many other small, dark Scotsmen with big noses —just look at me, for example—Will Fyffe did look faintly Jewish, as, for that matter, did the Aberdonian Harry Gordon. But Will Fyffe was born in Dundee, the son of Jack Fyffe, who ran a penny geggie and was Scots to the core. He told me that he had sent a postcard to the columnist saying, 'Walter Winchell is a liar'. He added happily, 'And I didn't put a stamp on it.'

Well, I published this story and, in due course, got a letter from a girl who said she was Walter Winchell's secretary. She said that Mr Winchell was very annoyed about this story, because he had never said that Will Fyffe was a Jew. I wrote back, giving the details of my interview, but I heard no more about it.

That was, however, my second run-in with Walter Winchell. I have mentioned the enterprising publicity man who wanted me to have Roy Fox's wife kidnapped by Glasgow gangsters. While I explained to him that that could not be done, I did agree to interview her. She had been a show-girl on Broadway and she told me a story of how Walter Winchell had taken her out to lunch one day to a celebrated New York restaurant. Its windows looked on to the street and, naturally, Walter Winchell and the Mrs Fox-to-be had a window table.

This was right in the middle of the Al Capone era, and the lady asked Mr Winchell if he knew any gangsters. (I can only assume that she was not a regular reader of his column!) He replied that there was a famous gangster having lunch only a few tables away. And just at that moment a car came cruising along the street and, as it passed the restaurant, men sitting in it opened fire from sub-machine guns.

Quick as a flash, Walter Winchell grabbed the girl and pulled her under the table. I don't remember now if the famous gangster was shot or not, but I imagine that that would be the end of the tale.

Never one to contradict a lady, I printed an interview with her in which I included this story. A month or so later I was sent a cutting from America which contained Walter Winchell's column. It mentioned my interview and went on to say that the gangster story was a lot of nonsense. It was one which various American starlets and show-girls had been telling for some time. Apparently it had now got to the stature of a folk-tale.

So I presume that's Walter Winchell and me one each.

Probably the founder of the 'keep it clean' movement among Scots comics was Harry Lauder. He was not the first Scots comic. As I have explained in *The Heart of Glasgow*, that honour goes to a tall, thin man named Harry Linn, who was famous for his song, 'The Fattest Man in the Forty-Twa'. ('The Forty-Twa' were the 42nd Highlanders.)

But Harry Lauder was the first comedian to establish himself internationally and he made the pattern for Scots comics for years to come. The odd thing is that he started professionally with an Irish song, 'Calligan, Call Again', because just at that time in the music hall, Ireland was considered to be the place where funny men came from.

For years now angry Scots have been inveighing against what they call 'the Harry Lauder image' of the people of Scotland. I can only assume that these hot-eyed chaps never saw Harry Lauder. I'm glad to say that I did. It was one of his last appearances at the Alhambra Theatre in Glasgow, and it was a remarkable demonstration of personality. It was in the days when the quick-fire revue was all the rage and everything on the stage was being done faster and faster.

Yet Harry Lauder presented his act in the way he had always done it—that's to say, a series of character impressions, with an interval between each one long enough for him to change his make-up and his costume. And the audience sat there and waited for minutes, while the orchestra played the introduction to the next number over and over again. These character impressions were brilliant. They were so well studied, so complete, and the songs were so well sung. Of course, Chaliapin said that when he wanted to hear a perfect singing voice, he put on a Harry Lauder record. Sir Hugh Roberton, conductor of the Glasgow Orpheus Choir, has said the same. He advised all his choir members to listen to Harry Lauder.

That night at the Alhambra was not the last time I heard him, but it was the end of his professional appearances. During the Second World War he was always ready to appear for charity. I recall him coming on at the King's Theatre one Sunday night when there was a Garrison Theatre presentation for the Scottish Red Cross. When the wee man wearing the kilt walked on, he was cheered mightily. He made a little speech about the war effort and then said, 'And now I've got to do my piece in the programme.' Voices in the audience started to shout for 'I Love a Lassie', 'Roamin' in the Gloamin', 'I'm the Saftest of the Family', and so on. But Harry Lauder said, 'Ladies and Gentlemen, this is the Sabbath.' And then, without accompaniment, he sang 'Rocked in the cradle of the deep'.

It was sentimental, it was corny, it was old-fashioned and out-dated, and it was supremely Scottish.

I met Harry Lauder at various first nights, particularly pantomime ones. He had a great habit of going round backstage afterwards to have a word or two with whichever Scots comic it was that was leading the show. He would give them useful tips on singing and presentation and, if the comic was young, he would invariably say, 'You're doing well now, son, but mind what I'm telling you. Watch the bawbees!'

This was very valuable advice to a young comedian because, once he moves up to a good-sized salary, the money is apt to go to his head. Many a young Scots comic (and some of the older ones, too) has gone off the rails because he made too much money too quickly. But the critics of Lauder would say that this showed, just once again, his desire to press the meanness or, putting it more politely, the canny thriftiness of the Scots.

True, Harry Lauder made jokes about thrift, though not to the extent that his critics make out. In his early days it really was a national characteristic, and I rather tend to agree with the people who wish it still was. But these stories were more in the great line of telling jokes against oneself. The Jews are famous for this. And the Aberdonians are credited with making up the Aberdeen stories themselves.

In private Harry Lauder was one of the most generous of men. This was a characteristic of his day. You put on a thrifty mask to the world, and hid your good deeds. I am reminded of one of the many stories about Harry McKelvie, the man who ran the Royal Princess's Theatre in the Gorbals for many years and then sold it at a bargain price to the Citizen's Theatre.

Harry McKelvie was a tall, saturnine man, who always wore a Stetson hat and smoked a cigar. The story goes that he was standing on the other side of Main Street, Gorbals, one day, looking across at the Royal Princess's Theatre, when a busybody type approached him and said, 'Mr McKelvie, do you realise that, if you gave up smoking, instead of just owning the Princess's you'd own the whole of that block of buildings?' (The block included another theatre, shops, a dance hall, and houses.)

Pausing only to take his cigar out of his mouth, Harry McKelvie replied, 'I do own the whole block.'

The classic story of McKelvie concerns a small-time Scots comic named Bob Merry, who asked the great man for an interview one spring day. Nervously he explained that he had a chance of running the concert party at Arbroath for the summer. He knew he could get a good company together, and he was sure he could make it a success. But he had to put down a deposit of £100, and he hadn't got £100. Could Mr McKelvie help him out and he would guarantee to pay it back by a certain date in August?

I can just imagine the impresario sitting there, listening to Bob Merry without a quiver of humanity on his long, thin face. Everybody knew he was a hard man, and Bob Merry felt inclined to get up there and then and walk out. After a minute or so, Harry McKelvie said, 'All right', and handed the comic £100.

Months passed and then, one afternoon in early August, Bob Merry turned up once again at the Royal Princess's Theatre. 'Well,' said McKelvie, 'what's the bad news? Your season's over early.'

'Oh, no,' said Merry, 'we're having a great season. We're going to run right on to September. Here's your £100, and thanks very much, Mr McKelvie.'

'Just a minute,' said McKelvie. 'You're a week early. The date you fixed for paying me back is not till Tuesday.'

'Yes,' replied the comic, 'but I can't manage next Tuesday and I didn't want to keep you waiting.'

'Humph!' grunted McKelvie. And he took Bob Merry's cheque for £100, tore it in small pieces, and dropped it into the waste-paper basket.

While he was quite happy to make a present of £100 to an honest comedian, Harry McKelvie moved ruthlessly against people he suspected of having done him, as I shall reveal when I come to the story of Tommy Lorne.

For myself, I met Harry McKelvie on only a few occasions. I found his grim exterior too difficult to penetrate. Once, however, I was working on a weekly series for B.B.C. radio which involved a comedian appearing in each show and telling the story of his life. Unexpectedly, Tommy Morgan let us down. He was annoyed that the B.B.C. had broadcast an excerpt from every Glasgow pantomime except his and, although I had already written the script, and he had approved of it, he suddenly took a fit of the sturdies and said he wouldn't do it.

What was to be done? The whole series had been worked out to the exact number of available comics. The producer suggested I should try the principal boy of the Princess's pantomime, Jeanette Adie. When she wasn't appearing in pantomime, Jeanette was a male impersonator so, by a little stretch of the imagination, she could qualify as a comedian. It was all very well for the producer to suggest this but he knew as well as I did that Harry McKelvie's permission had to be got for Miss Adie to appear, and Harry McKelvie was allergic to the B.B.C. He had only allowed his own comic from the pantomime, George West, to appear in the series after a lot of protests and arguments.

First I approached Jeanette Adie, who was delighted with the idea. But she said she couldn't do it without 'the Boss's permission'. So I went to see Harry McKelvie, who received me with his dourest expression. I thought I had better explain the whole circumstances, so I did. McKelvie's expression never altered.

Then he said, 'D'you mean that the B.B.C. is in a fix?' I said they were. 'Oh, well, in that case,' he said, 'it's all right. Miss Adie can broadcast.'

Harry McKelvie was quite unpredictable. The theatre had been passed on to him by his own boss, Rich Waldon. He had started there as a boy programme-seller (like Sir A. B. King) and had risen to become Waldon's right-hand man. It was expected that he would eventually hand on the theatre to his comic, George West, who had appeared in twenty-one pantomimes at the Royal Princess's. Instead, as I have mentioned, it went to James Bridie, Dr. T. J. Honeyman, and the other directors of the Citizens' Theatre.

2

The funniest Scotsman who has appeared on the stage in my time was undoubtedly the late, great Tommy Lorne. Words cannot express the effect that this tall, gaunt figure with the

craggy features and the big hands had on his audiences.
Unlike most comedians, he was funny even off the stage. I
once saw him walk across Renfield Street from the Pavilion
Theatre to Green's Playhouse. He was well dressed in a coat
and a lounge suit. But, as he walked these few yards, everybody in his vicinity started smiling.

I don't suppose we shall look upon his like again, but I
recall a performance by Duncan Macrae in *Let Wives Tak'
Tent*, a Scottish version by Robert Kemp of Moliere's *School
for Wives*. He walked from backstage down to where the foot-
lights used to be. And, though he was wearing the black
clothes of an elderly 18th century Frenchman, as he raised
one hand he looked amazingly like Tommy Lorne.

While I couldn't claim that my father, in the words of the
song, knew Lloyd George, I could claim as a youth that my
father knew Tommy Lorne. This put me high in the pecking
order at Riddrie. Tommy Lorne's real name was Hugh
Corcoran, and early in his life he worked at Blochairn Steelworks in the drawing-office. He was a gangling, pleasant
boy, but not overly interested in the work that was given
him. On one occasion, when the whole staff were working
late, my father heard odd sounds coming from the drawing-
office. He went along to investigate and found that Hugh
Corcoran and another boy were practising tap-dancing.

Even when Hugh Corcoran left Blochairn Steelworks to
try the stage as a career, he kept up a correspondence with
my father, although all that remains of it today is a single
postcard signed Tommy Lorne. The change of name came
about in this way. Corcoran started his stage career with
various partners under various names, but the time came
when he got a chance to go on as a comic in his own right.
He had to choose a name for himself. At this time he greatly
admired an English comedian called Tom E. Hughes, so
he decided he should be called Tom E. Lorne.

This name was 'phoned over to the bill-printer who interpreted it as Tommy Lorne and, after he'd seen it on the
posters, Hugh Corcoran decided to leave it at that. Surely
the bill-printer had a touch of genius, for somehow Tom E.
Lorne doesn't convey the magic of the man at all.

He was making some small success in third-rate theatres in Scotland when the Great War broke out and he was called up. He must have been one of the oddest-looking soldiers ever to wear uniform. However, the Great War ended and one day Robert McLeod, the conductor of the Royal Princess's Theatre orchestra, was at a pantomime rehearsal when he heard a familiar voice behind him, and here was Private Tommy Lorne, newly demobbed and still in uniform.

At an interval in the rehearsal McLeod told Harry Mc-Kelvie that Tommy Lorne was in the stalls and McKelvie immediately sent for him. He gave him money to buy a new suit and told him to come back the following week. And when Tommy Lorne came back, Harry McKelvie gave him a job as comic in a touring pantomime. In a year or two, McKelvie saw that Lorne was ready for the famous Princess's panto-mime. He put him into it with a notable 'feed', Bret Harte, a man whose sense of timing was so great that he was apt to push the comic into action and even shout 'Hurry up!' when he thought the comic was lagging.

Tommy Lorne was an enormous success at the Princess's. It got so that he just had to walk on to the stage and look at a bit of scenery and he had the audience in convulsions. He worked hard at the job of being a comic, and he was always going to odd places in Glasgow to get ideas for scenes and sketches. He took up popular Glasgow phrases of the time. When he cried in his creaking voice, 'In the name of the wee man!' or 'Ah'll get ye!', foreigners in the audience were amazed at the Glasgow reaction. Latterly he had only to say 'In the name!' and Glaswegians were prostrate.

Lorne spent several happy years at the Princess's. Harry McKelvie didn't bother about contracts. On the last night of the pantomime he'd go round the dressing rooms. If he looked into Tommy Lorne's and said, 'Comic, I'll see you in November', Lorne knew that he was re-engaged for the pantomime. If he didn't look into your dressing-room, you knew that you wouldn't be in the next pantomime.

Then some people got hold of Tommy Lorne and offered him a big salary to go into pantomime at the Pavilion Theatre. They pointed out to him that he had no contract with Harry McKelvie and was perfectly entitled to make a change. Unwisely he agreed and, when pantomime time came round again, Harry McKelvie found that he had lost his comic.

He lost no time in getting in touch with Tommy Lorne's new managers. He threatened to sue them and so terrified them that they agreed to pay to Harry McKelvie the salary which he would have been paying Lorne at the Princess's. So every week they had to send this sum to McKelvie and McKelvie in his turn immediately sent it to a charity.

Then came the accolade for Tommy Lorne—an invitation to be comic in the Howard and Wyndham pantomime at the Theatre Royal. There were critics who thought he would be too 'broad' for the refined Royal, but he proved them completely wrong. For the first time he played dame and was a greater success than ever. It was this success that caused his downfall.

For one of his Royal pantomimes Tommy Lorne received the biggest salary he had ever been offered. It was £250 a week, which would be worth at least £1000 a week now. Not only that, but it gave him a percentage on the gross takings each week. The pantomime was the customary success. It was packed out and at the end of the first week Lorne worked out that he should receive, between salary and percentage, £400.

But what he did get was £275. When he asked the manager if there wasn't some mistake, the manager pointed to some small print in the contract which Tommy Lorne hadn't noticed. True, it said there would be a percentage on the gross takings, but it added that in no week would his combined salary plus percentage exceed £275. So the pantomime went on its successful way, and the more successful it was, the more Tommy Lorne brooded over what he felt he was losing.

He had some bad friends at this time, and they encouraged him in his brooding. He started drinking heavily. This came as a shock to many of us because Tommy Lorne had been practically a teetotaller. I remembered an interview I had had with him when, after asking for my father, the first thing he had said was a warning against strong drink.

At this time his feed was W. S. Percy, an English comedian who found it more profitable to act as stooge to Tommy Lorne. During the summer-time Lorne appeared in revues and as he was as popular in the North and Midlands of England as he was in Scotland, he made extensive tours. But drink was getting the better of him and sometimes W. S. Percy found that he had no comic to feed at the second house and had to be the comic himself.

Tommy Lorne's pantomime contract was not renewed by Howard and Wyndham. He was forced to run his own pantomime and take it out on tour. But he had learned his lesson. He swore off drink and, when I saw his touring version of *Cinderella* at the Empire Theatre in Glasgow, I thought he was as good as ever he was. Howard and Wyndham took him back into the fold, and he signed a contract for their Royal pantomime for the season 1935–36.

Alas, he died in April, 1935, in his fifties. He was buried at Kirkintilloch, and huge crowds turned out for his funeral. He is still remembered fondly by those who saw him and the younger Scots comics today have often said to me, 'Of course, I never saw Tommy Lorne. I was too young. But everybody who did see him tells me that he was the greatest.'

Many of the Scots comics I have known have ended tragically. It seems almost an axiom that a man who makes people laugh should have a secret sorrow or a sad end. I remember Tommy Morgan in his last days. I was writing the script of a radio programme on the Princess's pantomime, and we wanted Tommy Morgan and his feed, Tommy Yorke, to do a short gag which they had done in the pantomime which followed Tommy Lorne's departure to the Pavilion. In his desperation to make up for the loss of Lorne, Harry McKelvie had, in Tommy Morgan's words, 'thrown on the comics in bundles of ten!'

Yorke and Morgan (the order of their billing then) were in the bundles, along with Syd Walker, Dave Bruce, Peel and Curtis, and goodness knows who else. They did only one act, and Tommy Morgan still had it among his scripts. It seemed simple enough for Yorke and Morgan, with the script in front of them, to recreate that scene in the pantomime.

But by this time Morgan had left the stage through illness. He was living in his luxurious Kelvin Court flat, looked after by his wife, and he seemed fine when I went to see him. But, he said, his doctor would not allow him out and he couldn't come to Broadcasting House to record his scene. Eddie Fraser, the producer, arranged for a recording van to go to Kelvin Court. Tommy Yorke (a feed out of work because his comic was out of work) came along. Each had a copy of the script and we started confidently enough.

After only a few lines, Tommy Morgan lost the place. He could not concentrate. He cursed himself and kept trying. Then, with his eyes wet with tears of rage, he said, 'Ach, they should take me out and shoot me.' We did not know then that he had had a brain operation. He wouldn't admit defeat and, through a long winter's afternoon, we kept on trying. At last we did it by recording small parts of the scene at a time and doing them over and over again if they went wrong.

All these small bits went back to the B.B.C., where the sound experts put them together in such a way that the little sketch sounded as bright and fresh as it had when Yorke and Morgan first did it at the Princess's. I listened to it, but I didn't enjoy it.

Will Fyffe died in a fall from the balcony of the hotel of which he was part owner in St Andrews. The strange thing is that, just at the time, he was learning his part for the next Alhambra pantomime in Glasgow, *Humpty Dumpty*, and his entrance line in the script was 'I fell!'

Of the tragi-comic comedians in Scotland the one I liked most was Wullie Lindsay, a man who might have been one of the greatest and who was defeated by himself. Harry Ashton, the manager of the King's Theatre in Glasgow for many years and a real man of the theatre, admired Wullie Lindsay greatly, but said that he was lazy. I think it went deeper than that.

Wullie started as an amateur with the famous Dennistoun Minstrels, a group which had a reputation as great in the city as any professional minstrels who had ever visited Glasgow. He was inclined at first to go in for conjuring, paper-tearing, shadowgraphy, and the other things that I practised too as a boy. I didn't study the 'Boys' Own Paper for nothing, you know.

When the Great War broke out, Wullie Lindsay was a member of the I.L.P. and refused to fight. As a conscientious objector he was sent to Barlinnie Prison and put in a cell with a light burning all night. At first he took it placidly, and then he saw what was obviously a peep-hole in the door. And through this little hole an eye was watching him. He paid no attention but, when he looked at the door again after a few minutes, the eye was still looking at him.

He started making faces at the peep-hole. Then he tried to sleep. But always his eyes were drawn to the door, and always the eye was there. At last he could stand it no longer. He threw himself at the door and burst into tears as he banged at the peep-hole and cursed the owner of the eye. And then he realised that it wasn't an eye at all. The part of the peep-hole which could be moved aside had a little dab of white paint on it, and this gave the appearance of an eye, to Wullie's overwrought imagination at any rate.

When the war was over, Wullie became a Scots comic. He moved up in the world sufficiently to be engaged by the renowned Florrie Forde in one of her touring pantomimes. He was to partner a man named Chesney Allen, and the act was called Lindsay and Allen. After one season, however, Wullie felt this was not his metier and bowed out. His place was taken by a chap named Bud Flanagan. And that was how Flanagan and Allen were born.

As a single act Wullie Lindsay kept going up in the small world of the Scottish music-hall. He was engaged as principal comic in a summer show at Dunoon, and that was doing well in those days. The show was a success. Wullie felt it was only a matter of time ere a theatrical agent would see him and book him into something bigger. One Sunday he took the steamer across to Gourock and, as he walked across the main street there, he was knocked down by a car. He was removed to hospital with a broken leg, and that was the end of the Dunoon summer show as far as he was concerned.

This accident virtually killed Wullie Lindsay's career. Physically all that resulted was a slight limp. But Wullie was

a defeated man. As so many defeated men do, he took to
drink. He was not a drunkard. I knew him well, and I never
saw him drunk in my life. But he would drink enough to
make him forget his responsibilities and among theatre producers he was not regarded as completely reliable.

Still, he got plenty of jobs because he linked up with J. A.
Cox, whom he called the Pantomime King of Scotland.
This odd-looking wee man would book up halls and small
theatres all over Scotland. Then he would enlist a cast for
each pantomime date by the simple method of going to
'Poverty Corner' and seeing who was hanging around.
'Poverty Corner' was the north-west corner of Sauchiehall
Street and Renfield Street, and it was known in the days of
the Depression for the number of out-of-work stage people
who were waiting there for something to turn up. Indeed, in
this connection, I remember once having lunch with
Andrew Stewart, then Variety Producer (I think) for the
B.B.C. in Scotland, now Controller of the whole jing-bang,
in Ferrari's Restaurant at 10 Sauchiehall Street. When
lunch was over Andrew, who is a kind-hearted man, decided
it wouldn't do for him to walk straight along Sauchiehall
Street past 'Poverty Corner', where all the out-of-works
would look pleadingly at him for a broadcast. So he took to a
lane which by-passed 'Poverty Corner' and got back to the
B.B.C. safely.

Well, J. A. Cox would go to the corner and, in a matter of a
few minutes, he would engage principal boy, principal girl,
comic, feed, specialty act, and anybody else he needed. He
would then give them a time and a place to meet the bus.
This bus took the cast to the town hall where the pantomime
was to be presented. During the bus runs J. A. Cox would
explain which pantomime they were doing that night and
leave it to his cast how they were going to do it.

They were all seasoned troupers and it didn't take them
long to write out a list of scenes and decide who was going
to do what in which. They had a pianist whom they could
consult on suitable songs, and they usually arrived at the
town hall in plenty of time to collect whatever they needed
in the way of scenery and props.

In these towns they had practically no competition. Their only rival was the radio and many people in the country places did not have wireless sets. The arrival of Cox's Magnificent Pantomime, *Red Riding Hood*, was an event. *Red Riding Hood* was the most popular among Cox's casts because the costumes were simple, with the exception of the Wolf, and there was always some sort of mask which would do for him. *Robinson Crusoe* and *The Babes in the Wood* were other easy ones.

Very often the artistes changed their professional names for these shows. A couple of comics might be Pettigrew and Stephens in one town and Marks and Sparks in another. This was because the comics were drawing unemployment pay and they did not want the employment exchange people to know.

Besides appearing in the town hall pantomimes, Wullie Lindsay took jobs wherever he could, and he also wrote scripts and songs. 'I was reading Schopenhauer in the public library the other day,' he told me once, 'and I got a great idea for a gag for Tommy Morgan.'

From one Glasgow library he borrowed an American study of comic scenes, situations, jokes and the like. It was just what he had been looking for for years. But he couldn't possibly copy out a whole book. So, after a decent interval, he went to the library and explained that he had been sitting beside the fire reading this book. He must have fallen asleep, because the next thing he knew, the book was in the fire and it was hopelessly burnt before he could do anything about it. The librarian said he quite understood, these accidents did happen, and fined Wullie 7s 6d, his estimation of the value of the book.

Wullie wrote many songs for a large number of Scots comics. In those days he was lucky if he got two or three pounds for the complete rights. Yes, lucky is the word. Colin Milne once told me how he had gone to visit a very famous Scots comic (but not Harry Lauder, I hasten to add!). The Scots comic was engaged and Colin was sitting outside his dressing-room door in the theatre when a wee man emerged and scuttled down the corridor.

Colin went in and said to the comic, 'That chap left in a hurry.' The comic was white with indignation. 'So he should!' he cried. 'Do you know what he's done? He's just offered me a sketch AND HE WANTS A COUPLE OF QUID FOR IT!'

Yes, Wullie Lindsay didn't get rich on the songs he wrote. That was often his own fault. He'd sell a song, literally for the price of a drink.

The Lindsay song which I remember best was one which was very personal. Wullie was in a fish and chip shop in Cambridge Street, then owned by a cheery chap from Grimsby. They were talking about the Scots comic of the day, Dave Willis, when the Grimsby man said, 'You know, he's getting more like Hitler every day.'

Dave Willis wore a small, Chaplin-style moustache, just like Hitler did. He was a tremendously funny comedian and had taken over Tommy Lorne's position in the theatre. Wullie immediately seized one of the paper bags designed to hold chips and wrote a song which he entitled 'I'm getting more like Hitler every day.' Dave Willis liked it and bought it.

But when he made his appearance as Hitler in a Glasgow revue and sang this song, the Government stepped in. They banned it because it was making fun of the head of a friendly state. However, it wasn't long before Herr Schickelgruber stopped being friendly to Britain and, after the war broke out, Dave Willis was able to sing the Lindsay song again without let or hindrance.

I had often seen Wullie Lindsay on the stage, because I loved shows in town halls and in second and third-rate music halls. But I didn't get to know him well until after the second war. He came to me at the *Citizen* office with some ideas about writing on old Glasgow theatres and how you could have a whole night out, including a theatre, a supper and ten cigarettes for just under one shilling.

He was a wonderful companion. Soon he became a central figure in the Express Bar in Albion Street, which was next door to the *Scottish Daily Express* office (and the *Citizen*) and gave Lord Beaverbrook a near fit because he didn't approve of the name. Here Wullie would tell stories and perform gags and do conjuring tricks and explain to anyone how thought-reading was done. He was doing it himself at the time in Sunday night concerts in such centres of sophistication as Bellshill and Larkhall.

In the middle of all this he suddenly got a week's engagement at the Empire Theatre, which described itself as the London Palladium of Scotland. I went to see him and, although he was second on the bill, he did really well. The audience liked him. He was given to understand that a very good report on him had been sent to London. 'And I gave the manager a bottle of whisky on Saturday night,' he told me, 'so I should be all right, Jack.'

But he wasn't. I have no idea why, except that Wullie had lost the power to go after things. He was sanguine about the future for a while, and then he seemed to dismiss the whole thing from his thoughts. 'What's the point of worrying?' he asked me. 'Every Saturday night, before I leave the pub, I buy a bottle of Eldorado. I drink one glass out of it, and then I get the bottle filled up again with a glass of brandy. That sees me over Sunday.'

The Empire bit over, Wullie settled back into his Express Bar life. Macdonald Daly, then editor of the *Scottish Sunday Express*, got into a fight with another member of the Beaverbrook staff. He sustained (wonderful word!) a black eye and he called in Wullie Lindsay with his make-up box to conceal it. Wullie did a great job and he might have started a new career if there had only been more fights among the Beaverbrook staff.

I arranged for him to give a talk on his kind of theatre to an audience of the Citizens Theatre Society. It was held in one of Glasgow's more magnificent buildings, the Trades House. The place was packed with douce citizens, but Wullie was a riot. Afterwards he said to me, 'This is going to be my future. I'll get a new suit on the never-never and start as a lecturer.'

So I got him a date at Barrie's town, Kirriemuir, to give the same lecture that he had given to the Citizens' Theatre Society. He didn't turn up. A big audience sat waiting for an hour and then had to go home. I saw Wullie only once after that, and neither of us mentioned this debacle. He was now 'writing' for another newspaper, but he confessed that he missed my touch.

Not long after that he died, alone in his little flat in the Gorbals. It was discovered that he wanted his body to go to Glasgow University for medical research. But, as he had made no official or legal arrangements, this could not be done. So, even after death, Wullie Lindsay was as inefficient as he had been in life.

He was a very funny man to meet. He had brilliant ideas about the minor variety stage. He could have been one of the great Scots comics and might have made an immense amount of money. It was just that he could always think of something else to do. I seem to have been meeting characters like that all my life. And sometimes I think it's a case of like calling to like.

4

Today there are not enough Scots comics to go round the theatres which want them. That's one good reason why I sometimes wish I had become a Scots comic. The money the top comedians make today is immense. But it doesn't match up to the money the big men made in the old days. I have mentioned Tommy Lorne's £250 a week in the 1930's. But Harry Lauder was making £1000 a week in his prime. Imagine what the equivalent of that would be today.

This lack of Scots comics has been going on for some time. It started something like a quarter of a century ago. At that time there was a very good double act going the rounds of the Scottish music halls—Jack Anthony and Bond Rowell. This was a song-and-dance act with great vitality. Anthony was small and lively. Rowell was lively too, but he was tall and buirdly and had a fine singing voice.

While they were successful in their own way, they realised they could never get beyond the level of a good supporting turn. One day they made out a couple of lists. One list was the number of summer shows which would be presented in Scotland that year. Opposite was a list of Scots comics. The number of summer shows was bigger than the number of Scots comics. And so they decided they would enter the Scots comic market.

Who was going to be the comic? Well, there couldn't be much doubt about that. You seldom see a big comic with a small stooge. Indeed, it's almost a law of life that comedians are on the small side. So Jack Anthony became the comic and Bond Rowell took the part of the straight man. The act was an immediate success, but what started as coming up roses ended as thistles.

It happens almost always that a comedy couple will start in perfect harmony, but inevitably the comic one will become more and more important to theatre managers and booking agents. So the time comes when Yorke and Morgan becomes Tommy Morgan in great big letters at the top of the bill and Tommy Yorke in small letters at the bottom. The same happened to the partnership of Jack Anthony and Bond Rowell.

Perhaps the best kind of comedy partnership to have is a married one, as exemplified by Gracie Clark and Colin Murray, unknown probably in England but tremendously popular in Scotland. Gracie Clark has been described by the critic Robins Millar as having a Chaplinesque quality, and this is no exaggeration. I feel it is rather sad that the English should be denied the opportunity of appreciating great comedy work, such as Clark and Murray provide.

I have, however, strayed somewhat from my point—that there are not enough Scots comics to go round. This is so different from the days between the wars. Scots comics were two a penny then, but there were far more dates to fill. Tommy Morgan told me that, when he was making his name, there were nineteen theatres in and around Glasgow which could be reached by tram-car. In other words, you could do a weekly show for nearly half a year without leaving the audience of Glasgow.

There was one story of a husband-and-wife act which had

come over to Scotland from America. They were immediately booked for the Glasgow circuit and worked for almost a year (with repeat bookings) without spending more than tuppence-ha'penny—then the maximum fare—on tramcars. Then they got a booking in Aberdeen, which happens to be 153 miles from Glasgow. All the Americans knew was that this was another Scottish theatre, so they approached a traffic policeman at Glasgow Cross and asked, 'Which tram do we take for Aberdeen?'

Even after the Second World War there were still eleven theatres operating in Glasgow. Now there are four, and even these are threatened. Moss's Empires, very unwisely in my opinion, gave up the Empire in Glasgow and it is now a skyscraper block of offices. But, as Bruce Forsyth has aptly said, 'When I was there last it was a theatre and it was half empty. Now it's offices and completely empty!' Perhaps 'completely' is not exactly true, but it is near enough.

And yet the Empire ended with record houses to see the Red Army Choir and Dancers and, shortly before that, it had its most successful season ever with the Andy Stewart Show. Andy Stewart has been described as the new Harry Lauder, and I'd go along with that, up to a point. The point is that Lauder was a beautiful singer, while Andy Stewart is a stalwart young man doing his best to conceal the fact that he has a limited voice range. That apart, Andy is a Scots comic of great personality and considerable gifts and, if the long cherished idea of a film on the life of Harry Lauder is going to materialise, he is the man who should play the part.

It's perhaps odd that Andy Stewart's first idea was to be an actor. His father was a schoolmaster in Arbroath, and young Andy came to the College of Drama in Glasgow to be trained. He didn't take much to the régime and my friend Colin Chandler, the director of the College, didn't take much to him. They parted from each other with mutual relief, and Andy started off as an impressionist in the music halls. He had made a big success as an impersonator in 'College Pudding,' the Glasgow Charities Week show run by the University and the various colleges of the city.

I saw him at the old Metropole Theatre in Stockwell

Street in a series of the transpontine drama. The particular confection I picked was *The Black Sheep of the Family*, produced by Harold Dayne who had been with the never-to-be-forgotten Denville Players whom I have mentioned in *The Heart of Glasgow*. Andy played the eponymous role and, I must admit, he wasn't very good. But the imaginative producer had included a night-club scene, to show to what depths people can sink, and in came Andy Stewart to present his impressions. Ah, yes, the days of the Crummles are not yet dead.

Then came the last of the Howard and Wyndham pantomimes at the Theatre Royal, before it was metamorphosised into the headquarters of Scottish Television. It was *Robinson Crusoe* and the star comics were Harry Gordon and Jack Radcliffe. Harry Gordon started the pantomime but had to leave because of illness, and Andy Stewart was brought into his place. It was a near-disaster. Not only had Andy never appeared in a pantomime in his life (and pantomime had ways and traditions of its own), but he was taking a part written for an elderly comic who specialised in representing the dame as a beautifully turned-out matron. Indeed, Harry Gordon was uncomfortably true to life in these dame parts.

Andy Stewart found his best medium was radio, although he still had plenty of stage engagements. I recall meeting him in an Aberdeen pub not far from the Tivoli Theatre, where he was appearing. I asked him about his future. 'Well he said, 'radio is a sort of long-term policy for me. I'm satisfied to go on with the 'White Heather Club' until I get the break-through I want on the stage.'

Within a year from that meeting, Andy Stewart had achieved his break-through, and it was due to one song that he had written himself. One afternoon in Broadcasting House, Glasgow, when they were rehearsing the *White Heather Club*, Andy had twenty minutes to spare. In a corner of the studio he sat down and wrote the words of a song which he called *A Scottish Soldier*, set to a bagpipe tune called *The Green Hills of Tyrol*, which had been based on a dance in the opera *William Tell*, which Rossini had taken from an Austrian folk song.

From the moment it was broadcast, *A Scottish Soldier* had the same effect on the life of Andy Stewart that *I belong to Glasgow* had on the life of Will Fyffe. Fyffe got his idea from seeing a slightly drunk Glasgow man in front of him in a train queue at the Central Station. He was looking for his ticket and at the same time crying, 'I belong to Glasgow—and Glasgow belongs to me!' At this time Will Fyffe was playing the minor music halls and, when he wrote the words of *I Belong to Glasgow*, he wondered which Scots comic he should try to sell it to.

Before he could sell it to anybody, he got a summons from the Pavilion Theatre in Glasgow to appear for a week in place of a variety turn which had been cancelled. So he sang *I Belong to Glasgow* himself. It brought the house down. More than that; in the audience was a London theatrical agent, who had just dropped in to see what was doing. Immediately he offered Will Fyffe a date in London, and that was Will Fyffe made.

There's another parallel between Fyffe and Stewart. Andy's first idea was to be a straight actor. Will Fyffe was brought up as an actor, in a penny geggie in which his father, Jack Fyffe, was leading actor. Young Will played infant and small boy rôles almost as soon as he could walk. He told me once that he might have stayed with the geggie until geggies disappeared, but for a storm.

The geggie was a portable theatre, made of wood and canvas, and the actors themselves were responsible for putting it up and taking it down. Once a storm blew up as they were taking down the geggie, preparatory to loading it for the next town. Young Will was up on top of the canvas when a mighty blast of wind blew the whole roof into a near-by river. The roof went sailing down the river, with Will Fyffe holding fearfully on to it. He was rescued when the roof went ashore. But it was then that he felt there might be a more secure life than a geggie one, and he started as a minor comic.

Anyone who ever saw Will Fyffe presenting his *Daft Sandy* act would agree that he was a fine actor. He introduced it as a solo spot in a Theatre Royal pantomime. In those days, before the conscientious English producers came along, the comic frequently introduced a scene which had nothing whatever to do with the plot.

Suddenly in this pantomime we were transported to a Highland glen and Will Fyffe, who had been appearing as Idle Jack or Billy Crusoe or some such part, came on as the village idiot. He played superbly on the audience's feelings, getting laughs and tears exactly where he wanted them.

I mention Will Fyffe's case because so many people think that it's a remarkable thing that there is a group of Scots comics today who were actors before they were comedians. Among them are Stanley Baxter, Rikki Fulton, and Larry Marshall. Obviously some knowledge of acting is a useful thing for a Scots comic.

On the other hand, there are the Scots comics who have turned to acting. The outstanding example is Jimmy Logan, brought up in the anything-goes variety atmosphere of the Logan Family, but able to play comedy parts with the greatest of ease. Incidentally, his tenure of the new Metropole has been one of the happiest things in the theatrical life of Scotland.

John Grieve, another actor who has played the Scots comic (though admittedly in the rather more rarefied atmosphere of the Citizens' Theatre Christmas shows), told me how he decided there was no way of making a living as an actor in Scotland and so he went to London. He was doing quite nicely there when he was given a chance to play in a television production in Scotland. This coincided with Jimmy's Logan's taking over of the Metropole, with a series of Scottish comedies. Now John Grieve, and a large number of other Scottish actors and actresses, has no need to bother about the London theatre or London television. They can get all the work they want in Scotland.

Jack Radcliffe, who started as a boy preacher and hymn singer in Bellshill, and became one of our best-liked Scots comics has played the principal role in Durenmatt's *The Fire Raisers* at the Citizens' Theatre. But I remember Jack as a bit of a rabble-raiser in his early days. Sometimes audiences in the music halls were inclined to be noisy, and Jack would take it upon himself to rebuke them. If the noise continued,

Jack would assume the classical stance of a boxer and shout,
'Any time you like!' He did this so often that eventually an
impresario put him into a touring revue with *Any time you
like!* as its title.

That's what I miss a bit in the Scots comics of today.
They are inclined to be too polite, although I will absolve
Lex McLean, Johnny Beattie, Chic Murray, and Billy Rusk
of that charge. But what I miss are the chaps like Power and
Bendon, whose *Mendin' a Door* was one of the minor classics
of Scots comedy, Sammy Murray, Charlie Kemble (who
sang a great rum-ti-tum song about people in the audience
he could see from the stage), Tommy Morgan, Dave Willis,
George West, Alec Finlay, and a man called Donald McKay,
who used to shed real tears as he explained how he was
nagged by his wife. I thought he was great, but he never got
anywhere.

We would take anything, of course, in the old days. I
recollect Tommy Lorne staggering across the stage with a
giant bottle of sauce, giving it a free advertisement. Indeed,
you expected the comics to include advertising gags in
pantomimes.

G. S. Melvin was not generally known to be Scottish,
although he came from Dundee and started his stage career
as a Highland dancer. He told me how, in his early days, he
had an act in which he included a joke about Scotch whisky.
One night a man came round to his dressing-room and
explained that he was the representative of, we'll say, Red,
White and Blue Whisky. (I've got to be careful here, for the
number of registered names for Scotch whisky runs into
thousands. If there is one called Red, White and Blue
Whisky, I'm only kidding!)

'How much are Haig's paying you to tell that joke?' he
asked G. S. Melvin. In some bewilderment Melvin replied
that nobody was paying him anything to tell the joke. When
he did tell it, he just mentioned the name of any whisky that
came into his mind. It was Haig's this night, but it had been
Johnnie Walker the night before, and it might be Black and
White tomorrow night.

'Well,' said the representative, 'if you'll always mention Red,

Iouse at arms. (The author is fourth from the right in the second row)

House meets Hood. (Lance-Corporal House and Captain Richard Greene, late of the Army Kinematograph Service)

White and Blue Whisky when you tell that joke, we'll pay you £10 a week and send you a case of our whisky once a month.'

G. S. Melvin thought this was a great idea and agreed at once. And so every night he told his whisky story about Red, White and Blue, and once a week a cheque for £10 arrived, and once a month a case of whisky was delivered to his home. In those days an act would last a comic for a year or two. But, in course of time, you had to have a change. So the time came when G. S. Melvin dropped the whisky story, especially as he was now doing one of his terrible funny female impersonations. But the cheque and the whisky continued to arrive.

And then one night, during the first house of a twice-nightly variety show, a card was handed into G. S. Melvin's dressing-room. It bore the name of the representative of Red, White and Blue Whisky and a note to say that he would call round to see the comic between houses. Melvin still had to do his first-house act and so, although it was completely foreign to the presentation, he introduced the story about Red, White and Blue Whisky.

When the representative appeared in Melvin's dressing-room, he said, 'I see you're still telling the story, Mr Melvin.'

'Oh, yes,' said G. S. 'It still goes down well.'

'That's more than our whisky is doing,' said the chap. 'The firm has got to retrench, and I'm sorry to tell you that we'll not be able to keep up the £10 a week. But we'll still send the case once a month, if that's all right.'

'That's perfectly all right,' said G. S. Melvin graciously. 'I was thinking of changing the act anyway, and the story might not be just as suitable. But any time I *do* tell it, I'll mention Red, White and Blue.'

So they shook hands on it and G. S. Melvin continued to receive his case of a dozen bottles until the whisky firm went out of business.

Ah, yes, when I think it all over, I do regret that I didn't take the plunge and become a Scots comic. Just think what I could have done with that great song, 'Arizona Aeroplane'!

E

Aerial Flights

Sometimes today I call myself the B.B.C.'s Forgotten Man. I have been broadcasting off and on, since the year 1928. But in recent years it has been more off than on. This is probably entirely my own fault and I bear no ill-will or resentment. But it occasionally strikes me as funny that I seem to get more to do for the B.B.C. in London than the B.B.C. in Scotland.

However, I take the view that it's amazing I ever got working for the B.B.C. at all, and I present the story of my first and second broadcasts as proof. In the early days of 1928, when I was still a Chartered Accountant apprentice by day and a free-lance journalist by night, I became interested in the Glasgow Historical Pageant which was to be held in June at Garscube Estate on the edge of the city. I went to the Pageant headquarters in Elmbank Street and offered to write publicity material.

My reason for doing this was obvious. I would get stuff out of the Pageant preliminaries which would make good gossip column paragraphs. I might even get enough to write articles for some of the wee magazines I had discovered in the 'Writers' and Artists' Year Book.' I did manage some paragraphs and articles, but I soon found that the Colonel who was running the Pageant was treating me as a Press Agent, acting, unpaid. I felt this was a risk I'd had to take anyway, and wrote whatever he asked me to.

One day he summoned me to his office and said, 'House, are you the chap who wrote that piece about the Prince of Wales's cattle appearing in our Pageant?'

I admitted I was. This was an article to be sent to the American Press and I knew they would be interested in the Prince of Wales, who was to attend the opening performance. It was very unlikely that any cattle of his would actually appear in the pageant, but one bullock is very like another and I didn't think anyone would actually pinpoint them.

'Good!' said the Colonel. 'The B.B.C. have asked us to nominate somebody to give an eye-witness account of the opening show and we want a man with imagination. You'll do!'

He told me I was to broadcast from the B.B.C. Glasgow Station 5SC, at seven o'clock on the opening night, and that was that. Nobody gave me any advice. Perhaps I should have contacted the B.B.C. but I was too shy. I felt even shyer when the newspapers came out on the morning of Saturday, June 23rd, 1928, with the announcement in the radio programmes:

'7.0. Jack House, C.A.—Eye Witness Account of the Glasgow Historical Pageant.'

I just hoped that the partners of Russ and Cree, C.A., my respected employers, wouldn't notice that somebody had upgraded me to the sacred rank of Chartered Accountant when I was a mere apprentice who wanted to leave the profession.

That Saturday afternoon I took a tram-car to Garscube and watched the Pageant. I don't remember much about it now, except that all the acting seemed very far off and the battles weren't as good as I expected. (The battles brightened up considerably during the following week, when the Territorials who were supposed to be beaten got fed-up with their lot and offered a more stubborn resistance on each successive night. I understand that, at the closing performance, it was anybody's fight.)

The performance was supposed to start at three p.m. and supposed to finish in the region of half-past five. It started late and it did not finish until after six o'clock. No transport had been laid on to take me back to Blythswood Square. All I could do was make for the line of trams, waiting at the terminus for the audience skailing. There seemed to be a solid line of cars all the way from Garscube Estate to the centre of the city, and we inched along in the most painful manner.

I tried to write out some sort of script but, between the joggling of the car and my worry about the time factor, I did not have much success. It was getting perilously near seven o'clock when my car reached the corner of New City Road and Cambridge Street, so I jumped off and ran over Garnethill, a considerable undertaking but I was fleet of foot then, down into Sauchiehall Street and up to Blythswood Square, where I found the announcer on duty standing on the steps of B.B.C. headquarters looking for me.

Panting heavily, I explained to him why I was cutting it so fine and suggested he should put on some gramophone records until I was ready. Brave chap, he withstood the shock of this suggestion and replied politely that that was agreed that I must start my eye-witness account at 7.0. and go on until 7.15.

He then sat me down at a microphone and there, with an opening paragraph, a Pageant programme and nothing else, I started talking. I should think that that was very probably the first unscripted broadcast ever given from Scotland. I kept going as long as I could but, at 7.12., I dried up completely. And then the announcer *had* to put on a gramophone record. 'Yes,' he observed, as I left with my cheque for three guineas, 'you were hardly ready.' I have always regarded the B.B.C.'s understatement as one of their nicest traits.

I was confident that that was my broadcasting career over —especially as on the following Monday a friend of mine said 'Did you hear that awful broadcast about the Garscube Pageant on Saturday? It was a shap with the worst Glasgow accent you ever heard in your life.' I never let bug it was me.

Of course, many years later, when I was making my first appearances in the *Round Britain Quiz*, I had occasion to go into the *Citizen* case-room one Monday morning after the quiz had been broadcast on the previous Sunday. A compositor from Paisley came up to me and said, 'Aye, ye done well yesterday, Jack, but ye've goat a helluva Glasga aahkcent.'

Going back to the eye-witness account, however, I hoped that sleeping dogs would be allowed to lie. I was amazed to get a call from Scout headquarters. Mr. Mackenzie, the secretary, said, 'We understand that you did the eye-witness account of the Garscube Pageant last Saturday.' When I admitted it, he said, 'Well, we want you to give a running commentary on the Rally at Hampden this Saturday.'

By which token I realised that nobody at Scout headquarters could have heard my eye-witness account of the Garscube Pageant.

I agreed to do this and then I had a problem to face. This Scout Rally on the sacred sward of Hampden Park was a very big affair. The inspecting officer was none other than the Chief Scout for Wales—the same Prince of Wales (now Duke of Windsor) I had seen at the opening of the Garscube Pageant on the Saurday before. All the Glasgow Scout Districts were putting on as elaborate shows as they could mount, and I had been given the job of putting on the Eastern one.

I had evolved a pageant of my own. Since this was Hampden, I proposed to show *The Evolution of Football*. Accordingly I had devised a show which started with pre-historic cavemen playing football with an enemy's head, Roman soldiers versus Picts, knights in armour, Wild Macgregors versus Impetuous Campbells, and ending in 2,000 A.D. with a couple of scientists playing football with robots by remote control. We had been rehearsing this for weeks.

It was obvious that I could not continue to produce the show and also give the running commentary, but I had a very good assistant (or so I thought) and it was agreed that it would be left to him.

Saturday, June 30th, arrived and this time I was glad to see that the newspapers announced the Rally broadcast as 'Running commentary by Mr Jack House, a Glasgow Scouter.' Nobody could argue with that.

That Saturday afternoon I arrived in good time at Hampden and was taken to a room where the High Heid Yins of the Scout movement in Glasgow were collecting to meet the Prince of Wales. The B.B.C.'s chief engineer in Glasgow was there and we got a place at the back. The sound of cheering outside warned us that the Inspecting Officer would be arriving at any moment.

The highest decoration in the Boy Scout movement is (or maybe was—I've been out of it for a while) the Silver Wolf, a small silver replica of a wolf worn on a green and gold ribbon around the neck. All those present entitled to wear the Silver Wolf were, naturally, wearing it.

In came the Prince of Wales, dressed, as became the Chief Scout for Wales, in Boy Scout uniform. He advanced towards Commissioner Young with left hand outstretched. (Scouts shake hands with the left hand.) Then he noticed the Silver Wolf round 'Boss' Young's neck. The Prince of Wales put his hand up to his throat and said, 'My God, I've forgotten my bloody dog!'

While presentations were taking place, the B.B.C. engineer took me up to the Press Box which had been turned into a studio. He explained that I would have to carry out the whole exercise by myself. Once the red light went on, I was to start my running commentary and keep it running for an hour.

'You may run out of material,' said the engineer, 'or there may be nothing worth describing for a moment. You see this switch?' I said I did.

'Well, if you want to stop or have a rest, just press that switch and the listeners will hear the Govan Burgh Band.'

The Govan Burgh Band were down below me, on the edge of the track surrounding the arena, and apparently they would be playing a non-stop programme for the whole hour.

He wished me good luck and left me. At 5.30 p.m. the red light went on, and off I went. This was very different from the Garscube Pageant. There was always something happening in the arena and, apart from that, I knew that I'd only to tell the listeners what the Prince of Wales was doing and all would be well.

Everything was going fine and it came to the time for my own show, *The Evolution of Football*. Full of confidence, for this was one item I knew all about, I started to describe this pageant of sport. And then I saw that everything that could go wrong was going wrong. Somehow or other, the cavemen were fighting the Macgregors and the knights were mixed up with the robots. The whole show was a complete shambles. To this day I don't know what went wrong, because I hadn't the courage to find out afterwards.

What was I to do? Should I tell the truth about this awful mess, and thereby discredit the Boy Scouts and particularly the Eastern District? Or should I lie and tell the listeners what *ought* to be happening? In the event I pressed the switch and they heard the Govan Burgh Band.

There ensued several years when I did not broadcast at all, unless you count a couple of Scout programmes I did for the Children's Hour with Auntie Cyclone, Kathleen Garscadden. One was called *A Day in Camp* and Kathleen and I were supposed to be watching a Scout camp in action. The day finished, of course, with a Camp Fire Sing Song and I had brought along eight or nine of my brightest boys to perform this part of the programme.

I didn't know what my fee would be because in those days B.B.C. people seldom mentioned indelicate things like that. However, at the end of the Children's Hour, Kathleen pressed an envelope into my hot little hand and I stowed it away in my sporran.

In order to compensate my Scouts, I had arranged to take them for tea to Craig's Tea-rooms in Sauchiehall Street. This was to be a plain tea, not a high tea, because I didn't think my fee would run to that. We sat down and I told the boys that they could eat as much as they liked. Compared with today, things were very cheap. Even French cakes, the pride and joy of Glasgow tea-rooms, were only a penny each, or tuppence if the place was very posh.

At last they finished and I called for the bill. It came to £1. 16s. 5d. Even after all these years I remember the exact figure. I paid it, left a tip, and took the boys to the tram. It was only when I got home that I was able to open the envelope and look at the cheque. It was for exactly one guinea!

2

Andrew Stewart, now Controller of the B.B.C. in Scotland, really brought me back to broadcasting. He suggested I should write scripts and he took them when I did. After I'd given an allegedly humorous talk or two I got an idea for a radio revue which I called *Fin de Saison*. Why I chose this French title remains a mystery to me, but the idea was that a number of people connected with the summer season—a landlady, a Clyde steamer purser, and so on—should reflect in song or sketch on what had happened on the Firth of Clyde.

It struck me that I might find it difficult to write the lot of this myself so I asked Allan MacKinnon to join me. Allan was still at Glasgow University at this time, but he had done quite a bit of broadcasting. I knew him best through his brilliant verses for the *Glasgow University Magazine*. He liked my *Fin de Saison* idea. We worked out the revue and apportioned the sketches and songs.

And that was the beginning of the funniest time of my life. We wrote all sorts of scripts for the B.B.C.—so many, in fact, that we used eight different names as authors. Well, it would never have done to have 'by Jack House and Allan Mac-Kinnon' appearing on half the pages of the 'Radio Times.' So we were among others, J. Morrison Bennett and some-times J. Bennett Morrison, and Alexander Carton Ross, and we kept Peter Solman for the satirical things that might have been written by a smart Jewish author.

Most of our work was produced by Robin Russell, a young man full of ideas. For example, he introduced a Saturday night revue which Allan and I wrote on Saturday morning and afternoon. It was as up-to-date as a newspaper, and it was acted by such stalwarts as James McKechnie (who later made such a success in London broadcasting), Ian Sadler, Willie Joss, Molly Weir and Eileen Herlie. Many of Robin Russell's ideas were later taken up by the B.B.C. in London and some of the most famous series owed their origin to Glasgow.

We would lunch with Robin and a great character called

Peter Keith Murray, who produced sound as if it were coming from outside and not from the studio. The lunch would be a gay one, and Allan and I would get back to our office at 35 Dundas Street, settle down to work, or to talk, and the 'phone would ring. It would be Robin Russell. 'Oh, Jack,' he would say, 'you remember that idea you put up at lunch-time. Well, it's fixed. Can you let us have a half-hour's script by next Tuesday?'

'Yes,' I would say. 'Certainly, Robin', and then put down the 'phone and ask Allan if he could remember what the idea was that we had put up at lunch-time.

Broadcasting was such a free and easy affair then. And the B.B.C. were quite ready to co-operate with us in any daft idea we had. We thought, for example, of putting on an imaginary 'life' of a Scottish poet who didn't exist. Andrew Stewart said it would be all right as long as we made it a leg-pull. So Allan wrote the poetry in various styles to show how the poet had advanced and I wrote his life story to go along with it.

When it was produced we had actors and actresses who could send up both the poetry and the life story. I remember particularly Nan Scott, a Scottish National Player, hamming the poet's lost love magnificently. But there was no indication in the *Radio Times* or in the opening and closing announcements that this was a hoax. On the day after the broadcast two Glasgow newspapers had straight-forward, complimentary stories about this forgotten Scottish poet. This was an 'Alexander Carton Ross' effort, and I sometimes thought that it was the author's name which gave it the ambience of authenticity.

One day Robin Russell 'phoned and suggested we should do a radio show on the cruise of an imaginary liner called the S.S. 'Glaswegian'. Cruising was all the rage at the time. The idea was that this ship should put in at various ports and each port would be the reason for a song or a sketch or both. We got to work on this and decided that the links in this revue would be made by a reporter from the *Auchenshuggle Bugle*, who would be sending back reports from each place the cruise liner touched.

We had to fix a name for this character, and, as I was looking out our office window at Dundas Street (as senior partner, I had naturally the desk nearest the window), I saw a man go hirpling down on the other side. 'There's a man with a gammy leg,' I said to Allan. 'Let's call the reporter Gammy.'

He agreed and we finished the script. When it came to the actual production I played the part of the reporter Gammy myself. Allan and I usually appeared in our own shows—at least, those written under our own names. The final scene in the show was the last-night-at-sea party when we made our reporter get rather gay on champagne, which was not his customary tipple in Auchenshuggle.

Next morning I had to take my 'Jingle' article into the *Citizen* office and, when I handed it over to Colin Milne, he said, 'What on earth was that you were doing last night?'

I was accustomed to remarks like that after our broadcasts, so it did not worry me unduly. But when he said, 'What was the idea of using Mr. Gammie's name?' I was horrified.

All of a sudden I realised that Gammie was the name of our deeply respected 'Churchman', who had a couple of pages to himself in the *Citizen* each Saturday. He had not long returned from a cruise to the Scandinavian countries and he had sent back reports from each port he had visited.

What was I to do? I could hardly go in and tell Mr. Gammie that we had chosen Gammy because I had seen a man with a gammy leg. I felt that that would just be adding insult to injury. But I did feel that I had better apologise right away. I went straight to 'Churchman's' room.

Mr. Gammie was a man with a long, Presbyterian face and a manner that fitted it. I went into his office saying rather incoherently, 'I'm sorry, Mr Gammie, but . . . .' He put up his hand and said, 'I don't want to speak to you. All last night ministers of the Church of Scotland were ringing me up and asking me if I had heard your libellous programme. I have already put the matter in the hands of my lawyers. There's nothing more to say.'

I retired in confusion. It seemed an open-and-shut libel case to me. Then the B.B.C. lawyers in London asked to see our script about the cruise of the S.S. 'Glaswegian.' Apparently they went over it with a fine tooth comb and reported that there was nothing in it which libelled Mr Gammie. And that was all we ever heard of it.

But it taught me a great lesson. I resolved in future to be much more careful in my choice of names for characters in radio scripts. Indeed, in the very next script I wrote, I named all my characters after colours—John Brown, Sarah Scarlet, I. P. Blue, Mrs Green, and so on. And in the one after that I called them by the letters of the alphabet in rotation—Mrs Alexander, James Blank, Jameson Carruthers, Sophonisba Dee, etc.

But such stramashes were unusual, especially considering the volume of work which Allan and I turned out. We worked amazingly well together, though we were so different in education and outlook, and it was a small pride to us that the B.B.C. entrepreneurs could not distinguish in our scripts who had written what.

At the same time, we carried on our own work. I was still writing a great deal, for the *Citizen* and for any other newspaper which would accept my work. Indeed, at one time I was writing radio columns in three different newspapers, the *Citizen*, the *Sunday Post* and the *Sunday Mail* under three different names. Allan's main work was for the *Glasgow University Magazine*. If the editor rang up from Gilmorehill and said there was a half page needing filling and what could Allan do, my partner would drop everything and concentrate on filling that half page. I have heard a B.B.C. producer, frantic with worry over a script of the Children's Hour which had been due three days before, being soft-soaped by Allan, who was at that moment writing a short story for the *G.U.M.* for nothing.

While I'm sure he enjoyed our partnership, I think Allan MacKinnon knew it couldn't last and he was looking for something more permanent. The job of Talks Producer for the B.B.C. in Scotland fell vacant and Allan applied for it. He got on to the short list and one day he left our office to face a 'board' at the B.B.C., still in Blythswood Square in those days.

When he came back, I asked him eagerly how he had got on. He said modestly that he thought he had done not too badly. His best moment was when one member of the board had asked him what he thought the job of the B.B.C. was in Scotland. To which Allan replied that the B.B.C. 'should act as a Maecenas to the arts in Scotland.' He said this seemed to go down pretty well, although he was doubtful if all the board knew who Maecenas was.

Then he added that one of the producers, who had been on the board, wanted to see me that afternoon. At the appointed hour I went to Blythswood Square and the producer made me welcome. 'I know you've been concentrating on humour and light programmes up till now,' he said. 'But I'd like you to try something serious. We've been asked to do a programme on the centenary of the Savings Bank of Glasgow and I want you to tackle it. After all, I think the job of the B.B.C. in Scotland is to act as a Maecenas to the arts.' I kept my face straight and said I couldn't agree with him more.

However, that was the beginning of a slight breakaway between Allan and myself. We continued to write revues and sketches together, but I was going in more and more for serious programmes. Allan had been turned down as Talks Producer—which was a great mistake of the B.B.C.'s, but probably was all to the good for him—and he was still inclined to look for pastures new.

One of his student friends had been Roger MacDougall, and Roger was now in London working on film-scripts. He asked Allan to go down and co-operate with him, and Allan agreed. Out of this came one of the best second feature films I have ever seen, *This Man Is News*, written by Roger and Allan, with Alastair Sim, Barry K. Barnes and Valerie Hobson in the cast. It was so good that it was sent out as a first feature film, and it would have been a great portent for Allan's future if the war hadn't come along.

3

But that was quite a while yet. Allan and I still kept in touch and wrote scripts together, though we were more than 400 miles apart. For myself, I tended to go more and more into the documentary world. I met James Fergusson (now Sir James Fergusson, Keeper of the Records of Scotland), who was on the B.B.C. staff and running, among other things, a programme called *Here Awa', There Awa'*. This was a weekly series in which some unusual Scottish character came to the studio and talked about his life and work. James suggested I might look for somebody to fill this bill.

Well, I heard that there was a thatcher working in Paisley, on the poet Tannahill's cottage, who was the permanent thatcher for Burns's cottage at Alloway. His name was Samuel Morrison and he was 84 years of age. By all accounts he was quite a character. Down I went to Paisley, hailed Mr Morrison on the roof of Tannahill's cottage, and he obligingly descended to give me an interview.

I explained what it was all about. I said I was there to talk to him and, out of that talk, I would write a script which he would deliver in the *Here Awa', There Awa'* programme from the B.B.C. in Blythswood Square, Glasgow.

He was delighted with the idea, and proceeded to tell me the story of his life. A lot of it was interesting, but he had two drawbacks. He would talk about the Zulu War, in which he had taken part, and he would tell dirty stories.

Neither of these things worried me. After all, I was going to write the script and I knew that I would be cutting out the Zulu War and, naturally, I would not include any dirty stories. We parted with mutual expressions of esteem, and I said that I would send Mr Morrison the script to his but-and-ben in Ayr.

Well, I wrote the script, sent one copy to Mr Fergusson and delivered the other one personally to Mr Morrison's house. All I had to do now was to make sure the programme was actually broadcast and collect my fee.

On the morning of the broadcast, I was surprised to receive

a telephone call from James Fergusson. 'Jack,' he said, 'we've got your Mr Morrison, the thatcher, here but we've run into a bit of a snag.'

'What's the snag?' I asked.

'Mr. Morrison can't read,' said James.

I'd never thought of asking Samuel Morrison whether he could read or not. I had explained to him fully about the script. I had delivered the script to him. And what he was going to do with it, if he didn't read it, I didn't like to imagine.

I was still in a daze when James Fergusson said, 'I think we've got a way out here. Mr Morrison has brought his son with him, and I've found out that he *can* read. So I think you'd better come up and work out some form of dialogue between the thatcher and his son that we can put over.'

So up I went to Blythswood Square and took my script back. The thatcher was not at all worried. I didn't like the look of his son, who was edging sixty, but beggars can't be choosers, as some Great Mind has said. I eschewed lunch and rewrote the script in the form of a dialogue, giving the son various leading questions and trusting that the father would provide the right answers. I delivered this second script to the B.B.C., but my worries were not yet over. James Fergusson had suggested that I should attend the afternoon rehearsal to make sure that everything worked all right.

The rehearsal was held at four o'clock and the thatcher stood on one side of a stand microphone, while his son, armed with the script, stood on the other. When James gave the signal, young Morrison spoke the first sentence, which was, 'Well, father, how long have you been a thatcher?'

Opposite him Samuel Morrison closed his eyes and intoned, 'Well, father, how long have you been a thatcher?'

We tried and we tried, but we couldn't get the Morrisons to work this dialogue out. Then the producer said, 'There's only one thing for it, Jack. You'll have to interview the thatcher yourself, and without any script.'

I was aghast. Unscripted interviews were quite unknown. I looked back nearly ten years to my dreadful first broadcast, when I had to give an eye-witness account of the Garscube

Historical Pageant without a script, and I was in the depths of despair. But what could I do? Either I interviewed the thatcher without a script or I lost my cheque. I agreed to interview the thatcher and there and then I made a list of questions which I read to him and which he agreed to answer. He was still in the best of spirits and didn't seem to think there was any trouble anywhere.

'Here Awa', There Awa'' was due on the air around 7.30 p.m. I went up at seven o'clock to make sure everything was all right. I was met by the announcer on duty, Howard M. Lockhart. Howard is now an international broadcaster and famous for his *Housewives' Choice* programmes and his broadcasts for hospital patients. Then he was just an announcer, very tall, very thin, and rather pale. It seemed to me that he was looking even paler than usual.

'What on earth is this that you're doing?' he asked me.

'Now, don't worry,' I said soothingly. 'This old thatcher is quite all right. Our only trouble is that he *will* talk about the Zulu War.'

'The Zulu War?' cried Howard. 'Just look at this.' And he handed me a message which he had received from B.B.C. Headquarters, which were then in Edinburgh. It said simply, 'If Mr Morrison becomes Rabelaisian, buzz him off.'

This took me aback somewhat, but I said, 'Oh, it's true that he occasionally tells a dirty story, but I'm sure he'll be all right tonight.'

Howard looked me straight in the eye and said, 'What I want to know is, how can you tell when a man is *becoming* Rabelaisian.'

And it's quite true. There is no outward sign. Chaps who tell dirty jokes don't usually signal them in any way.

I did my best to persuade Howard Lockhart that all would be well. I told him I was sure there would be no dirty stories, and our only problem was to keep the thatcher off the Zulu War. And just at that moment Samuel Morrison arrived, quite joco, completely unperturbed, ready to talk at the drop of a hat. It has always been my experience, by the way, that country people are much better broadcasters than city people.

I introduced the thatcher to a very wary announcer. Howard took us into the small studio, showed the thatcher where to sit, explained that he must speak into the microphone, and said that, when the red light went on, he must remain silent until I said, 'Good evening, Mr. Morrison', when he would reply, 'Good evening, Mr. House.'

Then I would ask him the questions and, when I saw that time was up, I would say, 'Good night, Mr Morrison', and he would say, 'Good night, Mr House', and remain silent until the red light went out. The thatcher said aye, aye, that was fine.

There was still nearly quarter of an hour to go to the broadcast, so I got him on to the subject of the Zulu War. He talked about the Zulu War to his heart's content, and I began to feel that he had got it out of his system and we wouldn't be troubled by it. All this time he did not say a single word out of place, or tell anything remotely resembling a dirty story, and the roses were beginning to return to Howard Lockhart's cheeks.

It was almost time for us to go on the air. Howard was standing at one side of the studio, ready to press the buzzer which would sound in the engineers' department, so that they could make the studio live. He gave a rasping cough, and, just to fill in an awkward space of time, I said, 'That's a rather nasty cold you've got, Howard.'

'Oh, aye,' piped up the thatcher, 'ye'll be lyin' ower faur frae the wife!'

Mr. Lockhart was a bachelor and this remark of the thatcher's combined with the warning he had got from headquarters, must have made him wonder whether he should allow the programme to go on at all. But he pressed the buzzer and on went the red light. Now he had to take a couple of steps over to our table, lean over me, and announce, 'This is the Scottish Home Service. 'Here Awa', There Awa',' etc.

He had just taken one step when the thatcher hissed to me, 'Dae we stert noo?' I motioned him to silence and Howard, visibly shaken, made the announcement. I said, 'Good evening, Mr Morrison.' The thatcher said, 'Good evening, Mr House.' And off we went.

It all seems so easy nowadays, especially with television. But this kind of off-the-cuff affair was quite unknown then. We were getting on fairly well, but the sweat was running off me. I was still wondering about dirty stories and the Zulu War.

We came to a question which the thatcher knew he was going to be asked. 'Now, Mr Morrison,' I said, 'will you tell us your age?'

Instead of replying that he was eighty-four, the thatcher leaned over and whispered to me across the microphone. I should explain that a whisper across a mike sounds much clearer to you at home than if a man sat back and bellowed. And what the thatcher whispered was, 'Oh, Ah'll no' gie ye ma real age, or Ah'll no' get ony mair joabs!'

Hastily I got on to the next question. At last I saw that this mauvais quart-d'heure was up and I said thankfully, 'Good night, Mr Morrison.' 'Good night, Mr House,' said he. Then Howard Lockhart had to take his couple of steps across to disannounce us. Before he could say a word, the thatcher cried, 'Are we feenished a'ready? Ah could go oan fur 'oors yet!'

Yes, the thatcher was indomitable to the end. That was more than could be said of Howard and me. I thought this must surely be the time when the name of House should be scored from the list. But next day I heard that a message had come from B.B.C. headquarters in Edinburgh saying that the *Here Awa'*, *There Awa'* broadcast had been a success.

One important official was quoted as saying that it had sounded just like two men who had been having an argument in a pub, still carrying on the argument on the pavement after they'd been thrown out. I took that as quite a compliment. Indeed, if I were a radio or television producer, I'd try to make more of my discussion programmes seem as if they were being conducted by two chaps who had just been thrown out of a pub still carrying on the argument outside.

4

All this time I was courting Jessie Miller, who was now Woman's Editor—or is it Editress?—of the best evening paper we've ever had in this city, the *Evening News*. We were married in Glasgow University Chapel on April 22nd, 1937, and Allan MacKinnon was my best man. It wasn't long after that that he got married to Jean Horn, a fellow student. But that took place in London, where Allan was now settled.

These were extraordinary days. We were all tremendously political, and most of us read the *New Statesman*, so you can guess which side we were on. We thought Ernest Hemingway was a great man, and we were moved by the Civil War in Spain. In Glasgow, though, the great event was the Empire Exhibition of 1938 and, when the Munich Crisis came along, there was a strong feeling in the city that, if the Nazis spoiled our Exhibition, they would suffer for it.

Glasgow is a great exhibition city. The first big exhibition was held in 1888 and since then there have been international exhibitions in 1901, 1911 and 1938. They have all been successful. Glasgow likes the idea of exhibitions, and it's interesting to note that, in the days of the British Industries Fair, more people went to the exhibition in Glasgow than to those in London and Birmingham combined.

We didn't have a good summer in 1938, but we had a great exhibition. I recall sitting on the balcony of the Coal Pavilion, on a warm summer night, looking across at the illuminated fountains, the great tower rising in the purple sky, the Guards' Band playing in their shell, the lighted pavilions everywhere. Glasgow was a mystical, wonderful place then.

I ran a radio show about the Exhibition every week. As I look back on it now, I'm amazed at the famous people we had in it for free. In those days personalities, comedians, characters were quite ready to do a broadcast without any thought of a fee. The only person I ever tangled with was the late Bill Tilden, the tennis player, who not only demanded a fee but wanted it in cash in his hands before he uttered a single word on the air. We turned him down.

While the Exhibition was on Lupino Lane brought up his show, *Me and My Girl*. It was an old-fashioned musical, even by our Glasgow standards, but it was completely electrified by the chorus and dance called *The Lambeth Walk*. The first time *The Lambeth Walk* was ever broadcast was on my radio programme. The singers were Lupino Lane and Teddy St. Denis and their accompanist at the piano was the composer, Noel Gay. And they did it for nothing.

Then there was the time that the B.B.C. informed me officially that they wanted a Roman Duke included in my Exhibition programme. I don't suppose you'll remember that there was a great international exhibition planned for Rome for the year 1940, or it may be 1941. This Roman Duke had come across to Britain to have a look at our exhibition in Glasgow.

The Duke was staying at the Central Hotel and I went there to see him and arrange what he could say in three minutes in my programme. From the moment I arrived in his suite, I realised that there was some error in protocol. The Duke received me as a representative of the British Government. He was surrounded by a staff of at least a dozen. As far as I could find out, only the Duke himself spoke English. I did my best for the Government, realising how I could let Britain down if I didn't play my cards carefully.

Luckily I had time to 'phone David Bernard, the producer, at Broadcasting House, and alert him to the fact that something approaching royalty was shortly arriving in Queen Margaret Drive. I couldn't do anything constructive myself, because I was now committed, as the representative of the British Government, to sit on the right hand of the Roman Duke in his journey from the Central Hotel to Broadcasting House.

It's amazing how fortune favours the brave. The Roman Duke's entourage consisted of three enormous cars. I was sitting in the front one with the Duke himself. We swerved into the old entrance to Broadcasting House, an entrance which was once part of Queen Margaret's College. Just at that moment who should be taking the air and having a quiet smoke but the actor who played the part of Inspector Harrington in a B.B.C. series that I recall only dimly. But I do remember that he was a tall, most impressive looking chap.

There he stood, puffing calmly away, as we drove up. Before I could say a word, the Roman Duke bounded out of the car. He knew the head of the B.B.C. when he saw one. He advanced on Inspector Harrington with every evidence of goodwill. And Inspector Harrington, blessings on him for ever more, sound actor that he was, responded in like measure. You never saw such a welcome given to anybody.

The Duke was whisked upstairs to a small studio, where an interviewer was waiting. When the red light went on he was interviewed. He did his bit for Rome. And he never knew that he was in the middle of a very light-hearted show that included Gipsy Petulengro talking nonsense before him and somebody singing a popular song after him. It didn't really matter, of course, because there was never any International Exhibition at Rome.

If that Roman Duke ever thought of an approaching war he certainly didn't reveal his thoughts. The ineffable Lord Beaverbrook was saying, 'There will be no war this year, or next year either.' I thought Lord Beaverbrook was the end, but I wanted to believe what he said. Perhaps that was Beaverbrook's secret, that what he wanted a lot of other people wanted as well.

At any rate, there I was, happily married, living a pleasant life, doing the kind of things I liked, going abroad for holidays, and generally enjoying myself. I was worried about Hitler, but I comforted myself with the memory of the visit I had paid to Berlin in 1932. I was staying in a very comfortable *pension* off the Potzdamerplatz. It was kept by an elderly Jewess, and I often wondered afterwards what happened to her.

One of the permanent guests was an Irish Professor who edited a monthly magazine of politics and literature published in English. I asked him about this chap Hitler and he said right away, 'There's nothing in it. Hitler and his National Socialism are as important as the Scottish Nationalists in your country.'

At the time that satisfied me, because nothing could have been of less importance than the Scottish Nationalists. But, when Hitler rose to power, I began to wonder about the Irish Professor—and about the Scottish Nationalists. And then, when the Second World War started, I saw my Irish Professor's name in the *Radio Times* as an advisor on Continental politics to the B.B.C.!

In August, 1939, Jessie and I went on a three week's holiday to the Shetland Isles. The weather was beautiful. Lerwick was enchanting. Hillswick was remarkable for having the only pub in the whole of the Shetland Isles. It was down by a voe and, when there were exceptionally high tides, the sea would come in and the drinkers would stand around the bar in their fishermen's high boots, paying no attention whatever to the elements.

The pub was kept by the Hillswick slaughterer and, if you went in and found it empty, all you had to do was shout in the direction of the slaughter-house, when mine host would appear, wiping the blood off arms and hands and signify that he would be with you on the dot. Sherry was sevenpence ha'penny a glass.

From Hillswick we moved up to the most northerly of the Shetland Isles, Unst, and stayed at what was then called the most northerly hotel in the British Empire, the Hotel Nord. We found right away that other tourists were not as sanguine as we were. In fact, everybody else had left the Hotel Nord, and we had it to ourselves, with the manageress, the waitress-cum-chambermaid and the cook. They were all Shetlanders, and in these islands the people use some thousand Norwegian words a day. We'd be having tea in the sun porch at the front of the hotel and we could hear them discussing something in the kitchen, and we hadn't the slightest idea what they were talking about.

This was rather worrying because it was the end of August and things were beginning to happen in Europe. There was no wireless set in the Hotel Nord, so we took to going up the hill to a house where they had radio and turned it on so loud that we could hear it outside. My father-in-law, Robert Bennett Miller, a Clydebank headmaster, sent us a telegram suggesting that we should return to Glasgow. Our waitress told us that her young brother had been called up. We decided that we had better get back home.

We just did it and no more. All the Shetland steamers were being transformed into hospital ships, and there was just one sailing from Baltasound, the port of Unst, at an early hour the following morning. We got aboard and I had my first drink for a week. We hadn't known that Unst was a 'dry' island and so had been forced to be teetotal for all that time.

Down we sailed to Lerwick, and then across to Kirkwall, the capital of Orkney. All the sailing programmes had been altered. There was a big crowd of people wanting to get back to the mainland. Jessie and I went ashore and had lunch at the hotel at the pier-head. In the afternoon we went back to the hotel for tea. Since lunch-time the hotel had been taken over as British Navy headquarters.

We left Kirkwall in the evening and the boat was packed. People were trying to sleep on deck, because every cabin was full. As we sailed out into the North Sea there was a magnificent sight ahead of us—warship after warship, stretched out right along the horizon. I had seen the British Fleet in films but never in reality. It looked wonderful, unconquerable, mighty. War had not yet been declared, but already we felt the stirrings within us. I remembered that, when I first saw *Journey's End* on the stage, I wished that I, too, could have experienced life in the trenches. It must be difficult to be a pacifist.

We sailed into Aberdeen on the sunny morning of September 3rd, 1939. As we disembarked, boys came running down the quayside bearing Sunday newspaper bills which said 'War Declared.' We went to the station and found there was only one train going to Glasgow that day. Like the boat, it was packed.

Down we went to our first black-out and the exciting news that the air raid sirens had sounded that morning. We'd been terrified at the threat of war in the days of Munich. Now we were almost glad that the waiting was over and it was here at last.

The Middle-aged Man on the Flying Trapeze

Soon after the war started I was asked to rejoin the staff of the *Evening Citizen*. I was given a daily column to do and I enjoyed it immensely. I could choose my own subjects and I soon learned that it's not the writing that is the trouble with columnists, it's getting the ideas.

So I found myself doing such things as trying to obtain a loan of £10,000 on note of hand alone (that's what the advertisements said, but it didn't turn out that way), walking from the Broomielaw to the source of the Clyde, being the hind legs of a pantomime horse, and acting as a waiter in the Rogano restaurant.

One big trouble about journalistic ideas of this kind is that they are so easy to conceive and turn out so hard to do. What's easier than being a waiter, you might say. But waiting is a much harder job than it looks. Not only that, but, if you're even just pretending to be a waiter, you have the restaurant's reputation in your hands. In the case of Rogano, I went to Don Grant, the chairman of the company which owned Rogano and one of the finest restaurateurs I have ever known. I thought it best to do the job in a friend's restaurant, and there was the additional advantage that a waiter's outfit in Rogano consists of a smart cream jacket with green trimmings and black trousers. In other words, I didn't need to wear the full rig, as demanded in the restaurants of railway hotels, for example.

I reported to Rogano around six o'clock in the evening and

was given my jacket and told that my station would be behind the sea-food bar. Rogano is the Prunier's of Glasgow and, while there are three restaurant rooms, many people prefer to sit on high stools at the sea-food bar. In those days Peter (now retired) was the head waiter behind the bar, and he decided that I should start by serving drinks.

This seemed to be simple. I merely took the order from the customer, wrote it on a pad, presented it to the bar, collected the drinks and placed them before the customer. Three girls took their seats and ordered gin and tonic. I decided that two tonics would be enough and put in my order. Then I placed a gin in front of each girl, lifted a bottle of tonic and said to the first one, 'Say when!' Obviously no waiter had ever said such a thing to her before, but she said 'When' all right.

Feeling rather self-conscious, I poured tonic into the other gins and, as I moved away, I heard one of the girls say, 'What an odd waiter.'

After that I was more circumspect, and felt I was doing not too badly. The strange thing was that none of the clientele seemed to recognise me, although I recognised several of them.

Then Peter decided that I should serve my first dish. A very young Naval Lieutenant was sitting at the bar and had ordered roast goose, sprouts and mashed potatoes. 'Now, Jack', said the head waiter, 'you'll serve him this and I want you to do it French service.'

I knew that French service meant using a fork and spoon in the right hand and I had never done anything like this in my life. When we had people to dinner at home I did a certain amount of serving, and I knew I wasn't very good at it. But I had another problem. On the last of my six days' walking up to the source of the River Clyde I fell in. It didn't matter very much because by this time the Clyde was a narrow burn away up in the Lowther hills. I was crossing from one side to the other, stepped on a slippy stone, and found myself sitting in the burbling brook. It was pouring and I was already soaked to the skin—I mean literally so— and I just sat in the River Clyde and laughed.

But, as I fell in, I hit the forefinger of my right hand on a small boulder. I felt no pain at the time and it wasn't until I got home that I discovered I had staved that finger. To this day I can't bend it properly and it is about half an inch shorter than the forefinger of my left hand.

So, when it came to French service, I was in a certain difficulty. Luckily the sea-food counter was high, so I was able to wedge the fork and spoon between my forefinger and thumb without, I hoped, the Lieutenant seeing this manoeuvre. I got his roast goose on to the plate without much difficulty, and the sprouts presented no problem. But the damned mashed potatoes stuck to the spoon and wouldn't come off. With much waving and jerking, I got a little on to the Lieutenant's plate and I could see that he was even more embarrassed than I was. When I said, 'Is that enough potato Sir?' he replied thankfully that yes, it was.

Afterwards Peter took me aside. 'I'm sorry, Jack,' he said. 'That was my fault. I should have told you that, before you serve mashed potatoes, you should hold the spoon under the hot water tap. Then the mash just slips off.'

I have cherished this information ever since, but I have never had any cause to put it into effect. Indeed, after this incident, I decided I had been waiting long enough, and retired from the scene. I had done the job for just a little over two hours and already my feet were burning and I was feeling exhausted. I have had a great regard for waiters ever since.

I suppose the silliest thing I did in those days was to go into a cage with a couple of lionesses. I was sitting in my room at the *Citizen* office one morning and wondering what on earth I was going to write about for the following day when Bailie John S. Clarke came in. John S. Clarke was a truly remarkable man. He had been an M.P. He was an Englishman who was an authority on Robert Burns, indeed he was President of the Burns Federation for a time and claimed to have proposed the Immortal Memory of Robert Burns more often than any man alive. When he lost his seat in Parliament, he turned to Glasgow Town Council and became a Bailie, or magistrate, in the course of time.

He wrote for the *Scottish Daily Express*, and occasionally for the *Citizen* as well, and he did a lion taming act twice a day

in a wee zoo in a former church in Oswald Street, belonging
to Andrew Wilson.

When he saw me sitting in my room with, no doubt, a
forfochen look on my face, John S. Clarke asked me what
was wrong. I explained that I had to find a subject for the
morrow, and he said, 'Why not come into the lions' cage with
me this afternoon?' Just at that moment I couldn't think of
any reason for refusing, so I said I would. John said he
would see me at the zoo at three, and I was left wondering how
daft I was.

I recollected that he did his act with a lion and a couple of
lionesses. I didn't know anything about the lion, but I
remembered that the lionesses had been a couple of cubs
originally trained by a sub-editor on the *Evening News*, Eddie
Campbell. Indeed, I had seen a picture of them about two
years earlier and they looked cuddly and kittenish. That
cheered me up a bit, and I comforted myself also with the
knowledge that John S. Clarke had been taming lions since
he was seventeen.

I decided to go down to the Oswald Street zoo about ten
minutes early, so that I could observe the scene. The first
thing I discovered was that the two lionesses I remembered
as frolicking cubs were now fully grown. They looked enormous and the cage looked very small. I felt more and more
nervous.

John S. Clarke arrived and said, 'Just one thing. One of
the lionesses is in heat so, before you come in, I'll put Rajah
into that other cage. If I let you into the cage with Rajah and
Nouri, he would treat you as a rival and he might attack.'
Apparently the lion wouldn't regard John S. Clarke as a
rival. Maybe it's something to do with being a Bailie.

Then John said, 'Now I'll go into the cage and take the
steam out of them.' And he did just that. He had that lion
and the two lionesses bounding round the cage and doing all
sorts of tricks, culminating in his holding a large piece of raw
meat between his teeth and Rajah, with his front paws on
the Bailie's shoulders, taking the food out of John's mouth.

Now he put Rajah into the small cage at the side and made
the lionesses, Nouri and Delia, stand facing the audience

with their front paws on small pedestals. There was an audience of forty people, who had paid thruppence each to get in. They didn't know they were going to see me, of course.

John came out of the cage and said, 'This is it. Take your coat off.' I was still wearing my overcoat, not only because it was a cold day, but also because I felt it might be some sort of protection if one of the lionesses took a playful swipe at me. But John S. Clarke was adamant. I took my coat off and, feeling very naked indeed, climbed the steps to the cage.

Those of you who have been in lions' cages will know that there is a narrow entrance cage before the big cage. This is so that the outside door can be closed before the inside cage door is opened. We squeezed into the entrance and then I followed John S. Clarke into the lions' cage. It seemed alarmingly small for two lionesses, John and me. The Bailie had a small whip made of parachute silk in his hand. This was to keep the lionesses in subjection. Most of the time it was lying on the floor of the cage.

He took me up to the first lioness and said, 'Delia, this is a friend of mine called Jack House. He's very fond of animals, particularly lions, and I want you to like him.' Then he said to me, 'Pat her on the head.'

I put out my hand timidly and touched the lioness's head lightly. 'No, no, no,' cried John. 'She'll never feel that. Give her a good hard thump.'

So I patted Delia's head slightly harder. She didn't seem to notice. She just kept looking out into the audience. John moved round to the other lioness and repeated the same introduction that he had made with Delia. 'Now pat Nouri on the head,' he said.

I put out my hand towards her head and the lioness turned round sharply and snarled at me. I was terrified. 'Tut-tut,' said John S. Clarke. 'That won't do Nouri. Temper, temper!'

He started a new act with the two lionesses, and I stuck to him closer than a brother. He seemed so confident, and yet I had heard of lion tamers being attacked by animals which had practically become their pets. And if Nouri and Delia attacked, there was absolutely nothing to stop them.

What worried me most was that Nouri, when she wasn't actually doing something to John S. Clarke's bidding, seemed to keep circling round in my direction. She was the one in heat, the one who had snarled at me already. I kept thinking of having read somewhere that what makes a wild animal attack human beings is that the human being emanates an odour of fear. When the animal gets this scent, it attacks. And I was acutely conscious that all sorts of odours were emanating from me.

After nine minutes or so John S. Clarke said to me, 'Is that enough?' I assured him that it was, and he let me out. I went back to the office, wrote the article about how it felt to be in a lion's cage, and it appeared next day. And the day after that I got the usual anonymous letters and postcards saying, 'Ha, ha! Tell us another. You never done that.' Well, they were not all couched in exactly those words, but that was the meaning.

I suppose I should have got over it by this time, but it still astonishes me that readers refuse to believe that newspapermen do what they write that they do. Nowadays I write two book criticism features a week, and people still come up to me and say, 'But you don't really read the books, do you?'

In the case of my adventure with the lions I should really have had a photographer there to record the scene for posterity. But I didn't like the idea of what a sudden flash might do to the beasts. Besides, it was war-time and papers were small and pictures were not encouraged. I'll tell you one thing, though. If somebody came along and suggested that I should go into the lions' cage today, I'd have no hesitation in saying no.

2

This was the time of the phoney war but, phoney or not, men were being called up steadily, and one man who left us was Colin Neil MacKay, who was film critic of the *Scottish Daily Express*. The job was wished on me, so I had a fairly full life, going to film shows most mornings, getting my material for the column and writing it six days a week, and acting as dramatic critic for the *Citizen*.

My editor at this time was the novelist, George Blake, and I have always been grateful to him for the opportunities he gave me. The encouragement too, for he was generous in his praise. I was sorry when he gave up his editorship while I was in the army.

The *Citizen* was officially owned between George Outram and Co. and the Beaverbrook Press, but it was produced in the *Express* office in Albion Street, and there was never any doubt in our minds as to who was the master.

One day the editor of the *Scottish Daily Express* came in and said, 'That film (and he mentioned its name), I see you were a bit hard on it. Wasn't it on the list?'

Every week I received a list of names of films, but nobody had ever told me what the list was supposed to represent, and I had got into the habit of throwing it away. He was horrified when I said so 'Good God,' he said, 'that list contains the names of the films shown at Lord Beaverbrook's country house. And they've got to be praised.'

As I digested this, he looked sharply at me and said, 'You'll be telling me next that you've never seen the White List.'

I had heard rumours that Lord Beaverbrook kept a White List of people who were not to be mentioned in the *Express*, unless to their detriment. But I could assure the editor that I had never seen it.

He took me to his room, unlocked a cabinet and picked out a fairly bulky document. 'Have a look at that,' he ordered, 'and give it back to me.'

So I took the document away and studied it. It consisted, as I remember it now, simply of a list of names, the vast majority of which were unknown to me. Certainly none of them swam into my ken. Even if they had, I doubt if I should have remembered that they were on this list.

As far as the list of films shown at Cherkley Court was concerned, I should, perhaps, have refused to go on being the *Scottish Daily Express* film critic. But I didn't take the job seriously and it didn't seem worth while to me to take a virtuous stand. Besides, there are different ways of 'praising' films. If I saw one I did not like, I wrote my criticism in such a way that, though it could be taken as praise, an intelligent reader would get my real message. And I reasoned that there must be *some* intelligent readers of the *Scottish Daily Express*.

The phoney war period ended and the real war impinged more and more on Glasgow. I went back to reporting for a day when Winston Churchill visited the city. What I remember best about that day was seeing the great man at a Civil Defence station in Dennistoun. It had been an arduous programme and, although Mrs Churchill was looking perfectly fresh, the Prime Minister was sagging a bit, and sat down rather wearily in a chair while tea was served. Then an elderly air raid warden stepped forward, had a whispered colloquy with Mr Churchill, and produced a flask. He poured something from the flask into Mr Churchill's tea, and in a few moments Caesar was himself again.

That famous French regiment, the Chasseurs Alpins, came to Glasgow and we grew friendly enough with some of the officers to invite them to dinner. Glasgow was renowned among foreign troops for its hospitality, and we did our small best to keep up the city's reputation. Then, all of a sudden, the Nazis drove into France and the Chasseurs were hurriedly recalled.

After Dunkirk we saw another group of foreign soldiers, the Poles. What remained of the Polish Army was reconstituted in the West of Scotland, and Glasgow was full of very smart Polish officers in unusual uniforms. The Polish Army Choir sang in the Athenaeum and became all the rage. Many of the Poles learned what they thought was English, and only discovered later that it was broad Scots.

One Saturday night in Ferrari's restaurant in Sauchiehall Street Jessie and I met a Polish captain and his American wife. He was Eddie Oppersdorff and was said to be a Count.

But then about half the officers we met were Counts or Princes or something of the sort. Mundi Oppersdorff, his wife, was good fun and sang to a guitar in the pleasant way that was done before electronics took over. We invited them home and soon became good friends.

Now it so happened that a young Glasgow couple we knew had invited us to dinner, and it was our turn to invite them back. I liked them well enough, but I felt that something extra was needed for the return match. So I suggested to my wife that we invite the Oppersdorffs.

When I asked Eddie Oppersdorff if he could come along, he said he and Mundi would be delighted to, but he felt it would be better if we could invite his Colonel and his Colonel's wife as well. We had already met them and found them a delightful couple, so four Poles were invited.

The general air of gaiety that the Poles affected must have got into Jessie's mind, because she then suggested that I should ask George Blake to this dinner, along with Frank Waters, the general manager in Albion Street. Then we felt we could hardly invite the editor of the *Citizen* and leave out the editor of the *Express*, so he was invited as well. And just to add to the atmosphere, Jessie was impelled to invite Guido Ferrari's young brother, Francesco, to the do. She argued that, since he could speak four languages, he could be a great help.

Thus our dinner for the young couple had turned into a feast for twelve instead of just for four. Jessie decided to take a day off to prepare the meal. It seems strange now, but we could then afford a maid and we were lucky enough to have an Irish girl named Kathleen, who was a good cook in her own right and absolutely doted on parties.

On the morning of that day I was working in my office when the telephone rang. It was Eddie Oppersdorff. 'I'm sorry, Jack,' he said, 'but the dinner is off as far as we are concerned. We've just had word that General Sikorski's daughter is arriving in Glasgow today, and we all have to be ready to receive her. We don't know what will be happening tonight, and all we can do is to apologise and hope to be with you another day.'

I was horrified. Here we had arranged this whole dinner on the assumption that our other guests were going to meet the Poles. The meal would have no savour without them. I said, 'Eddie, couldn't we invite General Sikorski's daughter as well? Then you could all come.'

General Sikorski, of course, was the hero who commanded the new Polish Army. As far as I could gather, his daughter was called Madame Sikorska and looked after the Polish Red Cross. Eddie Oppersdorff thought it was very doubtful whether an invitation to dinner would be accepted by Madame Sikorska or not. But he would consult and ring me back.

Within half-an-hour he was doing just that. They were coming to dinner. 'But I must warn you,' he said, 'that with Madame Sikorska there will be her lady-in-waiting, and also the Major attached to her person. There may be other officers, too. We do not know.'

By this time I was completely reckless. 'Let them all come,' I said, and then telephoned the good news to my wife. There would be at least twenty people, I said. What could we do? Jessie rose to the challenge. 'We'll manage,' she assured me. 'We'll make it a cold buffet.'

And so, around seven o'clock that evening, there we were, in our five room and kitchen flat, up two stairs in a tenement, waiting for Madame Sikorska and the rest of the Poles to arrive. The first people in were the young couple who were the unwitting cause of the whole brouhaha. Then came Francesco Ferrari, followed by the two editors and the general manager from Albion Street. All the non-Poles had arrived, but there was no sign of the important guests.

I was lashing out gin and sherry and whisky and trying to keep a look-out at our sitting room windows as well. Suddenly, round the corner of Clouston Street, came a procession of enormous black limousines, each flying a Polish flag on its bonnet. They drew up in a line fornenst our close and out jumped Polish soldiers who opened doors and stood at the salute. I just about had kittens.

Then up our ancient tenement stairs tripped Madame Sikorska, her Lady-in-waiting, the major attached to her person, and a fine assortment of Polish officers and their wives. Well, there was one great thing about the Poles. They took over any gathering they attended. There was no need for me to be the witty host or Jessie the charming hostess. The main thing to do was to see that the wine flowed freely. We

lleague of Coco (at Bertram Mills' Circus)

Private eye House (with Chicago's Deputy Chief of Detectives and the crime expert of the *Chicago Sun-Times*)

didn't even need to worry about seeing that Madame Sikorska was entertained. She had a sort of court that looked after protocol.

Then we invited our guests into our small dining room for the cold buffet. There were immediate exclamations of delight from the Poles. We thought it was a nice dining room but not all that nice. Then we discovered that what had caused the raptures was that we had the place lit with alternate red and white candles, and red and white are the national colours of Poland. We didn't dare admit that this was an accident. In fact, it was because we hadn't enough red candles for our candlesticks.

We had only one slight failure. I had brought in brandy, port and Drambuie to go with the coffee. The Poles had never tasted Drambuie and, when they were told it was a Scottish liqueur, they thought they would try it. Once they tried it, they wouldn't stop. After we were back in the sitting-room and I was being butler once again, I asked the major attached to Madame Sikorska's person what he'd like to drink, and he said, 'Some more of your beautiful Drambuie.' When I said that, alas, the bottle was finished, he beamed upon me and said, 'Perhaps you did not expect so many people.'

Next day I was asked in the office if the night had been very expensive. I calculated that I had spent just over £7 on the drink side, but that had been—except for the Drambuie —unlimited. So it was decided that I should have a regular allowance for entertainment. I may say I needed it, because we were hot on the entertaining then. We drank a fair amount too.

One day a shipping agent friend invited us down the Clyde to see a Swedish ship. We met the captain and the mate and they entertained us to a lavish smorgasbord. So we invited them home for dinner that evening. They must have mis-understood our invitation for, when we had given them drinks and were taking them into dinner, they bashfully admitted that they had had their dinner. But Swedes are almost as good trenchermen as Danes and they coped valiantly.

F

Owing to the black-out and certain restrictions they had to leave by half-past nine. I consoled myself for their departure with some Cherry Heering. And the next thing I remember was waking up in bed about seven in the morning with the dreadful realisation that life aboard a neutral ship was my subject for today's column and I hadn't written a word of it. Nor had I anything in reserve.

I jumped up, washed, shaved and dressed in record time and, refusing Jessie's pleas to wait for breakfast, hurried to the office. I went into my room and there lying on my table was the galley proof of the article I had written about life aboard a neutral ship. It was a good article too, as I found when I read it with some interest. I realised that I must have left home, gone down to the *Citizen,* typed my column, then subbed it and sent it to the case-room. But I couldn't recall any of it.

The war went on the uneven tenor of its way. I had my medical for the Services and was delighted to be found in perfect health. When one doctor asked me if I was handicapped in any way, I showed him my famous staved right forefinger, the injury sustained when I fell in the Clyde. He looked at it and said, 'Oh, you'll be able to pull a trigger with that all right'.

I was offered a couple of jobs in reserved occupations, but I turned them down. Not that I was a great patriot, otherwise I should have volunteered, like Allan MacKinnon, who went into the London Scottish on September 4th, 1939. I just felt that I should take my chance in the ordinary way. And my chance came along when my calling-up notice arrived. I had to report at the Gordon Highlanders' barracks at Bridge o' Don, Aberdeen, on March 17th, 1942.

I was a couple of months from my 36th birthday, and I felt that now I would be the middle-aged man on the flying trapeze.

Life in the Brig o' Don barracks that March was chaotic. While the barracks belonged to the Gordons, they were shared by the Cameronians and the Highland Light Infantry. Added to which, a new unit of the Army was formed, the General Service Corps. Officially, all of us in the intake of that day were in the G.S.C. and got badges which caused much perplexity to the Aberdonians, who peered at our caps and couldn't make out what we were at all.

We had no doubt what we were. All day long it was rammed into us that we were Gordon Highlanders. All our officers and N.C.O.'s were Gordons. The G.S.C. meant nothing to them. We got lectures on the history of the greatest regiment in the British Army, the Gordons. We were allowed by the Regimental Sergeant Major to buy Gordon ties, Gordon badges and even notepaper with the Gordon crest on it.

I have no doubt that this was happening in the airts where the Cameronians and Highland Light Infantry held sway. All General Service men in the Cameronian section were taught the fast riflemen's march, though they'd have to unlearn it immediately they were posted to another regiment. The Cameronians had different names for certain articles from the other troops. The Colonel in charge of the Brig o' Don was a Cameronian, and this was rather resented by the Gordons, who felt that, since it was their barracks, a Gordon should command the place.

We had a redoubtable sergeant named Tommy Dunbar, a lean, tough Aberdonian, who had been a barman before he went into the Army. He was instructing us in bayonet drill one day, when along came the Cameronian Colonel.

'Ah, sergeant,' said the Colonel, 'you're giving them sword drill.'

'Yes, sir,' said Sergeant Dunbar, 'we're at bayonet practice.'

'Have they had much practice with the swords?' asked the Colonel.

'No, sir,' said the sergeant. 'This is their first day with the bayonets.'

So the conversation went on, and every time the Cameronian Colonel said 'sword', the Gordon Sergeant said 'bayonet.'

When we marched the four or five miles to the rifle range, we saw a Cameronian platoon ahead of us, their legs twinkling as they marched at their quick step. Tommy Dunbar, marching beside us, gave us a look and said, 'Think you could pass them?' Some of us hadn't the breath to do anything but nod. 'Right,' he said. 'We'll march like Gordons and show the bastards.' And so we did, much to the chagrin of the Cameronian sergeant and corporal.

I started by hating every moment of life in the army, and by the end of the second month I was enjoying it. Conditions at first were horrible. We had nearly fifty men sleeping in a hut designed for twenty. The food was disgusting, though it gradually improved. Some of the N.C.O.s, particularly one or two of the P.T. corporals, should not have been allowed in charge of a creche, far less grown men.

But in our platoon I found a comradeship I had never known before. Most newspapermen consider themselves men of the world. In the immortal words of my first editor, Arthur Hedderwick, they can 'live with lowest, and yet know how the highest live.' (And if you can think of a more snobbish remark than that, I'll be glad to hear it.) I thought I had seen life in most of its aspects.

I must admit that I learned more in a few months with our platoon than I had learned in all my days as a journalist. We were a beautifully mixed bag. We had shopkeepers, clerks, miners, steelworkers, labourers, insurance agents, farm workers, and at least one man with previous convictions. We had also a poacher with crossed eyes. He confided in us that he was going to work his way out of the army because of impaired sight. But every time a rifle was put in his hands and there was a target in front of him, he got one bull after another.

Assault courses had just been introduced and, after a twenty-three mile route march, we returned to barracks and were immediately put over the assault course. Never in my life have I felt as fit. The only trouble was getting up in the morning. We were allowed to stay out until mid-night and most of us did. Reveille was 6.30 a.m. and that was just bearable.

But, owing to congestion at the barracks, it was decided that one of the three regiments would have to volunteer to have breakfast half-an-hour earlier than the others. Since it was the Gordons' barracks, we were allowed to 'volunteer.' That meant reveille at six o'clock. Since we were working on double-summer-time, we were actually getting up at four o'clock in the morning.

Our first item on the programme after breakfast was Bren gun practice, and it was held in a field of long grass on the edge of the barracks. The gun was placed in the grass and, on an order, you ran forward and threw yourself full length behind it. Since the weather was perfect, the grass was always soaking with morning dew. And I can still recall plunging into that long, wet grass and lying behind the Bren gun saying to myself, 'I hope I get pneumonia out of this. That'll teach the so-and-sos.'

My objection was not to Bren gun practice, but getting up at that terrible hour in the morning. I didn't get even a cold. I continued to be disgustingly fit.

One day Sergeant Dunbar called three of us aside and told us that we were to become lance-corporals, acting, un-paid. Oh, the thrill of it! It seems absolutely mad, looking back now, that a middle-aged man should feel so happy about a 'promotion' of this sort. But I was really immensely pleased.

At that time I felt I could be quite happy staying out the war at Aberdeen. There were all sorts of discomforts and there were the usual niggling army stupidities. But Aberdeen was handy and the Aberdonians looked for Servicemen to be hospitable to. I had made friends with a London Scottish corporal, who was an artist in private life. His name was Ian Eadie and he introduced me to artist friends in the Old Town of Aberdeen.

The fly in the ointment was that, after six months of train-ing, I'd be posted. A corporal in the Cameronians did come along and suggest that, if I liked to join the barracks concert party, I would be made up to corporal and live a life of cushioned ease thereafter at Brig o' Don, entertaining the unfortunates until the war was over. This was my big chance to become a Scotch comic. But I felt I was too old for it and I turned it down.

Then one day a letter arrived from Captain Allan Mac-Kinnon of the Army Kinematograph Service. He explained how he had gone from the London Scottish to the Royal Artillery and had now landed in this newly formed outfit, the A.K.S. He was making army training films. He reasoned that, at the age of thirty-six, I might not be looking forward to a career in the infantry, and he was suggesting that, if I was interested, he could arrange a posting for me to the A.K.S. in London as a script-writer.

I had already written one or two scripts for documentary films in Scotland. My first was for none other than Dr John Grierson. It was for a picture made by Stanley Russell in Glasgow and it was entitled *Sport in Scotland*. I can still recall the first sentence of my commentary—'Sport in Scotland flourishes like the heather on the hill.' At the time I thought that was great, especially as the accompanying picture showed a keen looking chap in a kilt striding over the heather.

So I wrote back to Allan and said I was interested. My six months of training were up and I went home on my first leave. By this time Jessie had gone back to reporting and was with the *Express*. As her holiday was longer than my leave, she arranged to come up to Aberdeen for a few days. But the morning I reported back, a sergeant said, 'We've been looking for you all over the place. You've to report to the A.K.S. at the Twentieth Century Fox Studios at Wembley.

4

I was walking along Piccadilly, my dubbined boots ringing out on the pavement. The sun was shining. I had just saluted a face that was in all the papers, General Montgomery, and he said, 'Good morning, corporal.' I wondered how lucky could I get? I was on my way to the offices in Curzon Street which the script department of the Army Kinematograph Service occupied.

Never for a moment did I think that, when I went into the army, I'd end up in London, doing a job which I actually could do. Not only that, but I was allowed to stay in private digs. The A.K.S. had taken over the Twentieth Century Fox

Studios at Wembley and a cinema alongside. But there wasn't room for everybody there, and soldiers on the production side were allowed to have billets of their own, provided they paid for them, of course.

The A.K.S. was divided into two sides. The production side was the smaller and was full of people who had come straight from the film world into the army and been commissioned right away. The big side was the exhibition one. Small teams were being trained to operate projectors, so that they could be sent anywhere and give shows to the troops. There was also a group of administrative officers, who had no experience whatever of film production or exhibition, and inclined to the belief that this outfit should first of all be the same as the rest of the army. This made for trouble at times, especially with the production side.

At first the script department was kept to Curzon Street, and it was only necessary for me to go to Wembley when I was working on a picture there or had to collect my pay of 14s a week. Each time I took part in a pay parade I heard the name Ustinov called out, but I never saw anyone appear. I had heard of Private Peter Ustinov, though. He was a fellow script-writer with me, but he was working on a very hush-hush picture about the coming invasion of Europe and he was with the director, Captain Carol Reed, and another script-writer, Lieutenant Eric Ambler, at Largs.

Word had indeed come through from Largs that, at a Garrison Theatre show one Sunday night there, a go-as-you-please competition had been held. Private Ustinov entered and won it hands down. Which was not surprising, of course, if you knew Private Ustinov even then. When I did meet him, I discovered that his principal aim was to steer clear of Wembley at all costs. With a name like his, he said, he was a target for sergeant-majors.

And indeed that proved to be so when our R.S.M., a young and nasty man, got a drill period instituted every Saturday morning at Wembley. Unless you were actually working on a production, you had to be there. Peter managed to be working on production quite a lot, but eventually he was caught. Thus I did one or two memorable drill sessions with Peter Ustinov, since he and I were the only two 'other rank' script-writers at that time.

Sure enough, the R.S.M. picked on him from his first order. I think he was anxious to try out how many different ways there were of pronouncing the name Ustinov. We drilled in the shadow of the Wembley Stadium and, as we marched uselessly up and down, I reflected that the last time I had been on this hallowed spot was when I was an Assistant-Scoutmaster at the Imperial Jamboree of 1924. I felt like shouting the words of the hero of *The Silver King*—'Oh, God turn back Thy universe and give me yesterday.'

On one parade Private Ustinov brightened the proceedings for Lance-Corporal House by outlining the plot of a play he was thinking of writing. He proposed to take a group of surrealist writers and artists who decide to opt out of civilisation and form their own community somewhere in the most remote valleys of the Welsh mountains. They buy or rent an old, dilapidated farmhouse at the back of beyond and they settle in, developing their surrealist ideas as best they may.

They have just settled down when, all of a sudden, the door flies open and in walks a tree. There are other remarkable manifestations of Nature, and things get worse and worse, until the poor writers and artists discover that their farmhouse is in the middle of a Battle School training ground. In other words, the British Army proves to be far more surrealistic than the surrealists.

Peter's plot had to be conveyed to me in the snatches when we were standing easy. I thought it was a very good one, because I'd had some Battle School training myself at Brig o' Don. But he never wrote this play, as far as I know.

By this time I had a large room on the top floor of a house in Notting Hill Gate. It was called Pembridge Chambers in its grander moments and I got the top floor very cheaply because of the constant air raids. Fortunately, I was fatalistic about air raids. Night after night London was raided and I didn't bother to go to the air raid shelter. I just stayed in bed and, as long as there weren't any bombs dropping near by, I often slept right through the raids.

I saw a lot of Captain Allan MacKinnon, his wife Jean, and

his mother-in-law, Mrs Horn, who lived in a top-storey flat in Knightsbridge. And not far away from my Pembridge Chambers lived Lieutenant Harold Cooper, another script-writer, who had come straight from working for Unilever advertising films into uniform as a lieutenant. We called him Bob, but it should have been 'Bov'. When young, he had looked very like that cheery-faced chap clinging to the Bovril bottle in the middle of the ocean, with the slogan, 'Bovril prevents that sinking feeling'.

Every Sunday Bov, his wife Joyce and I would go up to the Windsor Castle pub on Campden Hill Road, and often Allan and Jean would join us. Then who should I meet in the corridor of Curzon Street House but Captain Stephen Watts, now working for the Army Bureau of Current Affairs after serving in the Royal Artillery and the posh English Rifle Regiment.

He joined us as well. There were the constant air-raids, the food was poor and inadequate, you had to drink beer because there was nothing else, but I enjoyed living in London and I thought I was very privileged to get the chance of working with the A.K.S.

The production boys at Wembley paid no attention to rank. The first man in charge was Major Thorold Dickinson, and he spoke to Lance-Corporal House as a script-writer and not as an inferior in the establishment. Then there was one of the world's great cameramen, Captain Freddy Young, one of those gentle chaps with a will of steel. We didn't see so much of Captain Carol Reed, but there was a memorable occasion when, as orderly officer, he had to mount the guard on the triangular patch of grass just opposite the studio.

Like so many of the other officers, Carol Reed had come straight from civilian life and it was quite unfair to expect him to know the drill and give orders. I fancied that some of the admin. officers fixed this sort of thing up on purpose to show up the production men. However, one of our production sergeants, a cameraman, wrote out the orders on a small piece of paper, which Captain Reed concealed in his palm. He mounted the guard in a rather jerky manner, because he had to keep referring to his script, so to speak. The guard themselves, mostly production men, jumped to it, even though they couldn't always hear the Captain's orders, and what I think was intended to be a shambles came off quite well.

There had been some talk of my achieving an immediate commission, and Peter Ustinov too. But we were too late. Somewhere in the great Army mind, our A.K.S. establishment was being looked at and in the meantime we retained our other ranking. Sometimes this caused ridiculous situations. Various Generals would order films and these would often have to be discussed between General and script-writer. I was working on one script when it became necessary to have a consultation with the General involved.

Obviously a mere Lance-Corporal could not discuss a film script with a General. So the boys dug up a spare Captain, who was attached to A.K.S. but knew nothing whatever about films, and he took charge of me. We met the General in his room in the War Office. He lifted his eyebrows slightly when he saw me, but I didn't say anything. We got down to the consultation, which was conducted between me and the General with the Captain intervening. I thought it was rather like a husband and wife who refused to speak to each other conducting their conversation through their lawyer.

We had our troubles with the Generals. Naturally, they knew nothing whatever about the technical side of film-making. We produced a film showing the immense amount of work involved in producing the small emergency pack which every soldier would carry into action on D-Day. In order to impress our soldier audiences (who took a deal of impressing) we included a line of food vans bringing in the rations for the packs. Each van bore the magic of Lyons and, when the Generals saw the picture, the most senior shouted, 'That damned advertising will have to be wiped off those vans.'

When it was explained to him that the whole sequence would have to be reshot with plain vans or else cut the shots out altogether, he was amazed. Obviously he thought those film fellows could do anything.

Then there was the day we showed a Battle School training film to a clutch of Generals. This demonstrated what happened in a right-flanking attack by a platoon. At the end, when the lights went up, there was a bit of silence, broken by one General who said, 'Very good, very good indeed. But someone should have told you film fellows that we've changed our minds. Under the circumstances it's now a *left*-flanking attack.'

There was another silence, and then a second General said brightly, 'Tell you what. Why not just turn the film round? Then we'd have a left-flanking attack.'

It had to be explained to him that, while this was technically possible, all the soldiers would be wearing their equipment the wrong way round and carrying their rifles in the wrong hand.

Meanwhile the War Office had worked out our establishment, and it was now announced that script-writers must be officers. The scenario editor would be a Captain, and the writers Lieutenants. But that meant that Lance-Corporal House and Privates Ustinov and Browne (Tommy Browne had joined us as a script-writer. I'd known him as a newspaperman in Glasgow, and since then he'd become a playwright.) must go before a War Office Selection Board and, if passed, to a pre-OCTU and then an infantry Officer Cadets' Training Unit, so as to be fully trained as infantry officers before returning to do the same script-writing that they did as other ranks.

As the senior other rank, I was first on the list. I went for three days to a W.O.S.B. at Watford, where I was delighted to get the number 13. That's always been a lucky number for me. We were put through all the tests that had been devised for finding out if you were suitable officer material. The ones that worried me were the physical ones, for I soon discovered that my life in London had spoiled the good physical condition I had been in when I left Aberdeen.

As I was packing my kit to leave the W.O.S.B., Peter Ustinov arrived. He asked me, somewhat apprehensively, about the tests. He said he felt there was no future for him as an officer. And from what he told me later, I gathered that he had made no particular effort until he came to his interview with the psychiatrist. Obviously he had led that gentleman up and down the garden path and round in circles as well.

I asked him about one test in which a number of pictures are shown on a screen and each soldier has one and a half minutes to write down his impression of the picture. Most of the pictures have a morbid theme. The last is a plain white screen.

'Ah,' said Peter Ustinov, 'for that one I wrote, 'This delicate piece of chinoiserie represents the view from a carriage window of a train on the Trans-Siberian railway.'

Peter didn't pass. I did and before long I was arriving at pre-OCTU at Wrotham. I didn't see Private Ustinov again until I became an officer and Lieutenant Campbell Logan—later to present *Dr Finlay's Casebook* on the telly—took me to a military hospital to cheer him up. As you may imagine, he cheered us up, and it wasn't so very long before he was out of the Army.

The pre-OCTU was a dreadful place. As far as I could see, most of the officers and N.C.O.'s were rejects from good regiments. I can't remember a single one of them whom I respected. We were put through basic infantry training and then had a week driving trucks and a week riding motorbikes. I managed to get through a week of driving a three-ton lorry, having never driven anything in all my life and having been given virtually no instruction by instructors who didn't know their job. Then I was put on a motor-bike, again without a word of instruction, and, perhaps not surprisingly, I went straight into a barbed wire fence.

I felt no pain whatever from the barbed wire. Indeed, it amazed me that the staff were so worried about me, and that a sergeant took me on the back of another motor-cycle to the nearest military hospital. If you don't see your wounds, they don't worry you. All I was conscious of was that I had a large number of barbed wire scratches all over my arms and legs. What I didn't know was that the barbed wire had gone up through my mouth and broken the bone above my front teeth.

My first indication of this was when, to my surprise, I was taken to the dental part of the hospital and a Major who, fortunately, came from Dundee, had a look at me. We quickly achieved a rapport since I knew Willie Hunt and a number of other Dundonians who had made the grade in Glasgow newspapers.

The Major peered into my mouth and then shouted, 'Jimmy! C'mere! This is the most remarkable occlusion I've ever seen.'

A Captain dentist came through, also a Scot, and peered at my mouth, while I wondered what the hell an occlusion was. Later, of course, I found that it is the way one's teeth are set, and that my front teeth far over-lapped my bottom teeth. Ken Dodd, who probably wasn't born then but whom I met years later, has a very similar occlusion to mine.

The Dundee Major dentist assured me that he would do his best for me and he bound up my front teeth with wire. I realised then what a piano must feel like. After a couple of weeks he pronounced me fit to return to Wrotham and I'd just had a week's leave when I was posted to OCTU at Dunbar. How lucky can you get! I'd done my preliminary training at Aberdeen, and now I was doing my OCTU training at Dunbar, from which I could get home on a week-end pass every second week, and in which, in any case, I felt at home.

So I was trained to be an infantry officer—and I've got to admit I enjoyed most of it. One day, though, I had to report to the OCTU dentist, who had one look at my two front teeth and said, 'It's only a matter of time before they turn black and die.' That was twenty-three years ago and, although they're an off-white colour now, they're not dead yet. I've had a cast taken of them because I realise that these front teeth are important to me. If they disappeared for any reason, my upper lip would probably hang in folds.

I got a B pass through OCTU, showing I could lead infantry anywhere, and returned to London as a Second-Lieutenant to do the same script-writing as I had done as a Lance-Corporal. Life as an officer, I found, was very much easier. The Army Kinematograph Service had settled down fairly well, and there was not so much internecine strife as there had been at the start.

Stephen Watts had left ABCA and was now in a department of MI, the Secret Service. We got digs together off

Church Street, Kensington. One way or another, life was fairly pleasant, except for the constant air raids and the fact that I'd a lot rather have been at home in Glasgow.

The Army films we were making were much more interesting than they had been in my lance-jack days. Then we had a great number of aircraft-recognition pictures, a very important job but not one which caused much creative effort. There were young and energetic directors coming along in A.K.S. I enjoyed working with Ronnie Kinnoch, Phil Leacock and Roy Baker, all of whom were to repeat their Army successes in civilian films when the war was over.

Richard Greene swam into our ken briefly, and took part in a picture I wrote called *Officers and Men*. For a time, too, we had Lieutenant-Colonel David Niven in charge of the production side of A.K.S. and what a charmer he turned out to be. I use that word 'charmer' advisedly, because he didn't only hypnotise us with his stories about Hollywood, but he was able to persuade the administration side of A.K.S. that the production boys deserved a certain amount of consideration.

I worked also with Eric Ambler, whose thrillers I admire greatly but who remains in my memory as one of the most understanding administrators I have met. It's very unusual to find a creative writer who has also a gift for administration. But I have the feeling that, if Eric Ambler had ever decided to give up writing for big business, he would have been at least as successful in the business world as he has been as an author.

While I am name-dropping, I must mention Geoffrey Sumner, who has been a silly-ass-type on the stage and television, and was another man who kept the Army Kinematograph Service in the way it should go. And, of our A.T.S. group of continuity girls and cutters, I recall with great affection Angela Martelli, Phyl Crocker and Tillie Day. For years after the war I used to go to the pictures and, when the credit titles came up on the screen, I was able to say, time after time, 'I worked with him', or 'There's Angela again.'

Looking back, I know I missed some opportunities. Our

production group couldn't make all the films the Army wanted, and so Allan MacKinnon and Bov Cooper had to go to civilian units for help. I remember being in Bov's company one day when a civilian director said, 'There's one chap you must steer clear of. He's a mad Welshman and if you go out for a night with him, you're finished. His name is Dylan Thomas. Remember that name—a script-writer called Dylan Thomas.'

As it happened, I didn't get the opportunity to meet Dylan Thomas. I doubt if I'd have appreciated him anyway. My Calvinistic upbringing would have acted as a stopper. We like to get drunk in private.

But I did hear of an A.K.S. film made by a civilian unit, and the story was that Dylan Thomas was concerned in it. It was called *The Red Army* and it was issued just when General Montgomery was the top dog in, I think, Southern Command. At this time the Russians were beginning to make headway against the Nazis and a film liaison officer in Southern Command reported to General Montgomery that this new A.K.S. picture, *The Red Army*, was available.

Montgomery gave orders to get a copy at once. Then he ordered that it should be shown in a cinema at Slough to as many officers in his command as the cinema could accommodate. On a certain Sunday all the 2000 officers congregated in this Slough cinema. General Montgomery marched on to the stage and told them to stop coughing. Then he introduced a Professor from London University who was an authority on Russia, and the Professor gave a short lecture on the background of the Russian Army.

After that the lights went down and the screen was illuminated with the title, *The Red Army*. The officers present then saw what appeared to be snow-clad hills and across these hills a stream of creatures marched. When they saw the scene more clearly, the officers realised that these creatures were some form of insect. This, the more perceptive among them thought, was some clever trick of these film chaps, comparing the Russian Army with ants or something of the sort.

But it soon became clear that the snow-clad hills were just

a grey blanket and that the advancing army was composed of bed-bugs. In the East End of London at that time, bed-bugs were known as the Red Army. The clever film-makers had therefore given this title to their picture.From what we heard, all hell was let loose at Slough. Shortly afterwards we got a directive from the War Office that our A.K.S. pictures must be given titles which would indicate clearly what their subject was.

Oddly enough, as Paul Jennings says, I was concerned in an insect film myself about this time. The idea was to make a picture about the great new anti-insect drug, D.D.T. The Generals wanted something which would sketch the history of D.D.T., then show its application to modern warfare, particularly in the impregnating of uniforms which would be worn in and after the attack on the Normandy coast. The trouble was that the brutal and licentious soldiery were always wary of any idea of this sort. They immediately assumed that adding any form of drug to food, drink or clothing would make a man sterile. Well, even in Brig o'Don barracks we all knew that something was put into our tea to make us less susceptible to houghmagandy.

I was given this script to write and spent a considerable time travelling around the country collecting data on D.D.T. In particular, I went to a secret place some distance from London where experiments in D.D.T. were being carried out. Very soon I met an Army scientist who had injected himself with D.D.T. just to see what would happen.

'And what *did* happen?' I asked.

'I became sterile,' he said. But he added that he had got over it and, in any case, the amount of D.D.T. he had put into himself was immensely greater than any soldier could possibly absorb through wearing D.D.T.—impregnated battledress.

I decided to forget this revelation. Instead, I concentrated on another aspect, and that was the amazing effect of spraying D.D.T. on insects. At this station they were able to breed flies in huge numbers. I suggested to one of the scientists that we could have in our film the biggest cast in the world's film history. If he could breed 10,000 flies, we could show them being killed by a spray of D.D.T. He said that could certainly be done, and I wrote it into the script.

Phil Leacock was making this picture and one day he reported to me that I had made a big boner. I had this scene with 10,000 flies being killed by D.D.T. When he went to the research station, he was shown a container with only a few hundred flies and had to do the best as he could with them. I apologised and said I must have misunderstood the scientist.

There came the time when our picture, *The Story of D.D.T.* was shown in our Curzon Street cinema. It was considered highly successful and, when the congratulations were flying, one of the officers from the research station came up to me and said, 'I owe you an apology. I'm the man who talked to you about those 10,000 flies.'

'I always wondered what happened about that,' I confessed, and he said, 'Well, we were breeding the 10,000 flies just fine and they were to be transferred to another cage for the actual filming. What we didn't know was that some bright boy had cleaned out the cage using water that had D.D.T. in it. When we went along to make sure the 10,000 flies were ready for their film debut, we found most of them already dead. That's why you didn't get your cast.'

Most of the films I worked on were directed by Roy Baker, and I particularly enjoyed *Read All About It*, a picture made for the Army Bureau of Current Affairs to destroy two misconceptions on the part of the soldier—(1) 'I read it in the papers, so it must be true.': (2) 'You can't believe anything you read in the papers.'

In the course of time I became scenario editor of the A.K.S. and therefore a Captain. London was being pounded by V1s now and, though I still slept on the attic floor, I was worried sometimes when I was having a bath and I heard a V1 cut out on its approach. The trouble was that one side of the bathroom was a big window. As those who were in London then will recall, you felt safe while the V1 was roaring away. The cut out was the danger signal.

One summer's evening I went to listen to the band in Hyde Park, because it happened to be the Clydebank Burgh

Band that night. I was sitting in my deck chair, enjoying Kenneth Alford's *Musical Switch*, or whatever it was, when the sound of a V1 approaching in what seemed to be a dead straight line came to our ears.

It got louder and louder, and I saw the whole band, still playing valiantly away, steadily sinking in their seats. I have no doubt that we in the audience were doing the same. Everybody was waiting for the cut out. Then we saw the thing roaring overhead and it was still roaring when it disappeared to the North.

Yes, you felt you had some sort of a chance with the V1. But there was no chance at all with the V2, which dropped straight from the sky without more than a moment's warning.

Strange to say, the last film I wrote for the Army was on how to make and fire a V2.

On January 1st, 1945, I made a prophecy, a thing I am seldom given to do. I said that, before the year ended, the war in both Europe and the Far East would be over, and I would be out of the Army. Everybody who heard it laughed heartily. And it came true.

When the war ended in Europe, there was a race by the British, American and Russian troops to get hold of the men and material behind the V2 campaign. The Russians won the race, owing to geographical advantages. The Americans did not badly at all. But the British had to be satisfied with a comparatively small number of V2 engineers, not one of whom was an expert on the whole job.

The Royal Artillery decided right away to have a film made on the history of the V2 and to show a rocket in the making and, if possible, being fired. A Krupps testing works at Cuxhaven had been taken over, and I was recalled from leave in Glasgow to fly over to Hamburg with the Brigadier in charge of the ploy. (When I think of going on leave, I always remember that, coming up from Euston in the train, I would get out at the Central Station and walk into Gordon Street and take deep breaths of what to me was fresh air.)

The rocket assembly at Cuxhaven went surprisingly well, mainly, I think, because the German engineers were keen to show what a good job it was. I found my script much easier to write than I had expected, since I am not very good on technical jobs. And at last there came the day when our V2 was to be fired.

A clearing had been made in a wood and the rocket was set up on an iron table. It was due to fly up, curve over, and drop into the North Sea. It was operated from a bunker some distance away and the order of firing was that the first switch ignited the fuel, which must burn equally below the rocket; if the flame was not equal the second switch would cause the flames to be extinguished; if all was well, the third switch launched the rocket.

On the crucial day we had our cameras placed at various strategic points. I was slightly worried because, in my reading on the subject of the V2, I had come across plenty of cases where the rocket had blown up and killed the whole rocket unit, or had fallen off sideways instead of flying up, and careered along the ground.

It was a fine day for our launching. From our second camera, up a hill side, we could see the rocket unit finishing their arrangements. Then the Germans carried out their 'good luck' routine, which was to paste a pin-up picture (of a nude girl, if possible) to the side of the rocket and urinate over one of the legs of the iron table on which it rested.

Then the clearing emptied of people and there was what seemed to be a long, long wait. All of a sudden flame appeared below the rocket. This was it, we thought. It burned for a while, and then it went out. From the bunker the single figure of a man appeared. He walked across to the rocket and bent under the iron table. A few seconds later he seemed to throw himself from beneath the table and collapse. Then more people appeared and we realised that the rocket was not for firing.

Afterwards we learned what had happened. The flame under the rocket had not been even and, on the German engineers' recommendation, the second switch was put into action and the flame went out. Then one of the Germans—he must have been a brave man—volunteered to go out to the V2 and see what was wrong.

The V2 got its power from liquid oxygen and pure alcohol. When the engineer was under the iron table, he accidentally turned on the supply of alcohol. It spurted down and in a few moments he was dead drunk! He'd just managed to stagger from under the table before he passed out completely.

It did not take the engineers long to put the fault in the V2 right, and soon there was a successful launching of which the A.K.S. got some very good pictures. Indeed, for a long time afterwards, it was our rocket launching picture which was constantly used when such a picture was wanted in films of any kind. I can't tell you how many times I've seen it in Glasgow cinemas.

But then the atom bomb was dropped in Japan and the V2 became old hat. The second part of my New Year's Day prophecy came true, and the war ended in the Far East. Soon a directive came round us in the Army Kinematograph Service that, if any of us had employers who wanted us back, we were to get in touch with them at once. The Army didn't want a lot of film-makers hanging around doing nothing.

I had three offers to stay in London and continue working on films as a civilian script-writer. But all I wanted in the world was to get home to Glasgow. And so, on December 17th 1945, I stepped out of the Central Station once again, not on leave this time, but for good.

The Piping Days

I came back from the war imbued with high ideals. I suppose a lot of us did then. We'd voted Labour at the General Election and we felt a brave new world was opening up before us. I was, naturally, thirled to the *Citizen*, but I gave a showing of three of the A.K.S. films I had scripted at the Cosmo Cinema in Glasgow in an endeavour to persuade people that a Scottish film industry might be started. I explored the idea of founding a magazine which would be a sort of Glasgow *New Yorker*. If there was anything cultural to join, I joined it.

It took quite a long while for disenchantment to set in. Peace alone was so wonderful that you didn't worry about the various pinpricks and anomalies. New things were starting all the time and so your original ideas got lost or were submerged. I was forty now and I recollected a wise saying which Moray McLaren had quoted to me (I don't know who the original author was) that 'the Forties are the old age of youth; the Fifties are the youth of old age.' I think that is very true and the reason why so many men have a difficult time in their forties.

Not that I had much time to think about the old age of my youth. I was constantly asked to propose toasts at dinners, open pubs, give lectures, and write for all sorts of magazines. I tried to get back to my B.B.C. writing days, but I soon found that I had lost the touch. One radio revue was enough to teach me that the war had affected my sense of humour.

In any case, radio now meant appearing in quiz games and discussion panels, and talking paid better than writing. I was astonished to get a 'phone call from Gordon Gildard of the B.B.C. one day to ask me to be one half of a Scottish team in a new programme called *Round Britain Quiz*. Throughout the war there had been a famous *Transatlantic Quiz*, but the B.B.C. had run out of dollars, and it was proposed, as an experiment, to run a quiz confined to Britain. The Scottish team were to be the guinea-pigs, and my partner was James Fergusson, then a leader writer on *The Glasgow Herald*, now Sir James, Keeper of the Records of Scotland.

Our question master was a man I had never heard of—Gilbert Harding. I didn't take much to him when I met him. I didn't like his bristling moustache, his booming voice or the fact that he appeared to get drunk so quickly. He was also so terribly English, and I was terribly Scottish.

The very first *Round Britain Quiz* was a couple of rounds between Scotland and England. Lionel Hale was in charge in London, and the team there was Professor Denis Brogan and Hubert Phillips. A typical London team, I thought—a man from Rutherglen and a man from Wales! Gilbert explained that the London team had a bottle of whisky in the studio while recording and, he said 'What's good enough for London is good enough for Scotland.' So we got a half-bottle of whisky in the studio.

Sure enough, a glass would be poured for James and one for me, but we were so worried, strained, nervous and excited that we couldn't think of touching the whisky until the end of the recording when, by some strange stroke of fate, there was no whisky left in the bottle.

Originally we broadcast from the Glasgow studio in Queen Margaret Drive. Gilbert would sit on one side of the table, and James and I were on the other. We had in front of us all the questions that the London team were to be asked and the answers. In London Denis Brogan and Hubert Phillips had in front of them all our questions and answers. I think the idea of this was to give you confidence. You'd hear the London team getting nowhere with a question and you'd feel full of confidence. In actual fact, it worked the other way round. I'd be looking at a question that I couldn't answer in a month of Sundays, and I'd hear the London team get the answer in a flash, and all the confidence oozed out of my boots.

Each quiz was recorded, for the very good reason that, when a question was thrown at us, we sometimes said things we shouldn't say, such as 'My God!' or 'Oh, hell!' Recording the programme meant that these remarks could be cut out and so not insult the tender ears of the listening public.

I recall the London team being asked the question, 'What is the quickest way to Scotland and will you sing the answer?' We thought Denis Brogan would get that one right away and start singing (as only he can) 'Ye'll tak' the high road and I'll tak' the low road, and I'll be in Scotland afore ye.' But apart from saying that the answer must be a Scottish song, he couldn't help, and it was left to Hubert Phillips, who started to think aloud.

'Yes, I know it's a Scottish song,' he said, 'and I think it has something to do with death.'

In this he was right, of course, for the song is about a Jacobite who was executed at Carlisle. The Highlanders have a superstition that the spirit of anyone who meets sudden death travels under the ground to his home. That is the 'low road' referred to in the song. So when Hubert Phillips talked about death, James and I encouraged him from our end.

'Ah, yes,' he said, after he had assimilated some of our clues. 'It's not just death—it's the road of death. That's it— the road of death.'

'Of course,' said Denis Brogan. 'The L.N.E.R.'

I need hardly say that that was cut.

I had rather a similar experience when we were given a question about the famous man who was asked in America what he had to declare, and replied 'I have nothing to declare but my genius.' What names could he have declared, asked Lionel Hale.

Well, I knew that it was Oscar Wilde who had said 'I have nothing to declare but my genius.' I also knew that he had five names, but I could not at that moment remember what they were. However, I did recall that he was Irish and so, after trying O'Brien and O'Ryan and a few other names, I hit upon O'Flaherty, and that was one point.

From London Denis Brogan and Hubert Phillips tried to clue me. Denis in particular kept saying, 'Think of Mendelssohn—think of Mendelssohn.' He wanted me to think of *Fingal's Cave* and then I'd have got another of Oscar Wilde's names, Fingal. But each time he said 'Think of Mendelssohn', the only thing I could think of was the *Spring Song*, and I knew that neither Spring nor Song was in Oscar Wilde's name.

I had to give that one up. But the London team were still being generous with their clues, and eventually I stumbled on the right line. 'It's got something to do with cigarettes', I said. 'That's it—cigarettes', and so I got Wills. Two points, and on to the next question.

At the end of the recording the London producer came on and said, 'Really, Mr House, this free advertising will not do.' I explained that advertising had been farthest from my thoughts and that, in fact, I had never smoked in my life. He laughed and said not to worry, he would attend to it.

Two Sundays later this recording was broadcast, and I listened to it with more than usual interest. When the Oscar Wilde question was asked, I heard myself get O'Flaherty with some difficulty. Then I got nowhere at all with Fingal. And then there was a slight pause and my voice said 'Wills!' Every single word I'd said before that had been cut out.

I've often wondered what the listeners at home thought of that. I can just imagine the typical Glaswegian turning to his wife and saying, 'What amazing powers of ratiocination this man House possesses!' You know the way that listeners talk to each other.

Well, I'm now contemplating the twentieth *Round Britain Quiz*. Over the years the Scottish team is the only one which has remained the same. And I'm delighted to say that, in that time, James and I have won most of our contests. I think this is because we are so different. As I have related, I left school at the age of fifteen. James went to Eton and Balliol. Once, when Lionel Hale asked 'Was that James Fergusson or Jack House speaking?' I replied, 'You ought to know the difference. James speaks with a public school accent, and I speak with a public house accent.'

Most *Round Britain Quiz* teams were composed of a couple

of academics, though that is not so much the case now. But, as far as James and I are concerned, our areas of knowledge are wide apart. One day we were asked, 'If the Wizard of Dribble was heard to shout 'On, Stanley, on! where would he be and what would he be doing?' I replied that it would be Stanley Matthews shouting to Stan Mortensen to go in on his own at Blackpool.

James turned to me and said, 'How on earth do you know these things?' But the fact is that we could have gone out into Queen Margaret Drive and asked any one of the taxi-drivers on the rank there and he'd have got the right answer.

2

The biggest problem of the *Round Britain Quiz* was really Gilbert Harding. I miss him very much today. I think he was a man who had a great deal to bear. It's only now that I realise how good he was as a quiz master. But, as the spiritual says, nobody knows the trouble I've seen!

It became routine during the quiz recordings that Gilbert and I lunched together. Occasionally the producer at the Scottish end might be with us, but usually we were on our own. Nearly always we lunched after the recording, and for several years in Glasgow. Then when James went through to Edinburgh to become Keeper of the Records, we recorded there.

The trouble about lunching in Glasgow with Gilbert Harding was that I had to keep looking for new places because of the trouble he had caused in the last one. Then I thought I had found the answer. One bright noon we left Broadcasting House and took a tram-car into town. 'Where are we eating today?' asked Gilbert, and there was a twinkle in his eye, because he was fully conscious of the worry he caused me.

'The Bank,' I said, and Gilbert asked what was special about that. I explained that the Bank Restaurant in Queen

Street was run by Willie Maley, the famous former manager of the Celtic Football Club. Gilbert, as he never tired of telling everybody, was a convert to Roman Catholicism and a large part of the support of Celtic are Roman Catholics. He expressed himself as delighted that he would meet the great Willie Maley.

All of a sudden I remembered one thing about the Bank. It is in the centre of the 'rag trade' area of Glasgow and so was used very much by Jews in those days. 'Oh, by the way,' I said to Gilbert, 'I hope you don't mind a lot of Jews being there.'

Gilbert Harding then made a remark which I shall always treasure. 'Are you suggesting,' he said to me, 'that I am intolerant?'

Anyhow, we got to the Bank and I had already booked a table and told Willie Maley I was bringing Gilbert Harding along. Gilbert was not as famous then as he was to become, but he was well enough known for Willie Maley to be pleased too. At that time the front restaurant of the Bank was rather like a City chop house in London. There was a bar at one side and little tables for men only. Women were taken into some mysterious place at the back of the building.

Willie Maley and Gilbert got on famously. Mr. Maley had provided steaks when steaks were almost impossible to get. We chatted about the Celtic Football Club to our hearts' content. I thought to myself that I had found a haven at last. Gilbert had plenty to drink, but wasn't in the least affected. I bade him farewell about three o'clock and went back to my office with a thankful heart.

I used the Bank a good deal for lunch—or luncheon, as Gilbert said in correction—and next day I was there again. I was met by the manageress, Mrs Cook, with a face like thunder. 'Mr House,' she said, 'please do not bring Mr. Gilbert Harding back to this restaurant.'

I was dumbfounded. 'Why?' I asked her.' We had a very pleasant lunch here yesterday. What's wrong?'

'He came back in the evening,' she said. And then I learned that Gilbert had arrived at the Bank about six o'clock, already, as we say in these parts, well away. He had propped himself up against the bar and proceeded to dominate the conversation as usual. But then he had picked a quarrel with a small Jew, whom he insulted. The Jew took Gilbert out into Queen Street and knocked him down.

The Bank was a respectable restaurant and this sort of thing was out of the question. So yet another place was barred to us. At last I solved the problem by taking Gilbert to the Queen Anne, a lovely old Victorian place that has since been burned down. It was kept by the Bells, father and son, and they had a private dining room at the top of the building to which only personal friends were admitted. They took to Gilbert right away and he took to them, and for the rest of our recordings in Glasgow, this was the place we went to.

It was while we were still eating at the Queen Anne that our venue, as the best sporting writers say, was moved to Edinburgh. Gilbert decided that, when it came to the last recording in our series for that year, he would come to Glasgow first and have a last luncheon at the Queen Anne before going on to record the quiz in Edinburgh in the evening. This turned out to be the Harding day to end all Harding days.

He came up by morning plane and summoned me to an aperitif in the cocktail bar of the St. Enoch Hotel. In order to get time off to record the *Round Britain Quiz* I had to work very hard, and I just couldn't meet Gilbert's whims. I thought also that aperitifs in the St. Enoch Hotel were somewhat unnecessary, considering what would be waiting for us at the Queen Anne. When I arrived at the St. Enoch, there was Gilbert holding court in the cocktail bar. I prised him loose with some difficulty, and we stepped across St. Enoch Square and round the corner to the Queen Anne.

The Bells were waiting for Gilbert. They knew the importance of the occasion. They also knew what he liked to drink. So, when we entered their tiny office just inside the front door, they produced a bottle of gin and a bottle of Noilly Prat and told Gilbert they belonged to him.

At last, we made our way up to the top room for lunch. Gilbert was asked to name the drink for the occasion and he

said, 'What can we have but champagne?' And champagne it
was. We finished with coffee and a beautiful brandy. Then
I had to dash back to do some more writing, with the arrangement that I would meet Gilbert on the Central Station platform where the 4.30 left for Edinburgh.

I arrived on the platform at 4.25 to see Gilbert outside
the dining car, visibly swaying. The idea was that we would
have tea on our way through. Gilbert was in great form. He
had discovered that the dining car chief attendant was
named Dick Barton, and in those days there was a radio
character named Dick Barton who was a James Bond type
before James Bond was invented.

The tea came along and Gilbert fiddled about in a brief
case and produced a bottle of brandy which was about a
third full. 'We didn't finish the brandy after you left,' he
said, 'and Kenneth Bell insisted I should take what was left.
Have some in your tea.'

I said I liked brandy and I liked tea, but I did not like them
mixed. So Gilbert, sniffing a bit, poured a large dollop of
brandy into his tea, drank it, sat back, and went into a
sound sleep.

When we got to Princes Street Station, Edinburgh, I
shook Gilbert's arm and shouted, 'We're here!'

'What?' cried Gilbert. 'London already?'

I persuaded him that this was Edinburgh and that he had
still a session of the *Round Britain Quiz* before him, As usual,
he came back to normality in an instant.

'I have a room booked in the Caledonian Hotel,' he told
me. 'I don't trust these hotel people. Come with me, Jack,
and help me to make sure the right thing is done.'

My idea was that I would wait in the lobby until Gilbert
had got his room, then we could take a taxi to Broadcasting
House. But I knew better than to object. We strode together
into the hotel and up to the reception desk. 'Harding is the
name,' boomed Gilbert. 'You have a room for me.'

The girl receptionist looked up some file and said, 'Yes,
Mr Harding, room number so and so.'

'Has it got a private bathroom?' demanded Gilbert.

'No, I'm afraid it hasn't.'

'Well, my good girl, get me a room with a private bathroom. Don't you know I suffer from PILES?'

He roared this out, so that some American tourists at the back of the lobby looked quite horrified.

He got a room with a private bathroom and asked me to come along with him to see it. By this time, I was in a sweat. We were already overdue at Broadcasting House. And, sure enough, the first thing Gilbert did was to ring room service and order large drinks. I pleaded with him to get to the studio. He said the London team were always late and there was no reason to hurry.

At last we got a taxi and arrived at the B.B.C. late for Sir James Fergusson and our producer, but still in time for London. The whisky was produced and Gilbert poured himself his customary libation. Any ordinary man would have passed out quietly by this time, and I could see that even Gilbert was slumping in his seat in the studio. But the moment the recording started, he was in command of the situation. Perhaps he slurred his words a bit here and there but I think that I, knowing what he had already consumed, was the only one who noticed it.

At our last recording Gilbert had said that James, the producer and I must be his guests at a farewell dinner for the season. But when this recording ended, and we all went along for a drink at the Cafe Royal, it was obvious that Gilbert had forgotten all about his dinner. Soon James and George left, and Gilbert then suggested we should have dinner together. 'But first of all,' he said, 'we'll go along to the Arts Club and get thrown out.'

This idea did not appeal to me at all. At that time I was not a member of the Glasgow Art Club, and therefore not entitled to the reciprocal delights of the Scottish Arts Club in Edinburgh. If I had been a member, I hope I should have dissuaded Gilbert from this ploy. But I was weak and down into Princes Street we went.

It was a glorious evening and the setting sun had turned Edinburgh Castle and the Rock into a deep red colour, with a dark blue sky behind them. Gilbert insisted on standing in the middle of Princes Street, with the traffic performing all kinds of gyrations round us, to point out to me how magnificent it all was.

I got him on to the pavement and we climbed into a taxi which Gilbert ordered to proceed to the Scottish Arts Club. He looked again at the Castle and cried, 'You'll never see anything like this in the whole of Europe.'

The taxi-driver turned his head and said, 'Yes, it *is* nice, isn't it?'

'Who's speaking to you, you silly peasant?' shouted Gilbert.

Now, if it had been a Glasgow taxi-driver, the cab would have stopped at that moment and the driver would have thrown Gilbert out. But Edinburgh taxi-drivers are tolerant chaps. This one just clamped his mouth in a grim line and said no more.

When we arrived in Rutland Square Gilbert rang the bell, and, after a while, a young man in a white jacket opened it.

'Do you always keep your members waiting as long as this?' Gilbert demanded.

'Most of our members have their own keys,' replied the steward.

By this time I'd discovered that Gilbert's right to be in the Scottish Arts Club stemmed from the fact that he was a member of the Savile Club in London.

We went up to the bar, got our drinks, and went into the L-shaped lounge of the club. There was the customary exhibition of paintings. 'Let's go round the exhibition and see what's wrong with it,' said Gilbert. I declined. I took a magazine and sat in a corner. I could see that, fortunately, there were only three other men in the whole place and they were sitting together at a table at the other end.

Gilbert walked round the pictures, gazing fiercely at each and muttering under his breath. Then he suddenly wheeled round and came back to me. 'Jack,' he said, 'these three men are talking about me. Let's take the table beside them and listen to what they are saying.'

Ah, yes, it's easy to think now of how I could have stopped Gilbert being silly, or at least have extricated myself from the silliness. But weakly I went along with him to the table beside the three men. They paid no attention to us but went on with their discussion of the last subject to which any honest, free-born Englishman could object—cricket!

Gilbert was soon fed up with this. 'We must eat,' he declared, and led the way out into the street. He swayed in front of a car and the driver sounded his horn in warning. Gilbert immediately gave him the well-known Churchill sign. The driver stopped the car and I thought that the fracas which had been building up steadily was going to happen now. But there was a woman in the car with him and it was obvious that she was persuading him to drive on.

By now I realised that Gilbert had forgotten all about taking me to dinner. I said firmly to him that I had to get back to Waverley Station to get the train to Glasgow. He called a taxi and insisted on taking me to the station. Then he bade me a fond good night and said, 'I think I'll just take this cab to the Scottish Arts Club and be thrown out.'

And that was the Gilbertian evening's entertainment over for me.

I didn't worry so much when we settled down in Edinburgh for the recordings. There were plenty of troubles, but Gilbert became famous and all was forgiven him. Up till then he was just about the most insecure man I have ever met. The fact that he was a free-lance worried him. He told me he'd like to try writing and he actually wrote part of an article and sent it to me for advice. I'd hardly advised him ere he was being sought to write for all sorts of papers.

His turning point was the occasion when he misbehaved himself as question master of *Twenty Questions*. Next morning he was due in Edinburgh for our quiz and, when I met him, he had his sister with him. The papers were full of stories about the previous night's entertainment, and Gilbert's sister had come up to Scotland to keep an eye on him.

Gilbert himself was in a terrible state about it all and confided to me that this was him finished as far as the B.B.C. were concerned. But, of course, it all happened the other way round. He became a popular figure and, once he was actually seen on television, he could do no wrong.

One day we were lunching in the Café Royal oyster bar in Edinburgh. When we were having coffee Gilbert decided he

would like some port. The waitress pointed out that it was
after closing time and she could not serve him with alcohol.
Gilbert demanded to see the manager.

By now the oyster bar was actually closed and two women
cleaners arrived and started to wash the floor. Gilbert and I
sat there as they washed round our feet. He complained
bitterly to the manager that all he wanted was a glass of port
and that the stupid licensing laws of this city prevented him
from having it. At last the manager said that he would give
Gilbert some port for nothing, but he couldn't sell him any.

He went down to the cellars and came back with a dusty
bottle. Gilbert pronounced it just the thing, and the port
was poured out. It was a fine one. Gilbert beamed upon the
manager and insisted that he should have a glass of his own
port. Then he spied the cleaners. 'And these good ladies too,'
he cried. 'I insist upon it.' So the two cleaners rose from their
knees and were poured a glass of vintage port each.

These were the good days. But Gilbert became ill and
he would arrive at the studio with a mask and a cylinder of
oxygen. When he became short of breath, he would switch on
the oxygen and put the mask over his nose and mouth while
carrying on with the programme. He was a superb professional and no listener ever knew that this was happening
in the middle of the *Round Britain Quiz*.

Of course, he would not do what his doctor told him. One
day we went to the North British Hotel for lunch and Gilbert
revealed that he had been put on a very strict diet. I ordered
a Wiener Schnitzel and Gilbert said, 'That's right, Jack.
Make a beast of yourself!' Then he went into the almost
minute details with the head waiter about what was to be in
his salad and how it was to be prepared. As the head waiter
was about to leave us, Gilbert cried, 'No, no, no! I'm not
going to eat it. I'll have a tournedos Rossini with saute
potatoes and cauliflower.' And that's what he had, with some
good Burgundy, also in defiance of his doctor.

The last time I saw him was in that same restaurant. He
was very ill indeed and had had to stop several times in the
short walk from Broadcasting House in Queen Street to the
hotel. It was most distressing to see him trying to eat and

House and horse (in Glasgow, Montana)

Art critic House

enjoy his wine, and every now and then lean back and endeavour to catch his breath. At one point he said, 'Tell me some funny stories from Glasgow, Jack.' I was completely bereft of speech. If I knew any funny stories from Glasgow, they had gone right out of my head.

It didn't surprise me at all to learn from the newspapers next morning that, when Gilbert had arrived by aeroplane in London, he had been so ill that he was taken immediately to hospital. It wasn't so long after that that he died and ever since I have reproached myself for being so censorious of his failings. Gilbert Harding was a generous man—I don't mean generous only in the financial sense; he did give of himself.

3

We seemed to be quiz-daft after the war. At any rate, my life, outside newspaper work, seemed to be one darned quiz after another. *Any Questions?* had been started by the B.B.C. Western Region, and we had an equivalent in Scotland called *A Matter of Opinion*. If I say that I think ours was better, that's probably just national prejudice. But *Any Questions?* is still running as a radio show, and *A Matter of Opinion* has not been heard for several years. Perhaps that was national prejudice too.

A Matter of Opinion differed from other quiz shows in that a member of the public stated a definite opinion, and the panel argued about it. Our first producer was George Runcie and our first quiz master Neil Paterson, once a novelist likely to make a great name, but now a man who seems to confine himself to film scripts and makes good money. We went to small towns and villages and, since George was from the North-East, it was surprising how many of them were in Aberdeenshire, Banffshire and Inverness-shire.

Just as everyone thinks he would make an ideal editor, everyone thinks he would be a wonderful member of a quiz panel. All I can say is that it's very hard work. Of course,

G

if all you do is say exactly what you think, without any relation to other people, it's simple enough. And probably
helluva boring as well. But if, as with most quiz successes
I have met, you try to fit in with the rest of the team and
make things interesting and exciting for the listeners, then
it takes a lot of doing.

I always felt completely wabbit after every *Matter of
Opinion*. That doesn't mean that I did well in the programme.
It means that I was trying very hard. A great deal depended,
of course, on the rest of the team. If I was on the same
programme with Eric Linklater, Lionel Daiches (now
Sheriff Daiches), Johnny Bannerman or Douglas Young, I
felt all would go well. And later, when the urbane Noel
Stevenson took over as question master, things were inclined
to go so smoothly that I forgot to worry.

This could be dangerous. It was, I think, in Fraserburgh
that we were asked to express our opinion after a member of
the audience had doubted whether Billy Graham's visit to
Scotland would do any good. Billy had been in Scotland before, of course, but had made little impact. This was the
time that the bally-hoo was used.

If I remember rightly, Sir Compton Mackenzie and the
late Hector McNeil, then Secretary of State for Scotland,
were on the same panel. I don't recollect what anybody else
said, but I know that I said that I didn't approve of Billy
Graham and his style of evangelism at all. I thought one
good minister of the Church of Scotland could do far more
for our people than all handsome Billy's Bible thumping.
(And I mean that literally. Billy goes through Bibles like
winkie.) I added that I understood that this sort of evangelis-
tic campaign often resulted in an increase in the illegitimate
birth rate. And that was *that*.

Next day I had a 'phone call from a Professor of The-
ology (if I heard him aright on the line), who asked me to
prove what I had said. I got another call from a Glasgow
business man who demanded that I should prove I was right
about the illegitimate birth rate. Several letters came in on
the same subject, making the same request.

I knew that I had read this statement about illegitimate

births and religious revivals in a serious book on the subject, but I couldn't remember for the life of me what the book was called. However, the great Mitchell Library in Glasgow is my constant fount of information, and I got in touch with the Mitchell in the certainty that I could be proved right. The Mitchell did its best, but all they could produce was a number of books which suggested that revivals had the effect I had mentioned, but did not give any actual figures.

Quite unexpectedly a letter from Dr. Henry Farmer arrived. Dr. Farmer had been conductor of the Empire Theatre orchestra for years. He was also a distinguished scholar in Arabic. He said in his letter that he thought I might find some difficulty in standing up for what I had said about Billy Graham, and suggested I would find food for thought in the following list of books. It was very kind of him, but they were mainly the books which the Mitchell Library had produced, and I was still without statistics.

Another letter came in from the blue. It was from a school-teacher who wrote that he agreed with every word I had said about the effects of evangelism of the Billy Graham sort and that he had been assistant registrar of a parish in Dumfriesshire before the Great War. A religious revival was held there and, in the registrar's return for the following year, it was specially noted that the illegitimate birth rate had risen at the appropriate period after the revival.

I sent all the information I had gleaned to my critics. Those who wrote back said they were completely unimpressed.

Then Billy Graham arrived in Glasgow and started his campaign in the Kelvin Hall. By this time I was writing for the finest of all newspapers, the Glasgow *Evening News*. The editor, Jack W. Robertson, sent three of us to say what we liked about Billy Graham's opening night. He chose Angus Shaw, our News Editor who had been brought up in the Highlands, Jean Macauley, and me.

I tried not to be prejudiced—in fact, I leaned backwards not to be prejudiced. I admired the organisation and the presentation. I did my best to admire Billy himself, but he looked to me what he really is—a super insurance salesman.

I thought his preaching was poor. Indeed, he was a great disappointment to me. And then came the time when he called sinners to repentance.

Then it seemed to me that Billy Graham was using the same technique that Adolf Hitler had used at the Nuremberg rallies. There was the same insistent rhythm, the same repetition of words, the same technique of mass hypnotism. I'm not suggesting for a moment that Billy had modelled himself on Adolf. But it was a frighteningly similar performance.

Well, the poor souls came forward. I was truly sorry for them. I felt indignant that they should be misled in this way. I went back to the *News* and wrote exactly what I thought about Billy Graham.

It was then that I discovered how un-Christian self-called Christians can really be. I have been getting disgusting and disgraceful anonymous letters ever since I started writing for newspapers, but I have never seen any as disgusting and disgraceful as those which poured in upon me now. Then there were the anonymous 'phone calls. I grew quite accustomed to lift the 'phone and hear something like this.

'Are you the Jack House who wrote about Billy Graham?'

'Yes, I am.'

'Well, I hope you burn in hell!'

And that, I may say is a mild example of the kind of calls I was getting.

I'm not suggesting, by the way, that I was unique in this matter. It's possible that other people who had dared to criticise Billy Graham were getting the same treatment. However, it all died down, and in the end I found I knew more people who regretted the Billy Graham episode than favoured it.

I found this especially so among ministers of the Church of Scotland who had received lists of names and addresses of those who had come forward in response to Billy Graham's plea. One minister told me of receiving a list of 22 names, with the suggestion that he should follow them up and thirl them to the kirk. When he investigated the names, he found that twelve of them were already in the Boys' Brigade of his

church or in the Youth Fellowship. When he and his assistant went round the other addresses, they found that six had
changed their minds, and that the remaining four promised
to come to church. Two of these four did, once. He never
saw the others. Thus the twenty-two 'converts' of Billy
Graham did not mean a single addition to the church.

For myself, I should say that I think that Billy Graham
has been one of the worst things that has happened to the
Church of Scotland for many a long day.

But I am forgetting my point. All this started out of some
remarks I made in *A Matter of Opinion*. I said, you may recollect, that this kind of religious revival often ended in a
rise in the illegitimate birth rate. It so happened that I had
the opportunity to examine the official figures for the West of
Scotland for the year following Billy Graham's visit. The
illegitimate birth rate was up!

I think it is greatly to my credit that, until now, I have
never made anything of this fact. I might have renewed my
correspondence with the professor and the other letter-
writers. But, to tell you the truth, I have been so scunnered
by the Billy Graham business that I have never returned to it.

Until now—and I realise that I have moved some distance
from my subject, *A Matter of Opinion*.

I mentioned, among those with whom I have delighted to
appear, Eric Linklater. There was one occasion when four of
us were to broadcast from a district famous for its whisky. We
arrived together in time for lunch, and then our two com-
panions, who had had an arduous journey, decided to have
an afternoon's sleep. Eric Linklater and I went for a walk.
Soon we came upon a distillery, and felt we should pay it a
call. For domestic reasons, we were not entirely welcome.
True, we were shown round the place—very quickly, too—
but there was no dram at the end of it. I have visited twenty-
one distilleries so far, and that is the only one where I
didn't get a dram.

In the evening we did our *Matter of Opinion* broadcast.
We were slightly handicapped by the fact that one of our two
sleepers had taken sleeping pills and, even at that time of
night, he wasn't quite with us, although he made a most

valiant effort. At one point Eric made a somewhat derogatory remark to me, and I said, 'Don't you forget, Eric, that I took you to the distillery this afternoon.' To which he replied, 'And don't you forget, Jack, that I brought you back!'

Between this bit of dialogue and our sleeping partner's efforts, the idea got abroad that we were all drunk. I had the greatest difficulty in persuading my wife, when I got home, that we had been much more sober than any judge.

The difficult people to appear with on these quiz panel programmes are the professional politicians. For one thing, they are constitutionally suspicious. Even such a nice chap as Willie Ross, now Scottish Home Secretary, looks around him to see who is behind the arras at a panel broadcast.

And there was the time when Emmanuel Shinwell was in the same *Matter of Opinion* team with me. I asked Roderick MacLean, the producer then, whether there were 'any bans.' Mr. Shinwell bristled at once. 'What d'you mean, any bans?' he demanded. 'Who's banning us?' I think he thought that the B.B.C. were concerned in the banning, but we had to explain that the House of Commons had ruled that we must not discuss any subject which had been discussed in the House until sixteen days later. Although Mr. Shinwell was an accomplished Parliamentarian, he had apparently never heard of this rule.

I had a rather different experience with Harold Wilson in *Any Questions*. He was then just a Labour M.P., and I'd like to think that there was some aura of a future Prime Minister about him, but I must honestly say that I did not perceive it.

What I do remember very clearly was that Freddie Grisewood, our question master, said to us in advance that, if any of the four of us wanted to come in first on any question, we should raise a forefinger to signify this. Otherwise, he would just call us in as he felt disposed.

Now I don't think any panellist is daft enough to want to come in first—unless, by some strange chance, he has a special knowledge of the subject and wants to put it across.

On this evening, at any rate, I don't recollect any of us signifying that he wanted to come in first. But what I do recollect, and this very clearly indeed, was that if Harold Wilson was called in early in the proceedings, he indicated that he had not thought the problem out fully and would like to return to it later.

This meant that the rest of us, the three suckers, talked about the question and then our Harold came in. He was always last and he talked so long that Freddie Grisewood had to say, 'Well, thank you very much, Harold Wilson, but I think we'll have to go on to the next question.

So none of us ever had the opportunity to reply to Harold. It was only as the broadcast was ending that I tumbled to Harold Wilson's technique. I admired it tremendously. It didn't surprise me in the least that he eventually became Prime Minister.

All the same, talented though Harold Wilson may be in broadcasting, he doesn't hold a candle to Lady Barnett. I used to say Lady Isobel Barnett, but Gilbert Harding kindly pointed out to me that that was wrong. I have appeared with Lady Barnett only twice, but I can say that I have never known any broadcaster make such an impact on an audience as she does.

The first time was at the one hundred per cent Socialist town of Armadale. The team was Lady Barnett, Lord Greenhill, Professor Rex Knight and myself. Isobel, a real professional, was slightly worried about the audience. What would they be like, she asked. We did our best to fill her in on the subject. I dare say that the other men, like myself, felt rather protective towards her.

We needn't have bothered. From the moment we went on to the stage in the Armadale hall, we were conscious of the fact that the majority of the audience were women and that the entire audience had their eyes fixed on Lady Barnett. When the opinions were expressed and we started discussing them, I knew that nobody was listening to me, and I doubt if anyone was listening to Lord Greenhill or Professor Knight. But when Isobel parted her lips and leaned forward to speak, there was a lovely hush. This Socialist audience hung on her every word.

When the broadcast was over, there were scenes outside the hall. The police had to step in—to regulate the queue of people who wanted Lady Barnett's signature. The rest of us, the three men, crept quietly away. We knew, in the good old Glasgow phrase, when we werenae wantit.

4

Television arrived at last in Scotland and the B.B.C. asked me occasionally to take part in something or other. But it was all very small, and television didn't really get going in our country until Roy Thomson came along. As far as I could see, he started working the Theatre Royal in Glasgow on a shoe-string, but it wasn't very long ere the feeling was universal that S.T.V. was here to stay.

Naturally, Roy Thomson had engaged a Canadian as programme director. His name was Rai Purdy and, like most incomers to Glasgow, he was half horrified, half intrigued by the Scottish set-up. However, he wanted to establish himself and he took the normal way; he decided to put on a programme which he had already done with success in Canada.

It was called *I'll Buy That*, and the idea was that viewers should write in to suggest some extraordinary object that they owned and, if picked for the sacrifice, bring it along to confront the panel. There was a panel of four of us—Lady Huggins, Louise Boyd ('the operatic housewife') Larry Marshall, and me. Larry Marshall was the comic of *The One O'Clock Gang* (another Rai Purdy idea) and he was all the rage.

We were not allowed to see the object but each of us was allowed to ask five questions and each time we asked a question the contestant received £1. We had to try to guess what the contestant had brought along in the smallest number of questions. At least, that was what I thought, until one evening I suddenly got the idea, out of the blue, that the object was a penny-farthing bicycle. So, when it came to my turn, I said so. And it *was* a penny-farthing bicycle.

After the programme I was drawn aside by an executive. 'Jack,' he said. 'About that penny-farthing bicycle.'

'Yes?' I said.

'Don't you realise,' said the executive in a kindly way, 'that that contestant had a lot of trouble bringing that penny-farthing all the way from Naggiesburn? He deserved something for that trouble. But you cut him off with your very first question, and all he's going back with is £6. Next time you think you know the answer, string them along a little bit.'

It was a pretty ropey programme and I received a fair number of letters suggesting I should resign from the panel because it wasn't worthy of my position. I replied to all these letters pointing out that Gilbert Harding was a much greater personality and had more position than I had and yet he did all sorts of odd wee programmes, and advertisement on the commercial telly.

Certainly Scottish Television was having an effect on the local masses that had not existed in the B.B.C. telly days. I found that in most places where I visited in Glasgow, I'd be likely to have a group of boys and girls, of various ages, following me and shouting 'I'll buy that!' I took John Betjeman at his request into the Gorbals, and we hadn't been there long ere the chant of 'I'll buy that!' started.

It was very difficult to explain to Mr. Betjeman what this meant. He was quite incredulous when I told him. Fortunately, I didn't have to pursue the subject because John Betjeman was so entranced by Victorian Glasgow. 'The headquarters of the Victorian Society shouldn't be in London,' he said. 'They should be here. This is the greatest Victorian city in the world.'

Just a year or so later a conference of British architects expressed exactly the same opinion. Fortunately we have some lively organisations devoted to keeping what we can of the good Victoriana in Glasgow. And I believe that even Glasgow Town Council are beginning to realise what treasures lie under their noses. (You might think that this is not an apt phrase. How can a Victorian building lie under

a Town Councillor's nose? You don't know our Town
Councillors or their noses!)

To celebrate the second Christmas of commercial television
in Scotland, S.T.V. ran a pantomime one afternoon and
most of the regular performers were asked to be in it. The
subject was *Cinderella*, and it was written by Eddie Boyd,
who now writes those queer thrillers for Granada television,
and his assistant, who was Gordon Fleming then, but is
Gordon Flemyng now. Edith MacArthur was Prince Charming, Larry Marshall was Buttons, Louise Boyd was Cinderella,
and Michael O'Halloran and I played the Ugly Sisters. It
was our proud boast that as the Ugly Sisters neither of us
required make-up. A wig was enough.

Scottish Television seemed much more innocent then than
it is now. You'd be apt to meet a genial, short-sighted
buffer in the corridor who would implore you to 'call me
Roy', and you'd suddenly realise you'd met the boss. There
were plenty of growing pains, and it was all very rough and
ready compared with appearing on television for the B.B.C.

Yet I recollect that even B.B.C. television in Glasgow was
rather rough and ready at the very start. Early on, and this
was long before Scottish Television started, an evening programme fell through and it was suddenly decided to present
a television version of *A Matter of Opinion* from a Glasgow
hall.

Each member of the panel was made up as if he was a film
star. Make-up now hardly exists at all unless, like me, you're
bald. Then you have to get a matt finish applied to your
dome, otherwise you would literally scintillate. It was explained to me that my eyes were rather deep set. The make-
up girl's efforts to improve on Nature were such that I
could hardly see.

There was 'hospitality' first of all in a room off the main
hall, and I soon realised what a dangerous thing this can
be. I don't mean I'm against it. On the contrary, I think it's
very civilised, and often a help to worried people. But in
this case one of the panel asked the producer if viewers could
tell the difference between a glass of gin and a glass of water
on the screen. The producer, unsuspectingly, said they

looked just the same. So two of our panel took glasses of gin on to the stage with them.

This, plus the intense heat from too many lights, made it an interesting evening. For the first time, too, I learned of the intense mystique with which television boys imbue their work. Radio people are notably cool, calm and collected. Television types don't only let their hair down but are inclined to tear it as well.

I was in a Hogmanay show which had a cast of about forty, plus two bands. We were rehearsing in a Glasgow ballroom and the floor manager (well, I think that's what he's called—he's the chap who wears headphones and relays instructions from the top dog) was trying to get silence. 'If I don't 'ave 'ush,' he cried petulantly, 'I'll send you all home.' That would have been the day!

My own favourite television show was *Whigmaleerie*, an idea of Noel Stevenson's I think, in which for six months I appeared for ten minutes every Tuesday and presented some off-beat or instructive or satirical idea of my own. I followed *The One O'Clock Gang*, which meant that I had a ready-made audience of housewives who had just seen their children off to school after lunch and were now, presumably, relaxing.

Liam Hood started the series and then Philip Bray took over. We explained to the viewers what tartan was all about, how to behave in a posh restaurant, how to take care of books, what St. Kilda was like, and so on. I enjoyed every moment of it. But six months was enough for the S.T.V. Powers-That-Be.

I realise that I would never make a broadcasting executive, in either radio or television. The programmes I enjoy are the ones which are not brought back.

Still, as far as I can see, it's better to be on the fringe of television than actually inside it. The other day I met a man who had been a household name on television, until he decided to give it up and go into business. I asked him how things were going.

'Oh, very well,' said he. 'The difference between business and the telly is that nowadays I know who's stabbing me in the back.'

An Innocent Abroad

I was the happiest man in the world when I resigned from the *Citizen* in 1950. I just couldn't stand the stultifying hand of the Beaverbrook empire any longer. I had nothing to do, of course, with Lord Beaverbrook himself, praise be to God. I just admired him from afar when he visited the building in Albion Street and looked at the water buckets to make sure there was no dust on them. It wasn't likely that the noble Lord would find any dust on the top of the water, because our general manager himself made certain the water was all fresh on the morning of the Lord's coming.

Why people in London should imagine that they know better than anybody else in the country is something which I have never been able to understand. London is the most parochial place I know. I'll never forget seeing my first London newspaper bill. It was an *Evening Standard* one, as I remember, and it said 'Good News for South London Gas Users.' That, I think, is typical of London.

But it's worse when the people in London (I won't call them Londoners because most of them aren't) start spreading their parochialism abroad. How the Beaverbrook boys in Fleet Street worked out how we should be running a newspaper in Glasgow never ceased to surprise me. The fact is that they just didn't know. The ignorance of the English about Scotland is amazing, but the Beaverbrook eaglets (or whatever the latest silly word for them was) were the most ignorant I have known.

However, I was fortunate enough to be asked to join the *Evening News* in Glasgow, and I enjoyed myself immensely there. I enjoyed it all the more because on three occasions I was asked to return to the Beaverbrook fold. I was tempted to reply in the traditional manner, but I just indicated delicately that I was much happier where I was.

Being on the *Evening News* was too good to be true. Although the *News* was by far the best of the three evening papers, it had the smallest circulation. Then Jackie Robertson was appointed editor and things started moving. It was a really exciting time. C. Denis Hamilton came up from Kemsley House to inspire us to even greater efforts. His proposal was that we should raise our circulation to 200,000 from somewhere around 135,000. We buckled to, and we very nearly did it.

And then there was the great day, when Lord Kemsley and Sons handed us over to Cecil King and the *Daily Mirror*. We were assured, of course, that there would be no changes made. The three papers—the *Daily Record*, the *Sunday Mail* and the *Evening News* would continue as usual. Oh, yes, and the *Noon Record* too. I'm always forgetting the *Noon Record*!

We had a visit from the monolithic Mr King, who had sent up a chap named Suffern to inspire us. The office joke was that, if a man came up to you in the office and said, 'I'm Suffern,' you should not reply, 'So am I.' But the joke was on us. One morning in January, 1957, I walked into our marble halls, the entrance to the office, and I knew as I stepped through the door that the *Evening News* was dead.

It's a strange feeling being on a newspaper which has just been killed. We produced the first edition with the announcement that this was the end of a great newspaper. Then nobody on the staff bothered any more about what was happening in the rest of the world. Not one of us knew that the end was going to come like this. There had been rumours, of course, but there had been rumours about all the Glasgow newspapers for years. And, after all, ours was the evening circulation that was going up. If a paper were going to disappear, I imagined it would be the much inferior *Citizen*.

A miasma of the deepest gloom settled over the *News* office that day. Half an hour after I'd arrived, I was told by

Jackie Robertson that Sam McKinlay, the editor of the
Evening Times, wanted to see me at St Enoch Hotel. When I
got there, he offered to take over my *News* contract. I knew
Sam well. He had lived round the corner in Alexandra Park
Gardens when I was on my pavement in the sun at Kennyhill Square. I accepted his offer right away. Later I was told
that I'd been daft. Apparently I could have held the King
boys up to ransom. But I was so disgusted with the whole
business that all I wanted was to get away from Hope Street.

So I landed on the *Evening Times* and, at the moment of
writing, I'm still there. It's a pleasure to work for a Scottish
newspaper firm, and not a business controlled from London.
A few years ago a magazine called *Scotland* was running a
series in which various people were allowed to express their
own opinions. The then editor asked me to write mine. So I
wrote what I thought about the situation of the newspaper
business in Scotland. My article was returned, with a cheque
in payment of non-publication, and a letter from the editor
saying that it was essential that they should keep on good
relations with the Press.

But this chapter is called *An Innocent Abroad*, and not *An
Innocent at Home*, and it was my purpose to describe two of
the places I have seen under the aegis of my two good newspapers, the *News* and the *Times*. I have been led away by
natural indignation, and I must return now to my theme.

2

I have been very lucky in being allowed by two of my
editors to walk on pavements in the sun in both Russia and
the United States of America. I was on the *Evening News*
when, in 1954, I received an invitation from the Scottish-
U.S.S.R. Friendship Society to join a Scottish Cultural
Delegation to Russia. It was for a whole month, but Jackie
Robertson said I could go.

Visits to Russia were uncommon then. Stalin was not long

dead, and we thought that Malenkov was taking over from him. I doubt of any of us had heard the name Kruschev. One or two people told me I was a traitor to my country, going to Russia. And a great many who had never been in Russia told me what to expect when I got there. I would not be allowed to go anywhere on my own. But, if I did get out alone, I would be followed. Nobody would speak to me in the street for fear of the Secret Police. And so on. It seems daft now when so many people go on holiday from this country to Russia.

One or two persons who were invited to join the party actually refused because they were worried about what might happen to them. Most of the Cultural Delegation were attached to Glasgow University. By general consent we made Professor Atkinson (Spanish studies) our leader, and he was backed up by Douglas Percy Bliss, then head of the Glasgow School of Art. There was a University lecturer, Ronald Meek, and his wife, who could speak Russian. Joan Alexander, one of Scotland's finest woman singers and Agnes Walker, an accomplished pianist, were in the party and Agnes Walker's husband, Bill Maclellan. Our ten included also Farquhar Gillanders, from the University, and that remarkable old man, John Kinloch, a retired teacher and supporter of popular and unpopular causes.

Nowadays the flight to Moscow would be a simple affair. Then we had to travel by K.L.M. to Amsterdam, spend the night there, and fly next day to Prague. A second night there and on to Minsk by Aeroflot and then Moscow. The Aeroflot plane was very old fashioned and we sat in blue brocade armchairs and looked out through windows hung with white lace curtains. The stewardess wore a plain blouse and skirt. She was a student from Moscow University and was learning English. But she was too shy to speak to us. I noticed she was reading a novel by Jeffrey Farnol.

When we landed at Moscow airport the women of our party were still titivating and the first people to descend from the plane were the two members wearing the kilt, John Kinloch and Bill Maclellan. They were greeted by a woman and two men, our guide interpreters, carrying bouquets, and immediately each received a bouquet. Then, when our girls did appear, the bouquets were hurriedly snatched back and presented to them.

We drove the sixteen miles from the airport into Moscow and I was more impressed by seeing the shepherds out in the fields with their mixed herds of sheep, cattle and goats than I was with the outline of the new Moscow University which was towering on the horizon before us. These shepherds were wearing big slouch hats and cloaks and carrying long crooks. They reminded me of pictures I had seen in the *Boys' Own Paper* years and years ago.

It was a cold and windy April day when we entered Moscow and I wasn't struck by the appearance of the people. In fact, the street scene rather reminded me of Bellshill on a wet day. The men were wearing shapeless blue serge suits with baggy trousers, and the women seemed to go in mainly for equally shapeless jackets and skirts, with big boots. All the women wore headscarves, but not the gay kind of kerchief I was accustomed to. It was more like a cloot.

I was impressed by our hotel, though. It was the Savoy and Farquhar Gillanders and I shared an enormous Victorian suite—though not quite as enormous as the Meeks, which included a grand piano in one corner. The dining room reminded me rather of the Plaza Ballroom in Glasgow. It had a dance floor at one end with a fountain playing in the middle, and an orchestra which gave us such up to the minute tunes as *Smoke gets in your eyes*.

Right away we were taken to the Bolshoi Theatre to see the State Opera Company from Kiev. Our guides explained sadly to us that this would be a sort of second eleven affair, so to speak. The Bolshoi's own company had gone to appear in Kiev and the Ukrainians had come to Moscow. I am a compulsive counter and first of all I counted the orchestra from Kiev. They numbered eighty. In 1954 the Scottish National Orchestra numbered seventy-two.

The opera itself was about a Ukrainian hero and it had by far the biggest cast I have ever seen in any opera. They put a battle on the stage in one scene, with horses charging about in the middle of fighting men. As far as I could see, people were being killed right and left. But with a population the size of Russia's, I don't suppose one or two actors really matter. And all the while that this was going on, our guides were saying, 'What a pity you aren't seeing something really big.'

Next day we met our hosts, representatives of the Society for Cultural Relations with Other Countries. We talked over our programme and then questions were invited. Ronald Meek got up and asked if we would be allowed to go where we liked. The head man said certainly, but that they'd rather have some idea of where we were going, because of the difficulties which would be caused if we got involved in a street accident or something of the sort. But we were free to go where we pleased.

'In that case,' said Ronald Meek, 'what do we do about money? You can hardly go where you like if you haven't got any money.'

At this the Russians were quite taken back. They had been accustomed to *English* delegations—we were the first Scottish delegation ever to be there—and, naturally, the English had not mentioned the subject of money.

When he had recovered, the head man said that would be attended to, and at lunch time that day each of us was handed an envelope containing 250 roubles. We were told, too, that those of us who were broadcasters and/or writers would be invited to perform and would be paid for our performances. There was a slight catch in this, of course. We would be paid in roubles and these would all have to be spent inside Russia.

We were then taken on what I should think was a fairly routine trip through Moscow. We saw the new University, various art galleries and the Metro, with one station rivalling another in magnificence. After several days of this, the Meeks and I decided to go out on our own. When we told our guides of our decision they were not at all pleased. They said we were due to visit the most famous art gallery in the world and that we'd be missing something of high cultural value. We didn't care.

I felt quite excited at being out in Moscow on our own,

though we weren't chancing a great deal considering that Mrs Meek could speak Russian. We decided to have a whirl on the Metro first of all, because we wanted to see some of the stations we hadn't been shown. We felt, naturally, that we had been shown only the best ones. But, after riding around for a while, we got fed up because the stations we hadn't been shown turned out to be just as magnificent as those we had been shown.

I was beginning to pick up a little of the language and, at one station platform, I thought that a sign showed that the Botanic Gardens Station was not so far away. I asked Mrs Meek and I was right. I proposed that we should go there, for two reasons. First of all, I live near the Botanic Gardens in Glasgow and I thought it would be nice to be reminded of home. Second, I was wondering if we were being followed. I'd seen no sign whatever of that, but there is one sure way of finding out whether you're being followed or not, and that is to get into a wide open space, for then the person following you has got to get into the wide open space too. I was fairly confident that the Botanic Gardens would prove to be a wide open space.

We found the Botanic Gardens all right, with a statue of Stalin standing in front of the entrance with a welcoming arm stretched out. But behind the statue there was a cash desk and you had to pay a rouble to get in. However, the gardens, though not up to the Glasgow standard, were wide and open and I came to the conclusion that we were not being followed.

We left the gardens and were walking down one of the broad thoroughfares when we thought we'd try a side street. It was made of dirt and pocked with puddles and soon we found ourselves in what I imagine were slums in 1954. Most of the buildings were made of wood and were falling to bits. Some of them seemed to be sinking into the ground.

Ronald Meek started taking photographs, when an elderly lady approached us. She was wearing the usual shapeless jacket and skirt and big boots and she asked us (in Russian, of course) who we were and what were we doing there. Mrs Meek replied that we were members of a Scottish Cultural Delegation and were having a look at Moscow.

'But why do you come here?' asked the old lady. 'Why don't you visit—' and she named a number of the special sights of Moscow. Mrs Meek said we'd already seen these places and we wanted to see every side of Moscow. 'You have come here a year too soon,' announced the old lady. 'Come back in a year from now and you will see great changes.'

She waved her arms as she described how there was to be a new factory there and new buildings for the workers here and a big new road right in the middle of it all. I was most impressed. Either she believed implicitly what the Government told her, or perhaps the Government did carry out the plans which it announced. Alternatively, she was really a Government agent who had been alerted by walkie-talkie from our hotel that we were coming by that way and had lain in wait for us, so as to pump propaganda into us.

I wouldn't have thought of this last solution had I not read a brilliant series by a Glasgow sporting journalist who spent one night in Moscow attending a football match and came back to write five articles telling the truth about Russia. He made it plain that the whole Russian set-up consisted of trying to make you think you were welcome when you were nothing of the sort.

We went by night train to Leningrad, which I fell in love with. When I saw the Ambassadors' Hall of Catherine the Great's Hermitage, I realised where the designers of the Moscow Metro had got their ideas for stations. What was good enough for Catherine was good enough for Moscow commuters.

Then we flew to Tbilisi, the capital of Georgia, and found a new world. The Georgians are very independent. They insisted on making all their speeches in Georgian. Interpreters then interpreted it into Russian for our interpreters and our interpreters interpreted it into English for us. The Georgians seemed to pay no attention whatever to Moscow.

Almost the first thing we saw was a large poster announcing a Scottish-Georgian concert at which Joan Alexander would sing and Agnes Walker would play the piano. Nobody had thought of telling the girls. They were a bit temperamental about it at first, but agreed to appear, providing somebody could find them evening gowns. Naturally, they had not packed any evening dress.

The concert was a great success. Joan and Agnes had already made several recordings for Moscow radio and their reputations had evidently come South. We saw Georgian dancing for the first time and were most impressed. But the young Georgians in the audience seemed to consider it old hat and talked to each other while the dancing was on.

One night we entrained for a place called Gagra on the Black Sea. The carriage in which our sleeping compartments were was most magnificently Victorian. But when Farquhar Gillanders and I went on a tour of the train we found that the other carriages were not up to our standard. There were some about the level of second-class sleeping compartments on British Railways. Then there were compartments of plain wood, with shelves to sleep on.

When we got back to our own magnificence we said to our chief guide that we thought Russia was a classless society. He assured us that that was indeed the case. 'Then how is it.' we asked, 'that we are travelling in this luxury, then there are reasonable compartments, and finally just wooden shelves?'

'Ah, you don't understand,' he said, 'There are three ways of train travelling by night—hard, medium and soft. But there are no classes!'

We got to Gagra and were taken to see a collective farm. It was a very big one and grew tobacco and grapes for wine. These Georgian farmers appeared to be sorry for us. They knew that farming in Scotland was controlled by Dukes, who walked about with big whips, keeping the peasants in order.

The head farmer invited us to stay for a typical Georgian evening's entertainment. We had already been instructed in Moscow that an invitation of this sort must be accepted, because it meant that everything had been prepared and it would be most impolite to refuse.

So we were led into a big room where tables had been placed in horse-shoe formation. The only women who sat down were those of our delegation. The farm women served the meal, with the exception of three young girls who sat in the space in the middle of the horse-shoe and provided us with balalaika music.

I have never seen so much food in my life. But it wasn't the food that was worrying me. In front of each of us were two bottles of the farms' own freshly made wine. There was also a small glass containing a dark brown liquid.

The head farmer made a speech in which he explained that for an evening in the Georgian style it was necessary to appoint a tomada. (I'm not guaranteeing the spelling. That's what it sounded like.) And so he would be the tomada. It was one of the quickest appointments I've ever assisted at. As far as I could discover, a tomada was a cross between a chairman and a compere, something like the fear-an-tigh at a ceilidh.

Well, the tomada then explained that it was the custom in Georgia to open the evening with a glass of their own cognac. It was also the custom to drink toasts 'bottoms up', like this. And the tomada threw the entire contents of the glass down his throat with the greatest enjoyment. 'But,' he said, 'since you are unaccustomed to our cognac, the first toast will not be bottoms up.'

He raised another glass of the dark brown liquid and proposed, 'Eternal peace and friendship between the people of the U.S.S.R. and the people of Great Britain and Northern Ireland.' I will not swear that these were his exact words, but something like that. Once again he threw over the liquid in one fell swoop.

I thought that what a Georgian can do, a Glaswegian can certainly do. So I took a big swallow of my cognac. I'd got about half of it over when something exploded in my inside. When I had recovered, I sipped the rest.

The meal started. As I've said, there was plenty of food, but every now and again the tomada would rise, hold up a brimming glass of wine and say, 'Eternal peace and friendship between the people of Georgia and the people of Scotland', and it would be bottoms up again. However, the wine was pleasant and this was no hardship. The only trouble was that, as soon as your wine was half an inch from the top of the glass, some farm wench would come along with a bottle and top it up. Then, all of a sudden, they removed the glasses and substituted glasses twice the size.

And still the tomada was getting up and proposing eternal peace and friendship between the people of Gagra and the people of Glasgow, or something of that kind, and still we were drinking the toasts bottoms up. There was dancing and singing, in which we took part as well as we were able.

And then the head farmer's wife brought in a bull's horn. She presented this to the tomada and it was filled with wine. He lifted the bull's horn (and, as we all know, the Russians have the biggest bulls in the world) and said we would observe that the contents would have to be drunk to the very end, because you could not put the horn down on the table without spilling wine. 'And to spill wine in Georgia,' he said, 'is an unforgiveable sin.'

He proposed a toast, put the bull's horn to his lips, and drained it dry. It was then refilled with wine and passed to the first member of our Scottish Cultural Delegation. Well, I regret to say that our Scottish Cultural Delegation simply weren't up to it. Nobody got farther than a couple of inches or so from the top, and eventually it came round to me. I was the last member of the delegation and I realised that we were losing face. Somebody had to stand up (if that was the operative phrase) for the honour of Scotland.

So, when the bull's horn was topped up, I put it to my lips and I started drinking. No matter what happened, I went on drinking. I was conscious of the fact that the wine was dribbling down each side of the bull's horn on to my good suit, but I still kept on. At last I finished the last drop, to tumultuous cheering and shouts of 'He drinks like a Georgian!'

I then resumed my seat and lost all further interest in the proceedings. I could see and I could hear. But I couldn't speak and I couldn't move. I realised what it was to be wine-logged. And indeed it was a full fifteen minutes before I had another drink.

Thus we took culture round Russia. Perhaps I should say that I also made several broadcast recordings and wrote a long article about Glasgow for a Soviet youth magazine. I don't know whether the article ever appeared or not, but any Soviet youth who read it would undoubtedly think that Glasgow was the greatest place in the world. As, of course, it is.

I made around 2,500 roubles altogether and put it into a common fund for our party. I suppose, in the end, I spent around 1,000 roubles, but with great difficulty. In 1954 there simply weren't things to buy for presents.

I haven't been back in Russia, but I gather that there are a lot of changes. One point that strikes me is this. Four of us had been visiting the Patriarchate of Moscow to try to find out something about religion in Russia. Our interpreter was Inna, a clever and charming woman who, on the way back into the centre of the city, asked if we would excuse her as she wanted to get home to discover whether or not her two daughters had passed their school examinations. The results were out that day.

So this meant that the four of us were on our own from about five o'clock in the afternoon until eight. It was a boiling hot day and we all felt like a drink. Right in the middle of Moscow we found an open-air café with umbrellas and tables in the Parisian style. We sat at one of the tables and a waitress came over with a menu-cum-wine list. It was in Russian, but it was Greek to us.

Some genius had once told me that 'Beer' is an international word. All I can say is that it had no effect in Moscow. We just couldn't communicate at all. Then I saw some bottles of a pink-looking liquid at a nearby table and pointed to them. The waitress brought a couple over and poured them out. The liquid tasted like a rather wersh Coco-Cola. The waitress took one look at us and shook her head, then disappeared.

She came back with a chap in a black jacket and striped trousers, obviously the manager. He smiled to us and said, 'Champagnski!' We shouted 'Da, da!' and the waitress brought two bottles of Georgian champagne.

And the point of this story is that, when I got back to Glasgow, I couldn't get people to believe that four of us had sat in an open-air café in the middle of Moscow and drunk champagne.

3

It's odd how people doubted my stories about Russia, but accepted anything I told them about America. I've had three visits to America now, but my first was by far the most impressive. By this time I was working for the *Evening Times* and Sam McKinlay, my editor, said that, as I'd had a month in Russia, he thought it would be a good idea if I had a month in the U.S.A.

So it was agreed that I would visit the Glasgows of America. And then, all of a sudden, it struck me that, not only had I been in Russia, but I had also joined the Communist Party under the name of Alfred Abbott all those years ago. Even though I wasn't a card-carrying member (because I got nothing for that bob I paid over at Partick Burgh Hall), I had been known as 'Glasgow's Communist Scoutmaster.' I told Sam about this and he agreed that I should ask for an interview with the American Consul in Glasgow and explain all.

I met the Consul, a charming man with a twinkle in his eye, and the twinkle got even brighter as I told my story of my intromissions with the Communist Party. He didn't laugh outright, but he gave me a cup of tea and what he called a cookie and I call a biscuit. He assured me that I would get my visa all right and my impression as I left him was that he was going to have a right good laugh.

When I flew from Prestwick, I understood there were five Glasgows in America—those of Virginia, Kentucky, Missouri, St Louis and Montana. That's the way the tour was arranged. But, when I got to New York and looked up an American gazetteer, I found there were eleven Glasgows in the U.S.A. It was too late to change my elaborately-worked-out itinerary and, in any case, the Glasgows I didn't know about were very small indeed. Their populations ranged from 83 to about 140, and I gathered that, if you were in a fast car, you'd be right through some of these Glasgows before you realised it.

I flew into New York on the wettest St. Patrick's Day that

they'd had for fifty years. It was so wet that they didn't even hold the famous St. Patrick's Day parade. I had been booked in at the Hotel New Weston (if that's the right name) and had a room on the twenty-second floor. When I looked out of my window I got an acute attack of vertigo. But it was even worse to look at the bigger buildings across the way. Every one of them had a heavy cloud round its summit. I was accustomed to seeing mountains with clouds on their summits, but not buildings.

Everyone tells me that there is a wonderful tonic air in New York, that life seems keener and brighter. It didn't to me. I felt that New York was the same kind of gigantic ant-heap that Moscow was. Only the strange thing was that I felt more afraid in New York than I ever did in Moscow. Maybe it was all these reports in the paper about 'mugging' in Central Park and on the Subway trains that affected me.

I thought the New Yorkers would all be witty characters, especially the cab drivers. My first trip in a taxi was to the Rockefeller Plaza where I was to meet Henry Lowrie, now working in the New York *Express* office. The driver was a very handsome coloured boy and I made some remark to him about the weather. He didn't even bother to reply. He just nodded his head instead of making some wonderful New York wisecrack.

Indeed, I was reduced to remembering that, when I was interviewed by the immigration officer at Idlewild, he asked me what the purpose of my visit to the United States was. I replied that I had come to see the Glasgows of America. He looked at me sharply and asked, 'Are there many Glasgows in America?' Not knowing any better then, I replied that there were five. He shook his head, 'Well, well!' he said. 'That's one thing about my job—you learn something noo every day.'

I wasn't greatly impressed by the food in New York. They had the biggest steaks in the world, but they tasted like cardboard to me. Not that I have ever actually tasted cardboard, but they tasted what I imagine cardboard tastes like. On the other hand, I was very fond of breakfasts in the coffee rooms and drug stores.

One afternoon I'd been down on Wall Street and had taken the Staten Island ferry across the Hudson so that I could see the Statue of Liberty, and now I decided to walk back to meet Henry Lowrie by the Broadway route. I had a street map, but I hadn't realised what a very long thoroughfare Broadway is. At last I got into Fifth Avenue and was legging it rapidly towards Rockefeller Plaza, because I was already late, when I heard a female voice shout 'Jack!' I paid no attention, because I knew that my only acquaintance in New York was Henry. But again came the cry of 'Jack!' and I turned round to see Stella de Banzie running after me.

Stella was the wife of Eric de Banzie, Glasgow's leading columnist, who had left the *News* with me to join the *Times*. She was working as a receptionist at Simon and Schuster, the book publishers in New York. She'd been in a bus running down Fifth Avenue when she'd seen me from the window. So she jumped off and followed me. If I'd only studied my actuarial science a bit more when I was a C.A. apprentice, I could work out the chance of our meeting in New York like this.

The following evening Stella took me on a tour of New York which included dinner at the pub which was featured in the film, *The Lost Week-end*, and a drink in what I seem to remember was called the Peacock Alley (or maybe it was the Birdcage Walk) of the Waldorf Astoria. I don't think I was as impressed as I ought to have been.

The fact is that I was quite glad to leave New York and take the train to Washington, passing a town called Aberdeen on the way. While I wouldn't go as far as the Washingtonians, who describe their city modestly as the most beautiful in the world, I did like the place. I was made a member of the Press Club and there I had an extraordinary gustatory experience.

On several occasions I had started a meal with what the menu said were Jumbo Shrimps. These shrimps were certainly big, but they were always smothered in tabasco sauce, with the result that you tasted nothing but tabasco. On this day I had lunch by myself in the Press Club and I ordered Jumbo Shrimps. When they came along I observed that there was one jumbo in the middle untouched by tabasco. This was my moment. I would now discover what a Jumbo Shrimp really tasted like. I put in my fork and extracted it delicately. Then I ate it and found that it tasted like cardboard too.

I think I saw more drunks in Washington than anywhere else I went in America. It's certainly the only place I've ever been where I've seen drunk men falling out of a hotel entrance as half-past nine in the morning.

From Washington I went to my first Glasgow, in Virginia. In my book, *The Heart of Glasgow*, I have told something of my adventures in the American Glasgows. My biggest difficulty in them was to persuade the inhabitants that Glasgow, Scotland, was a somewhat bigger place than their own particular Glasgow—although the biggest (in Kentucky) had a population of only 7,000.

Glasgow, Virginia, was around the 1,500 mark. But it had a very big carpet factory and it was excessively proud of the fact that the red carpet on which Queen Elizabeth had walked when she paid her first visit to America as Queen had been made there. After this event, the firm got the carpet back and cut it into tiny pieces, which they distributed to their customers and their work people.

Sometimes, in America, I wondered whose Royal family ours was. I was often asked if I had met the Queen, and constantly whether I'd met Princess Margaret. At first I told the truth, and my questioners were most disappointed. Then I reflected that, although I had never actually *met* the Monarch or her sister, I had been very close to them indeed in the course of official visits. So, after that, when I was asked if I had met the Queen and/or Princess Margaret, I just said yes and everybody was satisfied.

At Glasgow, Kentucky, I was delighted to find that the local newspaper was the *Glasgow Daily Times*. Incidentally, to reach this Glasgow I went by Greyhound bus from Louisville, the home town of Cassius Clay. But I didn't know anything about Cassius Clay at that time and what occurred as most interesting to me was that my bus went through a great whisky distilling area, but Glasgow itself was 'dry'. The

editor of the *Glasgow Daily Times* told me that he was having
an investigation made at that moment as to why it was that
lorries taking whisky to the South always seemed to lose
cases as they passed through Glasgow.

My next Glasgow in Missouri, turned out to be the
typical small town of the American films. I expected to see
the Mickey Rooney of long ago come round the corner any
minute. It was on the Mississippi and the last of the stern-
wheelers was making a farewell trip down the river the week
after I was there.

I visited Glasgow Village, St. Louis, and discovered a new
housing estate with, as far as I could find out, no Scots. But
they use the coat-of-arms of Glasgow, Scotland, and they
call their streets by such names as Brigadoon, Dornoch and
so on. A small protuberance at one end of Glasgow Village
has been named Ben Nevis. The other day a resident wrote
to ask me if I could send her a photograph of an old Church
in Glasgow which could be used as a model for the new
Roman Catholic Church in Glasgow Village.

My last Glasgow was Montana, and I flew from St. Louis
to an alleged airport (it was really not much more than an
airstrip) called Wolf Point. This was the only Glasgow where
they knew I was coming. I'd been taking part in one of Bill
Meikle's *Scottish Magazine* programmes for the B.B.C. and
had met a man from Glasgow, Montana. So I told him I was
going to visit there, and he had evidently told the head men.

I was the only person to get off the plane at Wolf Point,
and there was a row of tall men wearing big hats and boot-
lace ties—a welcome committee. There was also a young
chap with a microphone who came up to me the moment my
foot hit the ground and said, 'Welcome, Jack, to our great
State of Montana. What do you think of it?' He then stuck
the microphone under my chin.

I could only say that I was sure it was fine, just fine, as far
as I could see, and I was looking forward to getting a good
look at it. Then the tall men came forward and shook me
solemnly by the hand. My host was Paul Campbell, owner of
the Central Hotel in Glasgow, Montana. He led me to a row
of long gleaming automobiles and ushered me into the first

one. The tall men got into theirs and off our cavalcade started at a furious pace.

We drove through an Indian reservation at about ninety miles an hour. Fortunately for the Indians, there didn't seem to be any about at the time. What interested me was seeing shiny big cars parked outside wooden shacks which looked as if they were going to fall to pieces any moment. I was told that some Indians didn't even have a shack. But they had a car and used it for sleeping in and eating in.

Paul Campbell was telling me that they'd been having some trouble with visiting cowboys at Glasgow. The night before they'd got liquored up and it had been necessary to throw one of them into the hoosegow. The others had threatened to break down the jail door and rescue their comrade. They had been dissuaded, but Mr Campbell confessed that he was not at all happy about the situation.

I was sorely tempted to pull out my notebook and take all this down. But I thought he might dry up at the sight of a notebook, as so many people do. So I committed it to memory and thought what a good story it was. Signs indicated that we were nearing Glasgow and the cavalcade started slowing down.

Just at the three-mile mark outside the city a group of cowboys suddenly appeared, riding towards us and firing guns in the air. 'It's these darn cowboys,' said Paul Campbell.

'Stop the cars!' the cowboys were shouting. 'This is a hold-up!'

'We'd better stop,' said Paul and did. Some of the cowboys had dismounted and, guns at the ready, were making my friends get out of their cars.

One desperado pulled the door of Paul's car open and shouted, 'Get out of the car. This is a hold-up.'

'Better do as he says,' muttered Paul.

So I got out of the car and the first thing I saw was a chap at the side of the road taking the whole scene with a cine-camera. I felt that a cine camera was not absolutely necessary for a hold-up, so when my cowboy stuck his gun in my ribs and snarled, 'Hand over your wallet', I gave him twenty-five cents and said, 'I come from Scotland and that's all I've got.'

He laughed, handed me back my twenty-five cents, and shouted, 'It's all right, boys. He's seen through us.'

It turned out that this was a 'Wild West welcome', specially staged for my benefit, and that Paul Campbell's story of the cowboy and the hoosegow was just a preparation. I was given a cowboy jacket and a ten-gallon hat to wear, and then I was asked to get on a spare horse that they had brought along, so that I could have my picture taken.

At this point Paul Campbell revealed that their plan was that I should ride the three miles into Glasgow City Centre with the cowboys, who were members of the Glasgow Rough-riders' Club. 'But we figured that you were a younger man,' he said, looking at my shiny pate. 'Just get on the horse and then you can get off again and drive back with me.'

Well, the last and only time I had ever been on a horse was when I was a boy on the sands at Prestwick. I had to be helped into the saddle by one of the cowboys but I didn't feel so bad when I got there because it was one of those cowboy saddles with a big pommel in front. I noticed that the cowboys were looking as though someone had stolen their scone, so I said I would ride the three miles into Glasgow. They seemed delighted and I cursed myself inwardly.

Off went the cavalcade of cars, and our horses followed. At first we were on the main road, but then the leader led us off across country and that consisted of a lot of ups and downs. I clung to my pommel like grim death (these old clichés are so exactly right, don't you think?), especially when we descended into what they called a coullee, and what I would call a ravine. Each time we went into a coullee, some-body produced a bottle of Old Granddad and passed it round. By the time we emerged from our third coullee I felt I was riding like a cowboy.

It must have had some effect. I'd been told that, when I got to Glasgow City Centre, I would be met by the Mayor and presented with the key to the city. And also there would be a woman who had emigrated from Paisley to Montana years and years ago and wanted to meet me to find out if Paisley was still the same. When we rode up to the City

Centre, there she was. She looked along our line of cowboys on horseback and said, 'Which is the chap from Scotland?'

I enjoyed Glasgow, Montana. They kept up an illusion of being Scottish, just like one or two of the other places I'd visited. Their Glasgow High School sporting teams were known as 'the Scotties.' Paul Campbell had a blown-up coloured photograph of pipers competing at some Highland Games as one wall of his cocktail bar.

Nobody could tell me why Glasgow, Montana, was called Glasgow. All the other Glasgows took their name from the fact that Scots and Scotch-Irish (people from Northern Ireland) moved down the Shenandoah valley and hived off to start settlements which were called after the place of their birth, or after a very powerful Scotch-Irish family whose name was Glasgow.

But in the case of Glasgow, Montana, it had been merely Stop No. 26 on the Chicago to Seattle Railway. One day a directive came forth from Chicago that the stations were to be given names instead of numbers. The story is that some clerk, knowing that about half of the directors were Scotsmen, thought to curry favour by giving Stop 26 a Scottish name and, for some reason of his own, chose Glasgow.

My last Glasgow visit was to Chicago, and perhaps I had better explain that. Among the denigrators of Glasgow, Scotland, are those who describe it as 'another Chicago', meaning that we have the same reputation for crime and gangsterism that Chicago has. So, if Glasgow can be described as a Scottish Chicago, then I think Chicago can be called an American Glasgow.

In fact, I enjoyed Chicago much more than New York and more than Washington. For one thing, the temperature suited me better. Then there was the same kind of vigour in the city which my Glasgow has. If I had never spent an evening with Detective Lieutenant Pape, I'd still be thinking of Chicago as a great place, much traduced.

The first afternoon I spent in Chicago, I met the editor of a golf magazine. He asked me what I was doing in the evening, and I said I'd been lucky enough to get a single seat for *My Fair Lady* at the Schubert Theatre, and then I was going out for the rest of the night with the crime reporter of one of Chicago newspapers. He said to me earnestly, 'When you come out of the theatre, take a taxi to the newspaper office. Don't walk or take any public transport.'

I thought this was daft as I had already done a recce. of the area and had found that the newspaper office was within easy walking distance of the theatre. However, after seeing a very good performance of *My Fair Lady* (Eliza was played by an American girl, who spoke perfect Cockney but lapsed into American when she was taught to speak English!), I spent a lot of time trying to get a taxi to take me to the newspaper office. By the time I did get one and arrived, I found the crime reporter had had to go, and had left word that he'd take me out the following evening.

By this time, of course, I'd dismissed my taxi. Around midnight I came out of the newspaper office, didn't see any chance of getting a taxi, and decided to walk back to my hotel. Well, it was a completely uneventful walk. I didn't even see a drunk about. I came to the conclusion that the golf editor had been kidding me on.

The following night I met my crime reporter friend in good time, and he took me to police headquarters and introduced me to Detective Lieutenant Pape, a keen, rather grim young man, who could have gone into a film detective's part at a moment's notice. My reporter pal could have taken a film part too. He tipped his hat back on his head and sat on Lieutenant Pape's desk, the while he chewed gum and exchanged wisecracks. I could just see that happening in Glasgow police headquarters.

I spent about four hours there, from eleven until three o'clock the following morning. We started off with a shooting in a social club. One socialite had pulled a gun on another socialite and, after a 'phone-call or two, Lieutenant Pape explained to me that this was a club for coloured socialites, and that the majority of the crime committed in Chicago was by coloured people. Thinking of the conditions in which they lived, I felt I could hardly blame them.

Anyhow, the colour situation was soon equalised. In came a report of a motorist who had stopped his car at traffic

House for the House? (The Woodside by-election 1962: with Colin Brown, Emlyn Hooson, Q.C., M.P., John M. Bannerman and George Mackie)

Miner House

lights. As he was waiting for them to change, a fellow (white this time) opened the opposite door of the car, hopped in, produced a revolver and ordered the driver to keep driving. They went far out into the country and, in a lonely road, the gunman made the driver hand over his wallet. Then he ordered him out of his own car and drove off, leaving the poor motorist in the wilds.

This interesting story was interrupted by a murder. It didn't take long for Lieutenant Pape to establish that a hard working man had come home to find his wife drunk. He'd given her a final warning about this, and so he killed her. At this point my reporter pal asked me if I'd like to see what was happening in the press room, where the crime reporters of the various newspapers worked.

I went through to the press room and there they were, working on the murder. Their trouble seemed to be a lack of information, because nobody connected with the family would talk. Then one of the reporters dialled the number of the murdered woman's father and said, 'This is the coroner's office. We haven't got just all the details we want about your daughter. Would you mind telling us. . . .'

I decided that, if it was like this every night, those films about crime reporters in the United States must be right after all. Of course, Lieutenant Pape had already explained to me that, in the previous year, they had had an average of a murder a day, not counting Sundays and holidays. I understand New York can beat this hollow.

And yet it's not long ago that Jack Webster, the hard-hitting radio commentator in Vancouver, was quoted as saying that, when he was a reporter in Glasgow, he was accustomed to covering 'the usual Saturday night murder'. No doubt the Canadians thought this was true, though my own feeling is that Jack was doing a bit of leg-pulling. The number of murders in Glasgow usually varies between a dozen and twenty a year, which puts us completely out of the Chicago class—indeed, just about in the Vancouver class!

I've got to admit that I was very much affected by my meeting with Detective Lieutenant Pape. Especially when I heard about an incident in a restaurant on Michigan Avenue.

H

A woman was having a quiet little meal on her own there, when a man came in and sat down opposite her. He put a newspaper on the table and his other hand was under it. He told her that he had a gun pointing at her and that she was to pass over her handbag and not move or make a sound until he had got right out of the restaurant—otherwise, he would turn round and shoot her.

She did as she was told and, when she could collect her courage, she gave the alarm. By then the gunman had disappeared. And what interested me specially in this case was that it had happened in the same restaurant in which I had had lunch that very day.

My crime reporter pal delivered me back to my hotel in the wee sma' 'oors (which is what they call them even in America!). I don't mind admitting that I was considerably shaken. I thought I knew something about crime, but not on this scale.

Just before lunch next day—well, it was really the same day, but you know what I mean—I went for a walk through the beautiful parkland on the Chicago lake front. It was a sparkling morning and, even though I'd been up late, I felt fine.

All of a sudden, I realised that a Negro was approaching me, and at the same time I saw that, in this part of the park, we were completely alone. If it hadn't been for my night in Chicago police headquarters, I don't suppose I'd have given it a second thought. In fact, I don't think I'd have given it a *first* thought.

But, after what I'd learned from Lieutenant Pape, I looked at this approaching Negro with grave doubt, tinged with fear. He looked bigger than me. He might have a gun or a knife or a cosh. All I had was traveller's cheques! So, without trying to make it too obvious, I set my course to steer well clear of him.

I was in the process of doing this when I suddenly realised something peculiar. The Negro was obviously setting his course to steer well clear of me. We were scared of each other.

I'm not one for drawing morals, and I don't intend to draw one here. But the truth is that I feel safer in Glasgow than in any other place I've ever visited.

On Being Paid to Enjoy Oneself

On my 59th birthday I refereed a football match. I record this in no spirit of vainglory. Indeed, it's just the opposite, because I was a referee without a whistle, with very little knowledge of the game, and with the drawback of speaking, approximately, English.

The game was on Glasgow Green and it was played between the staff of the Sorrento Restaurant in Buchanan Street and a motley collection of proprietors, chefs and waiters from other Continental restaurants in the city. Among the nationalities represented were Italians, French, Spaniards, Greeks, Irish, and others I didn't go in to.

It all happened because Enzo Rippa, who runs the Sorrento and Vesuvio restaurants along with Mario Romano and Umberto Cavalodoro asked my wife and me to a picnic. It was only when we got to Glasgow Green that I discovered it was a football match. True, at half time the boots of various cars were opened and cold chickens, bottles of beer and Chianti, salami, sausage, rolls, butter and what not were produced. But I'd already spent nearly an hour running up and down the field, and I realised I had about another hour to go. (Yes, I know it's forty-five minutes each way officially, but this wasn't official).

It did strike me afterwards that my achievement, taking it merely from the physical and not from the Scottish Football Association point of view, was a good one. True, I have never smoked in my life, but I eat and drink manfully. I have a pot belly, though I flatter myself that it doesn't show much. I can walk ten or twelve miles without any pain. All in all, I'm a very lucky man, and I attribute that to the fact that my pavement has been so often in the sun.

I have sometimes said—though I know it's tempting fate—that I am particularly lucky because, for years, I have been paid to enjoy myself. Most of the things I have wanted to do, I have done. And I point out, at the risk of repeating myself, that I have been paid to do so.

For example, my ambition for many years was to appear as a clown in a circus. For a time I cultivated the acquaintance of old Mrs Pinder, who ran Pinder's Royal No.1. Circus, which came every Glasgow Fair to the carnival on the same Glasgow Green I have just mentioned. Her son-in-law was the clown, under the name of Koko, and I hoped I might be allowed to go into the ring with him some time.

And then Bertram Mills' Circus came to Glasgow for one of its tours and I was able to arrange that I would go on as an assistant clown to the great Coco. Well, it's one thing to fix an arrangement like this with the management. It's quite another fixing it up with the clowns themselves. Coco, one of the world's most famous clowns, is a perfectionist. In this show he was doing an act with his son and, when I saw it, I didn't know how I could fit in at all. It was an elaborate affair involving the papering-a-wall act, the equivalent of the custard-pie act, and ending with a water scene.

Coco said I could take part in the opening scenes, but I couldn't do the water scene, which involved a lot of acrobatics, apart from getting completely soaked. This clown interlude lasted for nearly quarter of an hour, and I would be allowed on for the first five or six minutes. And for this appearance I had to rehearse with Coco and his son for nearly a whole day.

On the afternoon of my debut as a clown, I went along to the Big Top at Bellahouston Park to be made up as a clown by Coco. He explained that all professional clowns had a registered make up, which nobody was allowed to copy. So he invented a new one for me. As he was applying it, he said admiringly, 'Ah, you have a beautiful face for a clown!'

It must have been a good make up because my wife was in the audience to see my performance, and at the end of the show she didn't realise that I had taken part at all. The three of us went on and did the paper hanging bit quite reasonably. I felt I was a very inadequate clown indeed, but there were plenty of laughs from the audience. Then Coco's son brought a gigantic birthday cake into the ring and chased Coco with it. Somehow or other, Coco got the cake from him and started chasing me. The climax came when he was supposed to ram the cake in my face.

This was where most of the rehearsal had come in. The elaborate cake was built up out of shaving soap and mounted on a wooden board. Coco pointed out to me that he couldn't possibly ram this in my face. If he did, he might easily break my nose. So the trick was that, while he appeared to shove the cake at my face, I would actually take the board from him and shove my face into the cake. So the quickness of the hand deceives the eye.

The other point Coco made was that, when I did shove my face into the cake, I must keep my eyes and my mouth shut. Otherwise the shaving soap might have a somewhat deleterious effect. And the moment I had removed the remains of the cake from my face, I was to blow out. Thus I would clear myself of shaving soap enough to be able to turn and run out of the ring with the remains of the cake.

I took up my position, as rehearsed, at the entrance to the ring. Coco came flying towards me, with the dazzling white shaving cream cake in his hands. Then he paused for a moment and I took the board from him and buried my face in the cream. I remembered to shut my eyes and blow out afterwards. It all seemed very artificial to me, but the audience were rolling in the aisles. I ran out, still half blinded, and just managed to dodge the Liberty Horses, which were the next act. Coco and his son went on to the really difficult water scene.

When they came off they were full of congratulations. And, by the time I'd got my make up off and had changed, Cyril Mills came round and said that he'd take me on as a clown any time. Alas, it's too late now. I'd be quite willing to be a clown again, but there's no Bertram Mills Circus.

2

In this same line of getting out the Walter Mitty in me, I have done a stint as a railway station announcer and I have appeared in the pulpit of a church. In each case I experienced an odd sensation of power, though in one case I was unseen and in the other seen only too plainly.

I should think, after my one small experience, that being a railway station announcer requires a lot of discipline. I know that, looking down on the station concourse, I could see little incidents which I'd have loved to comment upon. I was tempted to say, 'If that couple with the two weans don't hurry up, they'll miss the Gourock train at Platform 13.' As it was, I was delighted to see the way that the populace obeyed my every command. I had only to announce the departure of a train and half the people I could see moved rapidly towards the platform I'd mentioned.

Being in the pulpit was rather different. It was in Trinity Church, run at that time by the redoubtable Rev. H. S. McClelland. I had, at his bidding, to talk about Robert Burns. I was very nervous indeed but, once I stood up in the pulpit, and looked down on the congregation, I felt this notion of power. Ever since I have looked on ministers of religion in a rather different way from that in which I regarded them in the past. I'm not suggesting, of course, that ministers are powerful, but even the poorest, I should think, must be stirred by his position in the pulpit.

And religion brings me to flying. Another Walter Mitty idea I'd had for years was to fly round Scotland in one hour. I got in touch with the R.A.F. and they said it was possible, but I'd have to wait for the right day. All of a sudden one afternoon, the pilot rang me up from Renfrew and said that the sky was expected to be cloudless for several hours and could I come down at once. I said yes and took a taxi to the airport.

There I was dressed in the complete flying outfit, including parachute and inflatable boat, and given what I realised afterwards was a rather incomplete instruction on how to use all the various gadgets. I waddled out to a two-seater jet, got into the rear seat with difficulty, put on my helmet with its oxygen mask, and off we flew.

All this seems rather small beer today, but it was new when I did it. It was so new to me that, soon after the take-off, I looked down at the scene below and said over the inter-com to the pilot, 'Are those the Campsie Hills already?' He replied, 'No, they're the Grampians!' (I don't expect my English readers, let alone some of my Scottish ones, to get the point of this unless they look at a map of Scotland.)

We were soon above Dundee at 35,000 feet, and I was able to see the North Sea on one side of me and the Atlantic Ocean on the other. It was one of the most exhilarating experiences I have ever had. I have flown over the Alps, over the Caucasus, over the Rockies and over various other pieces of high scenery, but none of these could compare with that flight over Scotland. We moved round the North and I saw the Orkney and Shetland Isles, and then we came down the Western coast.

We were somewhere above Rothesay on the Firth of Clyde when the pilot announced to me through the inter-com that he now proposed to dive 25,000 feet and level out for the run in to Renfrew Airport. So he started to dive and the next thing I knew was a most terrible searing pain in my ears. I pressed the switch on the snout of my oxygen mask and told the pilot how I was suffering.

'I'm sorry,' he said back. 'There's absolutely nothing I can do about it.' And that was that. Even when we started levelling out at about 6,000 feet, the pain was still there. When we landed at Renfrew I found that I was very nearly stone deaf. I could just hear and no more. Apparently, the wax in my ears had been driven right in when we dived the 25,000 feet. I was deaf for about three months and, although my hearing gradually returned, it's never been quite the same. I'm rather given today, when I go to the theatre, to thinking that actors are not as audible as they were when I was younger.

3

Newspapermen are inclined to be critical of everbody and everything, but especially politicians and politics. I've always felt that this is rather unfair on their part, if they've never known anything of politics themselves. Once I thought quite seriously of standing for Glasgow Town Council as a Liberal. But I held back because I was afraid that I had too good a chance of getting in! It's not that I wouldn't like to be a Town Councillor, but I simply haven't got the time.

So my own personal experience of politics was confined to taking part in *A Matter of Opinion* for the B.B.C. and various similar programmes where a distinction was made between speakers for the Right and the Left. I was always chosen for the Left. For years I had supported the Labour Party and, indeed, when I was a film script writer in the Army, I joined the appropriate union and was a fully-paid up member of the Party for a while.

That rather odd organisation, Aims of Industry, ran a number of Brains Trusts throughout Britain and Northern Ireland, and I was repeatedly asked to represent the Left against such regulars as W. J. Brown, former Independent M.P. and bosom pal of Lord Beaverbrook's; Colin Brooks, once editor of *Truth*; Colm Brogan; and assorted M.Ps. For a long time our quiz-master was Ted Kavanagh, one of the most delightful men I have ever met, and once we had a quiz-mistress in the unlikely person of Nancy Spain.

Miss Spain turned up at the Christian Institute hall in Glasgow wearing a long black evening gown and a tartan sash, and was all sweetness and light. She staggered everbody.

I grew away from the Labour Party because of their

attitude to Scotland. I've said before—and I've no doubt I shall say it again—that I'd be a Scottish Nationalist if it wasn't for the Scottish Nationalists. I think they're a rather misguided lot, and their ideas seem to me to be based purely on emotion.

The Tories and the Socialists both pay a lot of lip service to the cause of Scottish independence when they are in Opposition, and then forget all about it when they are in power. So I joined the Scottish Liberal Party, which I found had a real and practical plan for self-government for Scotland.

Among the people I met 'at various broadcasts and television shows was Johnny Bannerman, then the leader of the Liberals in Scotland. Once, during a television rehearsal, I told him that I'd be glad to do anything I could to help the Scottish Liberal Party. I didn't know what I was letting myself in for.

In the autumn of 1962 I was on holiday at Lundin Links, getting material about the East Neuk of Fife for a book I was doing in the *Glory of Scotland* series. (At least, it was supposed to be a series. So far, the total is only two!) I'd gone up for a couple of days before my wife could arrive and on the second day she 'phoned from Glasgow to say that there was going to be a by-election in the Woodside Division of the city—in which I live—and the Liberals wanted me to be their candidate. A representative would 'phone me at the Lundin Links Hotel that night at 7.30 to get my decision.

I spent a day of agonising indecision. I knew it was Johnny Bannerman who was responsible for this and I didn't want to let him down. One the other hand, could I afford the time to fight a by-election? And was I really equipped for it? However, when the call came through at 7.30. I said Yes and the die was cast.

The date for the by-election had not yet been fixed but, as soon as I returned from holiday, I had a 'phone call from Eddie Fraser, the B.B.C. producer. I had not long signed a contract with the B.B.C. to write and take part in a twenty-six weeks' Saturday night show on radio entitled *This Old House*. This was a programme in which, assisted by three singers, a gaggle of actors and the B.B.C. Scottish Variety Orchestra, I reminisced about my youth and Glasgow. It was a very nostalgic affair indeed and we sang and played all my favourite songs and had scenes from my favourite plays.

Eddie was on the 'phone to point out that, now I was a candidate in a Parliamentary election, I would not be allowed to broadcast while the campaign was on. Would I come up and have an interview with Andrew Stewart, the Controller Scotland and James Millar, the Programme Director?

Andrew had the appropriate paragraph from the appropriate section of the Representation of the Peoples Act. It seemed to show that a candidate was not allowed to promote himself in any medium at the expense of the other candidates. He thought that my Saturday night show of *This Old House* might be taken by an opposition candidate as giving me an unfair advantage. I thought of pointing out that, if the programme proved unpopular, it might have exactly the opposite effect, but I felt I had better haud my wheesht, particularly as Andrew was pointing out that banning me from the air for nine weeks was for my own good.

The only alternative seemed for me to resign as prospective Parliamentary Candidate in the Liberal cause in Woodside. So I had to agree to the ban and, you might say, I lost my deposit before I even started.

I soon found that other pursuits of mine were affected too. Being a candidate is almost a full-time job. It was all the more so for me, since I had a great deal of homework to do on matters of Liberal policy and the like. It's one thing to support a Party. It's quite another to speak for it. I attended Liberal candidates' courses, went to various political meetings and got a kind word from Jo Grimond at a big Liberal Rally in the Usher Hall at Edinburgh.

Then the date of the by-election was fixed and the campaign started. I had five opponents—Norman Glen, a Glasgow business man who had had several unsuccessful shots at getting into Parliament, first for the Liberals, and then for the Tories; Neil Carmichael, the Socialist; a Scottish Nationalist whose name, I am afraid, I have forgotten; Guy Aldred, the dear old Anarchist whom I'd first heard talking at the entrance to Alexandra Park in Dennistoun; and Robert Vallar, who was not so interesting to me because he represented the Socialist Party of Great Britain as that his father had been Glasgow's most renowned tattoo artist, Prince Vallar.

It was an exciting by-election. The national Press were interested and I was constantly being interviewed by important journalists from London who were manifestly amazed that Glasgow was comparatively civilised. That was more than some of them were. There was a big and constant television and radio coverage. It was most peculiar to be at the receiving end of all this. My general impression was that Scottish newspapermen and television interviewers were even better than I had thought they were.

The then secretary of the Scottish Liberal Party, Arthur Purdom, was my agent. I was too naive to know it, but the party had mounted a pretty big effort on my behalf. We had wonderful meetings—I mean from the point of view of the size of our audiences. We were having hundreds when others were having half-dozens.

But I was very conscious of the fact that I was not a good political speaker. I've always tried to see both sides of the case, and that's fatal for a politician. I like to be light-hearted in lectures and after-dinner speeches and the like, and being light-hearted at a political meeting marks you down as a lightweight. I think I did better in our coffee mornings with the Press. We held them in our sitting room and sometimes my wife would give coffee to between twenty and thirty newspapermen and women.

There was a wee Irishman named Paddy Travers, a little wasp of a man who represented the *Daily Telegraph*. His methods were simple. He just kept trying to trap me. Sometimes he did and sometimes he didn't, but it never worried me. I knew the number of people who read the *Daily Telegraph* in Woodside was infinitesimal.

Yes, I enjoyed Paddy Travers, and I enjoyed, too, the hecklers at my meetings. One gentleman was thoughtful enough to approach me at one meeting and hand me a list of the twenty-two questions which he proposed to ask at the end of my speech. He was even more thoughtful in providing me with some of the answers.

Then there was the heckler who asked me a question about the Liberal policy as regards agriculture. I was being supported that evening by George Mackie, the Scottish Liberal expert on agriculture and a very successful farmer. So I said, innocently, that I'd pass the question on to him. At this the heckler, an elderly man with a foreign accent, bounced up and down in his seat, shouting, 'Answer the question! Answer the question!'

He looked so funny that I laughed—another very bad thing for a political candidate to do under such circumstances. Then I said I would answer the question if he would just shut up and give me the opportunity. When I had answered the question, a wee Glaswegian in the front row looked up and cried, 'Aye, Jack, ye're fairly enjoyin' yersel' the night, aren't ye no'?'

What I didn't enjoy, however, was canvassing. Not only does canvassing make you realise what a postman has to put up with, but so much of it seems a waste of time. There was the lady who said, 'Oh, yes, Jack, we're votin' fur you. We've aye been Socialist in this hoose.'

Then there was the lady with spectacles and a fancy hairdo who assured me that I was quite mistaken in my belief that a by-election was taking place in the area. She knew for a fact that there wasn't. She was so assured on this point that I began to wonder if I was maybe making a big mistake.

One housewife said she was sorry that she and her husband couldn't vote Liberal because they were Labour supporters. I said that was all right and moved to the next door on the tenement landing. All of a sudden, the Labour housewife opened her door again and said, 'Oh, Jack, could you gi'e ma wee girls your autograph? They never miss you on the telly!'

We'd arranged a rally in Partick Burgh Hall, the very same hall in which I had joined the Communist Party under the name of Alfred Abbott nearly forty years before. Jo Grimond was to be the principal speaker, but he was held up in Orkney by snow. Despite the fact that this was announced both on radio and television, we had an audience of more than five hundred. That was the night I made my worst speech. All the same, we were considerably heartened by the turn out and began to think we might have a chance.

It was the same on polling day. George Mackie took me round the thirteen polling stations in the morning, the afternoon and early evening. You notice odd things when you're a candidate. If people are going to vote for you, they give you the Big Hello. If they aren't, they pass by with averted heads.

In the afternoon one of the polling officers said, 'Is this you back again, Jack?' When I admitted it was, he said, 'I used to be in the I.L.P. myself. I remember fine when Jimmy Maxton was standing in Bridgeton. You know what he did on polling day? He went to the pictures and had a good sleep.'

Ah, well, I knew I was no Jimmy Maxton. That night I went to the Sheriff Court for the counting of the votes. It was soon obvious that it was going to be a close thing between the Tories, who had held the seat, and the Socialists, although I appeared to be a good third. On the television screen (I heard later) Professor Esmond Wright had just said, 'The Liberals have to get five thousand if they are going to show that they mean business', when the result was announced.

I got exactly five thousand votes, not one more or less. It was a victory for Neil Carmichael, Norman Glen was second, and I was third. In vainglorious mood I announced that I would be back fighting Woodside for the Liberals at the next General Election, whenever that took place.

Paddy Travers had described me in the *Daily Telegraph* as 'a political tenderfoot'. He was right in one way. When I was making up my income-tax figures for the year in which this by-election took place, I found that my income had dropped by almost exactly £1,000, and I can assure you that £1,000 is an awful lot to me.

However, I'd said I would stand at the General Election and, when the next one came along in 1964, I did—in Woodside again. So did Neil Carmichael and Norman Glen, another Scottish Nationalist, and the invincible Mr. Vallar who, when he received eighty-two votes in the by-election said, 'It proves that there are eighty-two sensible people in Woodside!'

This time there was no fanfare for Woodside. There could be no great support from the Scottish Liberal Party since they were now fighting on a wide front. We had very little money in our own branch because we had spent so much on the by-election. Fortunately, I had Denis Mitchell, a leading Young Liberal, as my agent. Denis is now one of the best interviewers on B.B.C. Television in Scotland. He is also no longer a Liberal, alas!

We soon found the immense difference between a by-election and a General Election. I was canvassing a list of people who had been marked as our supporters at the by-election and now some of them were saying, 'We'd like to vote for you, but we must keep the Socialist out.'

Well, they didn't. Neil Carmichael came first again. Norman Glen came second again. And I came third again—but with less than half the votes I'd got at the by-election, and a lost deposit forby.

And that was the end of my political career—although I am still a staunch Liberal and look forward to the day when the Liberals will give us self-government for Scotland.

Sometimes, of course, I wake up in the night sweating and wonder what on earth I'd have done if I'd got in!

4

I often think that we are not grateful enough to the late Lord Beaverbrook, who has given us such inestimable pleasure by starting some of the funniest journals in the Press of today. The funniest, of course, is the *Scottish Daily Express*, which leads its uncle in London and its cousin in Manchester by a short head. I never miss the *Scottish Sunday Express*, but that's mainly because of that great Dundonian,

John Gordon, to my mind the best humorous writer in the business, next to Jennifer in *The Queen*.

When I consider how many laughs I have got out of these comic papers, I wonder why I am not popular with them. It surely cannot be because I resigned and then wouldn't go back when I was asked. Yet it is the case that I am never mentioned in the *Scottish Daily Express* or the *Evening Citizen*. My books are not reviewed in their pages, for which, of course, I am truly thankful. When I am taking a leading part in some public affair, my colleagues are named but I remain anonymous in the Beaverbrook Press.

Perhaps the funniest occasion was when I was asked to be the guest of honour at a Junior Soldiers' Parents Day at the Winston Barracks at Lanark. This was quite an occasion, when I had to make a speech, tour the barracks talking to the Junior Soldiers, be shown round an exhibition of work by the boys, and generally be Exhibit No. One myself.

I was approached by the unfortunate young man who was photographer for the occasion for the *Evening Citizen*. He explained that his mission was to prepare material for a 'slip page' for the following day's paper. This is a page of photographs, with accompanying letter-press, about some local event, which appears only in the local edition. The idea is to whip up local sales of the paper.

The photographer said he couldn't possibly include me in any of the pictures. This didn't worry me, it was what I expected, but it did worry the military. However, I soothed them down and the poor young photographer had nearly to stand on his head in order to avoid including me in his portfolio. And next day the 'slip page' on the Junior Soldiers' shenanigans at Lanark appeared, with no mention of the guest of honour, and no picture of him either.

There has been one solitary exception to this. When my book, *The Heart of Glasgow*, was published, I met a *Scottish Sunday Express* man in the Art Club in Glasgow. He said it had come in for review, and I laughed and said I didn't expect to see a word about it in any Beaverbrook funiosity. He said he'd bet me he could get it into his paper. It's just as well that I didn't take the bet because he did. Mistakes will happen, even in the worst regulated newspapers.

Of course, the only time I've ever been sued for libel or defamation of character or something of the sort was by a nap hand of Beaverbrook boys. I was taking part in a Scottish Television panel programme called *Sense and Nonsense*. The chairman was Magnus Magnusson and my fellow panellists were Frank Lilley, then a Glasgow M.P.; Dr. Alan Thomson, a Labour M.P. and Councillor Arnold Henderson, a Clyde-bank Communist. The idea was the usual one of taking one or two items from the news and discussing them.

At this time a silly young couple from the South of England had come up to Scotland without parental consent and a story about them appeared, with photograph, telling how they were presenting their respective parents with an ulti-matum. If the parents did not agree, they would proceed to get married in Scotland.

What Magnus wanted us to say was what would our attitude be towards our children if this had happened to us. Frank Lilley was first on the list, but I'm afraid I didn't pay much attention to his reply. Arnold Henderson came next and, among other things, he said he felt the Press had some-thing to do with this situation.

I followed Councillor Henderson and agreed heartily with him about the Press. Indeed, I said that my attitude would not be so much towards my child as it would be towards the Press.

Alan Thomson made a joke and that was that. At the end of the video-tape recording we saw it played back and listened to ourselves, and nobody saw anything wrong with it.

But along came the five indignant journalists of the *Scottish Daily Express* and the *Scottish Sunday Express* and said that we had traduced them shamefully. Their case was that we had sug-gested that the newspapers concerned had acted irresponsibly and that the young couple's defiance of their parents was influenced by the reporters. It turned out that this brilliant story had appeared only in these two newspapers, a fact which not one of us knew when we were recording the pro-gramme. They were suing Arnold Henderson and me and Scottish Television for £1,500 each.

There was some to-ing and fro-ing between the defence team of lawyers in Glasgow and our counsel in Edinburgh. We got the impression that we had a good defence to the claim by the Beaverbrook boys. Then I suddenly realised that I was going to the South-West of England for an *Any Questions?* broadcast and I would be in hailing distance of the town where the young couple came from. I volunteered to stay over an extra day and see what I could find out.

I was very fortunate. I found out a great deal and I came back and wrote a report for the information of counsel. More enquiries were made and everything seemed to be going our way. Then the blow fell. My lawyer told me that the other side were prepared to settle the whole thing out of court for a sum of £45 instead of £1,500—plus a letter of apology from Arnold Henderson and me!

Well, of course, that was that. I couldn't take on the Beaverbrook Empire in the light of this advice. All I had to do was agree to the terms of the letter. It didn't cost me anything and I found out afterwards something which I had long suspected—that hardly anybody reads the letters of apology in *Express* newspapers.

But that wasn't my jousting with the Empire Crusader over. I am the book critic of the *Evening Times* and I write two articles a week on books. The Monday one is called *Book of the Day*, and deals with a volume published on that very day.

Along came *Men of Power* by Lord Beaverbrook. I must confess that I had never been an admirer of the Lord's prose style. But this seemed even worse than usual. Since I am accustomed to saying exactly what I think in my book reviews I indicated that *Men of Power* was, to put it politely, not very good. I pointed out that Lord Beaverbrook seemed to be so intent to be 'with it' in the political-style books that he had gone in for footnotes in a big way, for footnotes are the thing nowadays. He even had one footnote which indicated that Constantinople was now called Istanbul.

But what puzzled me about the book was that I felt that the beginning and the end seemed to me to be by one hand and the middle by another. The middle, in fact, was the only

good bit in my opinion. I wondered, in my review, if Lord
Beaverbrook had a Maconachie, who had taken over when
he got tired.

A few days later I was summoned to the combined presence
of our then managing director, Sir John Spencer Muirhead
and my editor, S. L. McKinlay. I was shown a letter from
Lord Beaverbrook which said that I had suggested, in my
review, that he had not written the whole book himself. He
was afraid he would have to take legal action, much as he
would regret doing so against his old friends of the Outram
Press.

It was obvious that the Lord didn't know who Maconachie
was. He hadn't remembered one of J. M. Barrie's famous
speeches, in which he revealed that he had suffered from
writer's cramp and had to teach himself to write with his left
hand. But he explained that what he wrote with his left
hand was never quite the same as what he wrote with his
right. He attributed this to his theory that his left-hand
writing was taken over by an alter ego whom he called
Maconachie.

So it was arranged to acquaint Lord Beaverbrook of this
strange omission from his omniscience. I can well imagine
the welcome he gave this information. At any rate, another
letter arrived, saying that the Lord did not accept this ex-
planation and that he felt he had to take action. And that
was all we ever heard of it, as far as I know.

5

It's an odd thing to live the life that, as a youth, you
dreamed of living. I was always a hedonist and I saw myself
as being rich, well-known in Glasgow (I didn't care whether
or not I was well-known anywhere else), a member of clubs,
an after-dinner speaker, a journalist and maybe an author,
and a chap that head waiters welcomed and gave nice tables
and special attention to. And, *mirabile dictu*, I am all these

things, with one exception. I am not rich. I spend all my money on riotous living, and I enjoy every moment of it.

Glasgow is just about the ideal place for living my kind of life. I dare say there are other good places, but Glasgow suits me perfectly. If anyone says it's because I want to be a big frog in a small pond, that's absolutely all right with me. I couldn't stand being a small frog in a big pond. As for being a big frog in a big pond, I realised long, long ago that that was not for me. I don't want success. I just want to enjoy myself.

So I live in a pleasant city, where I can walk to work in the morning, if I feel like it, by the River Kelvin, through Kelvingrove Park and along Sauchiehall Street. I have a sheaf of good restaurants to choose from for luncheon or dinner—the Vesuvio, the Malmaison, the Grosvenor, the One-O-One, Ferrari's, Epicure's, Sorrento, Rogano, the Skandia Bar for smorrebrod, Sans Souci (for Chicken a la Kiev and Retsina Wine), and a wheen others, including the Eagle Inn out at Bishopbriggs and the Old Eagle Tavern (for the best hot bacon rolls in Glasgow) in Howard Street.

I belong to the best club in Glasgow, the Art Club in Bath Street.

Some of the older members tell me it isn't what it was, when the great whisky drinkers stayed up till all hours night after night. Maybe that's so. I don't miss them.

Then I'm a member of some of the odd sodalities which exist in Scotland. I'm one of the Thirteen, a club consisting of thirteen members which meets in Glasgow around the thirteenth of each month, and has just celebrated its seventy-fifth birthday. What I like especially about it is that it was started by a group of newspapermen in a Dennistoun hostelry. This means that, though I did leave school at the age of fifteen, I now consort with Harry Barnes, the director of the Glasgow School of Art; Fred Rimmer, Professor of Music at Glasgow University; Professor Bill Fletcher of Strathclyde University; Ross Higgins, who occasionally sells my books; Colin Chandler, director of the College of Dramatic Art in Glasgow; Christopher Small, dramatic critic of *The Glasgow Herald*; and other chaps who know more than I do.

Then there's the All Saints Club which I had the honour to help to found. It consists of Edinburgh and Glasgow men, approximately in equal proportions, and it exists to keep the feud between Glasgow and Edinburgh in good repair. We meet for dinner three times a year and have supped in such places as Provand's Lordship, the oldest house in Glasgow; Stirling Castle; Charles Rennie Mackintosh's library in the Glasgow School of Art; the Surgeon's Hall in Edinburgh; the City Chambers in Glasgow; the Tolbooth Jail in Edinburgh; and the studio of the Glasgow artist, Bill Crosbie.

Our members include Lord Birsay, who was recognised as a Saint by the Moderator when he became Lord High Commissioner at the Assembly of the Church of Scotland; Alastair Dunnett, editor of *The Scotsman*; Stuart Piggott, the archaeologist; Sir John Boyd, the lawyer; Moray McLaren, author and wit (and the only man who has met me half way between Glasgow and Edinburgh); 'Bingo' Mavor, who leads the Arts Council in Scotland and is a son of the late James Bridie; Emilio Coia, the caricaturist who introduced me to Sir Max Beerbohn on the top of a mountain above Rapallo; Angus MacDougall, the Glasgow plumber who knows more about claret than any man I've met; Nigel Tranter, the novelist; and so on, and so on.

Am I name-dropping? You bet your life I am! And I could go on for 'oors yet, as the old thatcher said to me at the end of that broadcast.

Then there are the Nomads, another old Glasgow club, composed mainly of business men who meet every second Monday to listen to papers given by the members and then a discussion. Our honorary president is Sir Compton Mackenzie, and my standing in the Nomads went up considerably when Sir Compton saluted me on both cheeks in the French fashion at the cocktail party before our last dinner. I mentioned this to show that we are quite accustomed to Continental ways in Glasgow!

Other small clubs come and go, and I think I belong to most of them. It seems to me that a modern Dr. Strang could come along and write a new book on Glasgow clubs which could be just as fascinating as that famous old one.

Of course, in all this social activity I'm inclined to get out of my depth occasionally. For instance, I am vice chairman of the Scottish section of the Society of Authors and also a member of the Scottish P.E.N. Club. This means that I meet such distinguished authors as Oswald Wynd, Cliff Hanley, Marion Lochhead, Lavinia Derwent, James Allan Ford, Alistair Mair and a dozen more who make me feel an amateur. I don't mean they intend to do so. It's just the awesome effect they have on me.

But a newspaperman learns early in life never to give himself away. And I never have until I wrote this book.

Apart from this sort of social life, there's the great swirling, bustling life of Glasgow itself. It's a wonderful city to live in.

There are so many things to do in Glasgow, so many things to see. There are theatres and concerts and entertainments of every kind. There are Glaswegians, the salt of the earth. There are the odd places and the strange corners. After a lifetime here, I am still finding things I've never known before.

Just the other day I was lunching in Ferrari's when an obvious Londoner came in (it was the time of the Scottish Motor Show at the Kelvin Hall), greeted another Londoner and said, 'Why did nobody tell me about Glasgow before? What a time I had last night!' Well, of course, that could mean all sorts of things, but at least it doesn't mean that Glasgow is the drab, industrial place which some people try to make it out to be.

In my old age I am even beginning to think that Glasgow Town Council is not so bad after all. There was a time when I felt that the whole attitude of Town Councillors was to look for something lovely and old in Glasgow and ding it doon. But there seems to be a change of heart in George Square. Good buildings are being preserved. And, although there's still a tendency to build barracks and call them housing estates, such a new complex as the one which has replaced Duke Street Prison is really worth while.

Yes, I'm getting optimistic about the city I love. I wish I could be as optimistic about the newspapers I love. There are so few of them. I realise that I was lucky enough to see the great days in Glasgow, and I only hope that the present days become no worse.

I headed this chapter *On Being Paid to Enjoy Oneself*. In these last twelve months my newspaper has sent me to Italy, Ireland, Canada, Israel and France (Paris to be exact), in that order. I live the life of Reilly and no mistake. All this and Glasgow too!

I am well aware that this display of euphoria may gar philosophic people greet. They have my permission to do so. As far as I am concerned, the sun is still shining on my pavement.

Index